Ramblin' Rose

Ramblin' Rose

The Life and Career of Rose Maddox

Jonny Whiteside

with a previously unpublished foreword by

Woody Guthrie

The Country Music Foundation Press

& Vanderbilt University Press

Nashville & London

First Edition
97 98 99 00 4 3 2 1

The rose motif appearing on the title page and chapter openings is a
computer simulation drawn from one of Rose Maddox's classic
Nathan Turk costumes.

This publication is made from recycled paper and meets the minimum requirements of American National Standard for Information
Sciences—Permanence of Paper for Printed Library Materials ∞

Library of Congress Cataloging-in-Publication Data
Whiteside, Jonny.
    Ramblin' Rose : the life and career of Rose Maddox / Jonny
  Whiteside ; with a previously unpublished foreword by Woody
  Guthrie. — 1st ed.
        p.   cm.
    Includes bibliographical references (p.   ), discography (p.   ),
  and index.
    ISBN 0-8265-1269-0 (cloth : alk. paper)
      1. Maddox, Rose. 2. Country musicians—Biography. 1. Title.
  ML420.M13863R36   1996
  782.42'1642'092—dc20
    [B]   96-34377
                                                       CIP
                                                       MN

in loving memory of my hero, **Fred Maddox**

CONTENTS

ACKNOWLEDGMENTS

Working on this project was a pleasure from start to finish, primarily because everyone associated with Rose Maddox was as friendly and forthcoming as they were helpful. I would like to thank the various branches of the Maddox family—Kitty, Tyrone, Sandy, Don and Nila, Benny, Alta Troxel, Barbara Hale, and Donnie Maddox—all of whom cooperated with the hard-headed charm peculiar to this singular clan. Thanks to Ronnie Pugh, Bob Pinson, and the staff of the Country Music Foundation, who provided as much encouragement and guidance as they did invaluable information; also to Charlie Seemann, formerly of the CMF, now with the Fund for Folk Culture in Santa Fe, New Mexico; to Chris Strachwitz, Patrick Milligan, Rich Stivers, and Otto Kitsinger, and to Loretta DeBiaso at Capitol Records and Tina McCarthy at Columbia Records for discographical information; to Nora Guthrie at the Woody Guthrie Foundation; to Kim Pickens for whom more thanks are due than I can possibly express; to Chip and Tony Kinman, Dave Keen, and Keith Storer for making me listen up; to Steve Bataillard, Diane McCarthy, Barry McBride, Dan Nishimura, and Jim Howie for undertaking numerous, occasionally hazardous long distance trips hunting Maddox lore; to Glenn Glen, Paul Bowman,

Wesley Tuttle, the late great Hank Penny, and the late, just-as-great Jolly Joe Nixon; to Glen Mueller, Billy Leibert, Johnny Russell, Truitt Cunningham, Bud Duncan, Juanita Albright, Ralph Hicks, the late Bill Boyd, and Fran Boyd at the Academy of Country Music, all of whom greatly enhanced my understanding and knowledge of country music in general and Rose Maddox and the West Coast scene in particular; to Dean and Kim Moore, Merle Haggard, the staff at Hag Inc., and the entire Strangers organization; to Wanda Markham, Jim Shaw, Paul Groah, Johnny Bond, Chris Simon, Tex Whitson, Murrell Counts, J. D. Rhynes, Red Simpson, Ken McKnight, T. J. Meekins, Inez Savage, Bobby Jobe, Richard and Linda Thompson, Mack Owen, Gene Moles, and Henry Sharpe, all of whom assisted in minor but thoroughly indispensable ways; for steering me in the right direction, great gratitude to Peter Guralnick, Kit Rachlis, and R. J. Smith; to Bill Malone and John Morthland; to my very patient agent Mitch Douglas; to my fine editor Paul Kingsbury; to Alan Eichler, Don Waller, and John Lomax III; to Brad Benedict and Vicki Arkoff at Capitol Records; to the generous staff at AFTRA and the Society of Singers; to Ronnie Mack, Gary Lambert, Ray Campi, Rene Engel, Lloyd Martin, and Jimmy Koo; and to everyone else who has booked, recorded, or listened to Rose Maddox.

FOREWORD

In 1949, Woody Guthrie—then already well-known as a folk-singer, songwriter, and author (Bound for Glory)—*wrote the following letter and addressed it to the Maddox Brothers & Rose, care of 4 Star Records in Pasadena, California. Though Guthrie may have had some self-interest in heartily endorsing Rose and her brothers (the Maddoxes had recently recorded his song "Philadelphia Lawyer"), his colorful, stream-of-consciousness letter nevertheless tells us much about the Maddoxes' standing among their musical peers during their heyday. The letter is rendered exactly as it was written, typographical errors and all.*

The Maddox Bros. & Rose are Four Bros. (count 'em) and one lone sister. I don't guess I could call her very much a 'lone' sister, with those 4 bros. circling round all about her. They are sober, serious, wide awake, and best of all, they're young. Young in body and young in spirit. They are the best Hillcountry String Band in these 48 states of ours.

I've been listening to records all of my natural life, and, have cocked my ear to the horn and speaker to listen unto several tens of thousands of songs on records. I went to the Library of Congress several trips and sat and played through their piles of commercial and non-commercial recordings, the famous Lomax shelves, and heard a dozen songs about everything from a wild cyclone to a gambling hall shooting craps, good and bad men, good and bad women, fast and slow horses, shipwrecks, boat races, train wrecks, floods and the shouts of the saints and the sinners. My life has been glued to a song on a record for as long as I can recollect.

I've been a worshipper for long years at the tuning keys of the well known Carter Family. They came closer to being my model of a singing Family than any other tribe on waxy discs. In such pieces as "Worried Man Blues", "My Little Darling", "Coal Miner Blues", "Will You Miss Me When I'm Gone", the Carters are at their tip top best in their spiritual and sadly tragic pieces. It is on the funny, humorous side of things that the Carters are at their weakest, and, the quiet running sunnymountain harmony which the Carter Family used with such genius is not any too well suited for the clowning laughing side of the hill.

Rose Maddox leads her four brothers on a sad, true story biblical hymn, "Tramp On The Street", which, for story content background, as well as for pure force, is for my money, the absolute perfection so far hit and reached by stringband folksingers. You hear in Rose Maddox's voice a depth of sympathy for three men in history, born to rock in their mothers arms, then to be left to die like a tramp on the street.

I've heard several dozens of songs and ballads, poems, about the poor lost tramp dying, starving, freezing out in the cold. The story is old in my mind, but what caught my ear and shook my feelings most was, as I said, the womanly sympathy, and the warmth of the bitter pity in the rise and fall of every word from this young lady, Rose Maddox. Her brothers again back up her feelings with their strings in a way that touches of the mood of her story. Rose and her brothers rock the old spiritual, "When God Dips His Pen Of Love In My Heart". The same deep religious idea rings here, but in the lighter vein. The shuffle and stomp is more on the regular beat. The fingers snap and the head rolls from one side to the other, and the true religion of the neighborly love seems to sound and to abound on every leaf and stem, rock and stone. Even if a small measure of giddiness of the young, the youthful. You forget and forgive the Maddoxes if they sorta overdo things on this one. "The Milk Cow Blues" may seem an odd coach-car on the firefly Maddox train. You may think, or ask, what on earth are they doing away over here in the blues part of the world, anyhow? Well, the blues sing and try to tell you what all is wrong with your world; the same way that spiritual songs tell how to fix it better. There is a link chain between the spiritual song and the blues. It takes a singer and a backup band of wide range. There aren't any too many bands on the music trail today that master such a wide range, wide enough to do the "Milk Cow Blues" as well as Sister Bessie Smith, and, "Tramp On The Street", in a way that outdoes the classic Carter Family. Rose Maddox and Bros. make this jump as nimble and light footed as a wayfaring stranger drifting through your part of town. These Maddox people take the "Milk Cow Blues" and make it their very own private and personal property. Like their own rockhouse they built with their own hand to suit their own notions. When you can take a good song and put your own feelings into the old words, you are a real artist by any yardstick. The closest I've heard the Maddoxes come to singing cheapened posey poster art songs, is whilst they sing one of their best sellers, "Time Nor Tide". But, as weak as the words are to this song, Rose and the boys make the thing stand up. Even when they perform a down right badly written song it soundeth good to the soul; and, when they got their hands onto a number with some goodly meat on it, they take it and make history out of it; but however they choose a song in the A number One box, well, old or new, they make it a classic thing. I composed a ballad some ten years back by the name of "The Philadelphia Lawyer", (The Reno Blues) which I sung for quite a long spell over my KFVD program, before I, like all odd folksingers, drifted back to New York City. The Maddox Brothers and Rose made a record of this song on a 4 Star label, and, when the 4 Star man, Don Pierce, took me into his little plywood booth and touched his needle to this "Philadelphia Lawyer", my ears wiggled just out of pure, pure joy. I didn't just LIKE the Maddox recording, I fell in love with folklore, folktales, folk poems, folk sayings, and folk of every size, shape, and color all over again. Already, a free sample record of this "Philadelphia Lawyer" has been sent to each and every radio station in the U.S.A.

What they have done on the "Philadelphia Lawyer" of mine, is a jamup job of mimeing (mimicking) of folkballad. It has always been one of the chief kinds of pasttime and entertainment in the Isles of Britain, I know, to act out or to dance out (in high color costumes) this form of longstory ballad. The Maddoxes are digging in a vein that the entire human race has for untold centuries used to laugh at, and forget for the minute most of your debts and burdens. In taverns, in schools, in houses, on stage, in halls and walls of all humanly kinds, this form of monkeyshines has carried us on toward the friendly labors of a newdawning day.

They work in more than a dozen blazey colored changes of shirts, pants, skirts, hats, props, and properties. They ride from stage to stage in four big slick Cadillac sedans. The ladies get loud when they hear the spidery fingers and lonesome (or Clowny) strings picked and plucked by the four brothers; whilst the boys in the crowds got even louder in their cheers at the sight and sound of sister Rose. Five thousand is just an average nightly crowd for the Maddox Brothers and Rose. They are a family of youngsprouts. They work hard and they love their work. They jump up just a minute or so ahead of the new-morning sun, and, they work till the midnight oil burns out. I might not ever get close enough to them to shake their hands, so I can tell my own two cents worth right here.

Just always remember that you are handling a power in your music and in your singing that is older and stronger than any known or unknown form of atomic energy. Your songs can rest and comfort the living heart and soul of the human race. You can make a person feel like trying to build up a whole new world but here, all by himself, single handed. You can cause workers to work, and the sick to feel better, the heart to laugh, and the lovers to multiply the earth. You can sing and teach living history, past, present, and future, in ways that a thousand sour lectures and sermons can never do. Your work can sing on the wings of the clouds from this end of the world unto the other end. And, if you see this, and try your best to always pick out the best song your inner conscience tells you, then, a thousand years ahead of this day on your calendar, as long as there are voices to sing and hearts to listen, your work, your songs, and your labors will spread to bless and fertilize the land. I could not safely tell you that you are the best family of singers I've heard, unless that is really what I think of you. You are this because of the fact that you have lived and grown, argued and joked, played and sang as a family. That's your greatness if there is any greatness in your talents. Keep on being your family and let your songs heal, protect, awaken, and give full dignity to your larger family of all shades, and shapes, and sizes of bank accounts, who dwell under the leaves of the world and look to you to draw this family a little closer around the welcome table for the next meal.

—*Woody Guthrie*

©Woody Guthrie Publications, Inc.

PREFACE

The walls inside Rose Maddox's living room are jammed with
twenty-six eight-by-ten framed photographs, the cozy chaos of a
fifty-eight year career in country music. There in the singer's living
room—decked out in blond wood paneling and tooled-leather wag-
onwheel furniture—the memories dominate and seem almost to
overwhelm the present. Among the department-store portraits of
grandchildren are a mess of old c&w promo shots. There is a
jumbo 1947 studio portrait of four strapping young men clustered
around a pert young woman in her twenties, all clad in elaborately
decorated western costumes. "Maddox Bros. & Rose," it reads.
"The Most Colorful Hillbilly Band in America." In smaller type:
"Heard exclusively on 4 Star Records, Pasadena, Calif."

Here is another, in color, which shows the boys onstage, perspir-
ing, hands blurred, wearing purple satin shirts; on their backs,
embroidered coyotes howl beneath a golden-thread moon. Rose,
dancing centerstage, wears a flamenco outfit complete with veil and
castanets. There, a large portrait, from 1967, shows Rose at the
microphone, hair stacked in a country music queen's honey-blond
coiffure, living up to her nickname: the Sweetheart of Hillbilly
Swing. At the time the photo was taken, she had just been awarded

a square in the Country Music Hall of Fame's Walkway of Stars, one of the few formal recognitions that Nashville has ever accorded her.

Clear as a bell comes her mule-skinner's shout from the back bedroom: "Hang on, I'll be right out." Even her speaking voice has a kick. She walks into the room, movements stiff but purposeful, and settles into the leather couch. Though she is slight of build, with a cascade of silver-gray hair framing a face dominated by her eyes, the way she carries herself demands attention. Her forthright manner, buggy-whip tongue, and dry humor are those of an indefatigable, self-assured rural grande dame. Yet Rose, now seventy-one, is a modest woman, more concerned with her next booking at a local tavern than with any past glories. Between jobs, she grows restless and finds little consolation in reviewing yesterday's triumphs. For Rose, any time not spent singing is wasted time.

Although she grew up a country music star (she has sung professionally since age eleven), Rose Maddox carries her fame without a trace of haughtiness—as long as you stay on her good side. "Don't go pokin' in that fireplace," she barks. "I don't like outsiders messin' with my fire."

Charm and grace alone have not taken her this far. Fending off drunken rounders since adolescence, Rose learned to get tough at an early age. She does not shy away from confrontation. She meets it the same way she does her music: head on.

Perhaps her headstrong attitude, characteristic of the Maddoxes, at times worked against her best interests. Back in the 1950s and '60s, a woman with an aggressive style was often poorly received by the country music chieftains in Nashville, though on the West Coast, Rose's lifelong base of operations, such hardheadedness fit right in. When Rose's career blossomed, Los Angeles was home to a thriving country music scene, with a small army of performers, dozens of dancehalls, nightclubs, radio and television shows; and many independent record labels hoping to cut hits with the consistent impact that Capitol Records seemed to manage so easily.

Rose Maddox did not worry about hits. In the early 1950s she was such a hot property that Columbia Records held three separate contracts with her—one for her act with her brothers, one for duets with her sister-in-law, and one for her solo act.

In her heyday, she commanded the respect and admiration of the biggest names in the music business. "I remember seeing a television interview with Bing Crosby, years ago," Rose recalled. "They asked him who his favorite country singer was and Bing said, 'Rose Maddox.'" Hank Williams once sat alone in the empty Riverside Rancho ballroom, waiting for promoter Marty Landau to introduce him to Rose. "I never thought I'd get a chance to meet you," Hank told her. The Hillbilly Shakespeare and the Sweetheart of Hillbilly Swing talked for hours, mostly of music and mutual friends. "You are as important to hillbilly music right now," Hank said to Rose, "as Roy Acuff was ten years ago."

Forty years later, she still commanded the respect of her peers. During the taping of CBS-TV's "Women of Country" special in 1992, Pam Tillis, Suzy Bogguss, Trisha Yearwood, and Lorrie Morgan all clamored for Rose's approval, as well they should have. Rose Maddox was country's original, high-kicking firebrand. As leader of the Maddox Brothers & Rose from 1937 to 1957, she exploded the previously inconsequential role of the 'girl singer' in country music, established herself as one of country music's first national female stars and set the tone for every woman who followed her. A member (briefly) of both the "Grand Ole Opry" and "Louisiana Hayride," she reached national radio audiences. Her recordings on the 4 Star, Columbia, Capitol, and Starday labels constitute one of the most influential and groundbreaking bodies of work in country music history. Strongly rooted in traditional gospel singing, her fiercely declamatory vocal style was, and still is, a pure blast of Southern soul. After seventy years of living, that voice is as strong, sassy, and beautiful as ever—a fact that the music industry acknowledged in nominating her 1994 Arhoolie album, $35 and a Dream, for a Grammy in the Best Traditional Bluegrass Album category. Though she did not take home the award, and though most of the prestige she once enjoyed may be gone, the mark her family made on country music remains indelible.

The Maddox Brothers & Rose were among the most influential performers of their day. Fred Maddox's ferocious, intricate slap bass rhythms laid the bedrock on which rockabilly was to be erected, while his rowdy sensibilities helped the band to develop and further the popularity of honky-tonk style country music. The shaking guitar and mandolin leads of Cal and Henry Maddox often looked even further down the line, seamlessly entwining sacred, blues, western, and old-time songs. All the Maddoxes excelled in harmony singing. And with Rose in the spotlight, they were anything but a simple hillbilly band.

But an examination of the music they played—or rather the spirit they lent their music—only hints at what the Maddox Brothers & Rose were all about. Their stage show, for instance, was legendary: a breakneck, nonstop barrage of patter, clowning, and visual jazz. (Indeed, Don Maddox spent as much time cracking jokes and rifling through his trunkfull of props as he did fiddling and singing.) Their strikingly colorful stage attire set new standards for country music years before rhinestones had become de rigueur in Nashville. As Tennessee Ernie Ford once said of the Maddoxes, "Their costumes would make Liberace look like a plucked chicken." Yet they were never so much innovators as interpreters who always pushed the recognized limits and revealed new possibilities which their peers snapped up as quickly as they figured out what the Maddoxes were driving at. What they achieved was a new synthesis, which fed audiences who were hungry for the new, yet afraid of giving up the familiar.

For all these reasons, this opportunity to set the record straight about Rose Maddox and her contributions to country music is a distinct pleasure, made all the more so because this biography has been an authorized and closely collaborative venture from the start. Rose Maddox is a woman of rare character and dazzling talent, a natural folk artist whose contributions, achievements, and influence still echo through recordings being aired on country music radio stations around the world.

The story of Rose and the Maddox family ought to be as familiar as the Joads of Steinbeck's *Grapes of Wrath,* yet their legacy and Rose's own extraordinary achievements have slipped in and out of obscurity. Although Rose never stopped working or recording, brief scholarly examinations and occasional popular rediscoveries have been the extent of her limited recognition. Largely isolated from the Nashville establishment due to her career-long choice of the West Coast as her base of operations, Rose Maddox is a prime example of the manner in which historical accounts have underreported, if not ignored, numerous important contributors to country music.

Above all, though, Rose Maddox's story is a fascinating account of a boxcar-jumping, dirt-poor little girl who helped thousands of Dust Bowl emigrés adjust to their new home and who grew up to become a living symbol of outspoken proto-feminist independence and strength in post-war America. Her meandering path from poverty to stardom and back again is one of country music's greatest and most characteristic journeys, one that began in a desperate and altogether challenging place and time.

Ramblin' Rose

CHAPTER ONE

Boaz, Alabama is a small, isolated town some ninety miles northeast of Birmingham. Although located close by the musically fertile Sand Mountain region (home to the Delmore and Louvin Brothers, who later became two of country music's greatest duos), Boaz itself was a place where few residents ever set their sights on musical stardom. During the 1920s, as postwar prosperity swept the United States, it bypassed the rural South, or rather was unable to manifest itself. Sharecropping was still the only recourse for many Southerners.

So it was for the Maddox family. In the hills outside town, Charlie and Lula Maddox reared their family and tended a cotton patch, which belonged to Lula's brother, who took a standard 60 percent of the patch's yield. Both Charlie and Lula were natives of Boaz. Lula Gertrude Maddox was the daughter of the Reverend Jackson Smith, who had built his own church (known as Smith's Chapel in the Piney Woods) and a considerable reputation in Boaz. The Smiths, who counted among their number landowners, a schoolteacher, and Lula's preacher father, were evidently a cut above the Maddoxes in social standing when Charlie Maddox lied about his age in order to get a marriage license to wed Lula in 1910. Somehow no one seemed to mind Lula's marriage to the less prosperous Charlie, so they set up housekeeping, reared their children, raised cotton, and picked banjo when the sun went down. Tough as times were, the Maddox family character—equal parts humor, pride, resilience, and a peculiar brand of benign mysticism—supplied spirit enough to carry them through.

On the fifteenth of August, 1925, Lula and Charlie rejoiced at the arrival of newborn Roselea Arbana Maddox. One wonders if rejoice is the appropriate word, for Charlie and Lula had already delivered four sons and a daughter, and had suffered through a miscarriage and also the death at eighteen months of another girl. Yet they warmly received another hungry mouth into their fold.

To Lula, family was all that mattered. A woman of considerable self-confidence, Lula knew her children were destined for greatness. Accordingly, they all received grand handles: Clifton R. E. Maddox (born in 1912), Gertrude Alta May (born 1914), John Calvin (born November 3, 1915 and named after President Coolidge), Fred Roscoe (born July 2, 1919 and named for Lula's brother), Kenneth Chalmer, better known as Don (born December 7, 1922), and the youngest, Henry Ford (born March 19, 1928). These last two sons, of course, were named for leading automobile moguls of the day.

The Maddoxes' world, a wooden shack on a few acres of land, began and ended with immediate family—a curious, exclusive realm inhabited by Maddoxes and Smiths alone. To young Fred, Boaz seemed "a hundred miles away—come to find out later, it was only three!" The Maddoxes remained independent of townsfolk by mutual agreement. This was not so much a social rift as an inability to see eye-to-eye, initiated by Lula and upheld by all involved.

Lula was never the conciliatory type. She was small—standing just under five feet tall—but stout, with close-bobbed brunette hair and a pair of intense, dark eyes. Maverick and independent almost to a fault, Lula possessed a high, stubborn spirit and fierce drive that was too far advanced to fit the standard of gentility that even the poorest of hill women were expected to uphold. ("Mama had a lot of ideas that she couldn't use," explained eldest daughter Alta, "because of the way things were in that part of the country.") As fiercely protective of her brood as a mother lion, Lula was a born leader. Family was all she had to follow her. Charlie never sought the upper hand in marriage, instead surrendering all authority to Lula.

Part of what kept the Maddoxes apart from the community was Lula's well-known ambition to explore the West. Devouring dime-novel accounts of the West's glorious bounty and proud inhabitants, she nurtured an obsessive dream of a land of milk and honey. Her almost child-like naiveté transformed the Western states into a paradise of biblical measure. In Arizona, Lula often told the family, "the air is so pure, they ain't got no flies there!"

It was her dearest wish to go west, a burning ambition she had entertained for at least a decade prior to Rose's birth. To her friends and neighbors, who both cherished fierce native pride for the South and were well-grounded in conservative common sense, such ideas were a sign of madness.

"Mama had always wanted to come out here, for as long as I can remember," said Alta. "When she read, she read only western stories. It just sounded so good to her, it was exactly the way she wanted her life to be." Such a journey was unheard of, particularly for a family with small children. This was the only notion of Lula's that Charlie flatly refused to go along with.

Isolated from Boaz by distance and thought, the Maddoxes happily built their own world. They relied on family to provide what sustenance and spirituality they needed to keep discontent at bay. Both sets of grandparents were remarkable, touched by a sense of divinity and the mystic. Lula's mother, Arcany, as her name implies, was well known as a seer and healer. She used faith, laying on of hands, and a variety of backwoods methods with reportedly legendary success. Fred recalled a childhood bout with diphtheria, cured by Arcany's use of a pencil wrapped with red thread. He credited her with saving his life. Later generations of Boazians would recall Arcany as a witch, an assertion that brings a snort of derision from the Maddoxes. "She was really more of what you'd call a prophet," Fred maintained.

As a young man in his native Georgia, Charlie's father, R. E. Maddox, heard a call from the Lord too strong to resist. Taking up his fiddle, he wandered the lost highways of war-torn Dixie Land, "just a-preachin' and a-playin' his fiddle," according to Alta. Riding Reconstruction's tide of unrest, Maddox was probably the only source of contact and news from the outside world for many of the tiny communities he passed through.

Though he offered fiddle tunes and sacred selections for entertainment, it was the grave young man's skill at oratory that really moved his audiences. Families touched by his sermons would compete to provide R. E. Maddox with food and lodging. This is how he met, wooed, and wed his wife, whom he took immediately back onto the road with him. Clearly a charismatic and compelling character, R. E. Maddox epitomized the essence of folk musicians: the messenger-performer making the best of troubled times, both for himself and for those he played to. This specific social role was passed on to succeeding generations of Maddoxes, who embraced both its easy ways and its considerable responsibilities.

How and where R. E. learned to play fiddle is unknown, but he did so during a crucial period in America's musical development. The nineteenth century saw the first wholesale blending of European melody and song with African rhythms and the call-and-response chants of black slaves. This combination became the basis for virtually every type of American popular music to evolve since, and the two streams of music first joined in religious music. The most effective and dramatic results appeared as slaves began rocking old world psalmody with their native beats, creating the fiery gospel of the "Negro spirituals." Not only had Africans created the banjo, they readily took up the white man's fiddle and created a musical framework used to this day. Maddox was straddling a critical line and was himself contributing to the development of a new folk music that would later color his grandchildren's contributions.

Upon reaching Alabama, the Almighty relinquished his grasp on Maddox, and the couple settled down to life on a farm seven miles outside of Boaz. They raised seven children there (Charlie being second youngest). Though he had quit preaching, R. E. Maddox retained a reputation as a speaker of great pith and insight. It remained his duty to address Boaz's citizens in times of crisis and civic concern.

He did not abandon his fiddle, however, and passed on a great love of music to his children. Alta recalls a visit to his farm in the early 1930s. It was late in the evening, and she found her grandfather in bed but not averse to socializing. She asked how long it had been since he had played; in a single fluid motion he shot one hand beneath the bed, producing fiddle and bow as he leapt from under the blankets, commencing to dance and play all over the floorboards, nightgown snapping between his bony knees.

Of particular renown and popularity in Boaz was Charlie's younger brother, Foncy. Foncy Maddox grew to become a performer and music teacher known throughout the Southeast. By all accounts, he was musically gifted, able to pick up and master virtually any instrument in a few moments' time. He performed at every type of social gathering, always packing the schoolhouse or home set aside for his use.

"There was no instrument in the world he didn't play, or couldn't learn to play," Alta recalled. "When he was onstage, he'd use the guitar a lot, but he'd swing off and use a fiddle or banjo, to make the different things he did sound better. He was a showman from the word go. If he opened his mouth, the people laughed!

"He sung ever'thing. He did a lot of blues, he did a lot of jazz, and he did country, of course, but more folksy country. Back then, they didn't have music category'd into so many different things, and whatever you did, it was a part of you."

Foncy often appeared in blackface, as did many country musicians (Jimmie Rodgers and Bob Wills among them) in the years prior to World War II when the practice was generally reserved for traveling medicine shows. Foncy's blackface differed from his commercial theatrical and medicine show counterparts in that he would don the burnt cork to sing spirituals, rather than to sell snake oil or to burlesque the oafish Jim Crow and wily Zip Coon characters so widely popularized on stage in the 1840s and 1850s.

"When he did blackface, he'd sing the old nigger spiritual type songs,"

Alta recalled. "They called 'em that when they had slaves, you know. You could see his eyes rollin' in there. He'd sing those and people, I tell you, the tears would be a-flowin' like rivers. He was so great, you couldn't imagine."

Foncy traveled throughout Alabama, Georgia, and Tennessee, presenting a program of songs and down-home patter. Usually appearing at a schoolhouse, he also offered musical instruction to locals who attended his show. "Why, he'd teach 'em whatever they wanted, for money, so he could go on to the next place," said Alta, "and he would travel up to Memphis, where they had colored entertainment.

"Colored people wasn't allowed in our part of the country, because if they was caught around there after dark, why, they probably never would have left there at all. It was just a thing left over from the war days, you know, so Foncy would have to go to places like Memphis."

According to Alta, Foncy sought out black musicians not only to play with but also to learn from. This connection to Memphis musicians—playing alongside sympathetic Beale Streeters—seems especially significant, given the Bluff City's rich contributions to all forms of popular American music. Blues and jazz became staples for Foncy, yet he always came back to their source, gospel music.

Alta's descriptions of Foncy's music making are intriguing. His singing style was apparently similar to the well-crafted hokum of Emmett Miller, the yodeler whose 1928 recordings of "I Ain't Got Nobody" and "Lovesick Blues" deeply influenced Jimmie Rodgers, Hank Williams, and Bob Wills. One wonders, if Foncy had responded to the numerous public auditions for field recordings by New York record companies (as Jimmie Rodgers and the Carter Family did), what a sharp-eared record company scout like Ralph Peer or Art Satherley could have made of him.

But Foncy Maddox's musical career ended abruptly in the late 1920s after he got married to a strong-willed woman, whom the Maddoxes now characterize as an "uptown gal." "She wasn't no country gal," recalled Fred Maddox. "She was so damn tight! She always called him 'Maddox,' like they do in the army . . . 'Come here, Maddox!' and 'Now, look here, Maddox!' and she really got him down, because he wasn't the cowing-down type. And I think he kinda went off the deep end, up here," Fred said, tapping his forehead gloomily.

"He was a musician," recalled Don Maddox. "I don't know much about him, but I do know that he turned to preaching in later life."

Alta saw it as one of the saddest turns any Maddox made, then or since. Just why Foncy abandoned music (virtually never to play again) is a mystery. Yet on at least one occasion Foncy's reputation trumped that of his famous niece and nephews. Following an appearance in Southern California, during the early sixties, Rose was giving a late-night radio interview. An eager group of native Alabama musicians phoned the station to find out if this "Rose Maddox was any relation to the famous Foncy Maddox" who had tutored them as kids! Although he passed away in the late forties, Foncy is still remembered in Boaz as one of the greatest native talents ever to spring from that city.

Foncy was not the only musician in his immediate family; brother Charlie was a banjo player of great skill. "I don't care who you mention that plays a banjo—five string—nobody that I ever heard, and I've heard a lot of them, ever played like Papa," Alta maintained. "He noted ever' note of it, didn't chord at all, and he didn't play anything but the regular, old-time banjo pieces, like 'Shout Lou,' 'Boil Them Cabbage Down,' and 'Shortnin' Bread.' He played the best banjo I ever heard." Lula was also proficient at both banjo and mandolin but played only at large family gatherings, whereas Charlie often played for his own enjoyment.

When their firstborn, Cliff, was of an age to take up the family tradition, Lula asked the boy which instrument he wanted to learn. His choice, the mandolin, was immediately ordered from Sears Roebuck. Foncy began instructing him and would instill in Cliff all the technique and knowledge he had gained through his travels. As he grew, Cliff took to performing with Foncy, who was often joined by a musical trio of sisters from a nearby farm (one of whom, Gordie Whissenant, later became Cliff's wife).

By this time (the late 1920s), Jimmie Rodgers had begun recording for the Victor company, and Cliff, like so many other young Southern musicians, became a disciple of the Singing Brakeman, the most influential country singer of the day. He and Foncy mastered Rodgers's repertoire, thus incorporating a vital, final twist to the Maddoxes' musical store. Alta recalls Cliff going to Gadsden when Rodgers appeared there and following the performance, even getting a chance to meet briefly with his idol. Such a meeting was the dream of every hillbilly from Virginia to West Texas, and from then on Cliff pursued a career in music, without the aid or encouragement of anyone but Foncy, years before any of his brothers had the slightest interest in performing.

His mother's well-known distaste for in-laws had forced Cliff and Gordie, after marrying, to live separate from the family. They also wondered at Lula's oft-voiced intentions to go west, and their doubts widened the gap between households. Alta soon married as well, and drifted away from Charlie and Lula for the same reasons, moving to Gadsden (where her husband worked at a Goodyear rubber plant).

At home, Charlie and Lula had to scratch and scrape to get by. "That Charlie Maddox—sorriest man in Alabama!" That's what Rose recalled hearing many a time about her father. "But he always took the greatest care of us," she said. "He was what's known as a 'get-around-guy.'"

Whatever surplus produce the Maddoxes raised would be taken into town and sold. Whenever he made these trips to Boaz, he would tuck a few quarts of his moonshine into a basket, cover those with straw, set a few eggs atop that, and while Cal and Fred sold vegetables from their wagon, Charlie would make the rounds of local merchants, asking nonchalantly, "Anybody need some eggs?"

"They all knew what he was doin'," said Fred, "and by the time he'd come back, we'd have sold ever'thing from out of the wagon."

Still, it wasn't enough. Time passed, the price of cotton dropped lower and lower, and life became accordingly bleaker as the kids got bigger. Sad and lean, Charlie watched his family spiral down into destitution. His wily methods were often thwarted by the execrable conditions of sharecropping. A particularly crippling incident took place in 1931, when the price of cotton had sunk to its lowest point since the days immediately after the Civil War. Charlie had learned of an imminent jump, from seven cents a pound up to eleven cents. Charlie, Cal, and Fred picked and

loaded a warehouse full of the stuff, awaiting the considerable increase—
only to have Lula's impatient brother, Roscoe Smith, sell it all at seven
cents. Sure enough, the price jumped just as Charlie had predicted. (Years
later, Fred's voice still resonated with shock as he related the story.) Angry
at this callous betrayal, Mama decided they should pull up stakes and
leave Boaz.

The family moved to Big Wills Valley, several miles south of Boaz, and
settled in a large sharecropping community. Owned and operated by
"Old Man" Harper, this mill town was home to several hundred souls
who worked his land, chopped his cotton, crushed his cane for sorghum
in the syrup mill and, naturally, spent their wages in his company store.
Here the Maddoxes saw an even sharper decline in their quality of life.
According to Rose, they subsisted on "potatoes, corn bread, and gravy—
and we were lucky to have that," while Charlie and Cal worked like dogs
for the landlord. The Maddoxes saw their relatives less and less and lived
in squalid conditions alongside scores of other disadvantaged families in
the Depression-ravaged countryside. Nevertheless, the Maddoxes spent
the next two years in Big Wills Valley.

Lula's discontentment grew acute. Early in 1931, she had resolved to
take seventeen-year-old Cal (her favorite, after Rose) and hitchhike to
California, leaving the others behind if necessary, showing just how
strongly she felt that urge to go west. Such an undertaking was plainly
absurd, yet she was dead serious. Charlie put his foot down. Faced with
her husband's adamancy and the daunting length of the journey, Lula
backed down.

As she appears in a photograph from around 1933, print dress hanging loosely from her, Lula was a heavy set, worn young woman, a quintessential Depression-era mother right out of a Dorothea Lange portrait.
But she was something more: an intense, dark-eyed dreamer sprung from
an oracular line, one who longed to cross the nation, by foot if need be,
to chase down her dream, ready to forsake all she had known, convinced
that a glorious and bountiful life awaited in the Golden State.

People who knew Lula unfailingly characterize her as domineering,
unbending, and iron willed. Yet her harsh methods often worked won-

ders and would catapult her and her offspring to the very pinnacle of their chosen field, hillbilly music. Indeed, given Arcany's reputation, one wonders how clear a premonition of their destiny Lula carried with her. Still, the time was not right. So she waited, certain that a chance to head west would come.

Charlie and Cal spent the winter of 1932–33 cutting firewood for "Old Man" Harper. "Papa and Cal, they cut cord wood all winter, for fifty cents a cord," recalled Fred. "Sawed it, split it and stacked it, and then Old Man Harper wouldn't pay them for it!"

The landlord simply refused to pay up—and who were they to argue? This was the final humiliation for Charlie. "He came home one night," said Don. "I guess the landlord had fired him. Anyhow, he said, 'How would you like to go to California?'" A grim, dark moment. To Lula, joy.

This was the chance she had been waiting for. She gathered together all their worldly possessions. "So we sold ever'thing we had," said Fred. "We sold two mules, got five dollars apiece for 'em. Sold a wagon, a milk cow, what little furniture we had, and we got thirty-five dollars for ever'thing."

News of their intended journey soon spread to Boaz, where it generated the shock waves of minor scandal. "Ever'one thought they was crazy!" said Alta. "And later, Mama said, 'Well, ever'body thought we was crazy anyhow, so there wasn't no difference!' That was just the way she said it. But she didn't feel crazy, said it was the happiest day of her life when they left and started west, because she was a-doin' what she had always wanted, and she knew it was better out west than it was back there."

CHAPTER TWO

If Boaz seemed a hundred miles from their cotton patch, then California might just as well have been on another planet. To everyone but Lula the prospect of walking and hitchhiking two thousand miles, with five children ranging in ages from five to seventeen years, was sheer folly.

"Mama's family thoroughly objected to her pickin' up all them kids and headin' for lands unknown," Rose said. "It was the greatest tragedy that had ever been! They tried every way to talk her out of it but she would not be persuaded."

Cliff and Alta, still hoping that Mama would undergo a change of heart, watched in amazement as the family prepared to leave. For Lula, it was all settled by the middle of March 1933. She ignored her married children's misgivings, spat at the tongue-wagging wives of Boaz, and took her family on the road, bound for uncertain glories in the distant West. She led them proudly.

The Maddoxes' journey west is a classic Depression-era tale. Although Rose was only seven at the time, the mark the trip left on her was indelible. Fred, then thirteen, would relate his vivid memories of the journey with great relish and colorful embellishment for the rest of his life. With winter barely over, the clan trooped out to the road and hoisted their thumbs. The first car to stop was a shiny new convertible belonging to yet another of Lula's brothers, Gideon Smith, a Boaz schoolteacher known to the kids as Uncle Gid. Told of their scheme, he burst out laughing.

"He thought it was the funniest thing he'd ever heard," Fred recalled. Uncle Gid carried them into nearby Gadsden, where they spent the night at Alta's. "I was scared—real scared," said Don. "I kept tellin' 'em we could just stay there with Alta. But we just kept walkin'."

The family walked all the next day—seven strangers was quite a load for most passing automobiles—and spent their first night outdoors in a pine thicket east of Birmingham. Beds were made up of pine needles for the kids, but Charlie spent the night bolt upright, tending a fire to scare off any would-be attackers or troublesome wildlife. Decades later, both Rose and Fred laughed at their father's fears—as if Charlie's reaction was unnatural, as if they had felt at home beneath the stars, under Lula's influence. Mama, for her part, slept like a rock.

"Then we headed to Birmingham, caught some rides and got into the city, which we had never seen," Fred said. "Got on a streetcar and naturally I had to get sick, stomach sick, from never ridin' in anything like that other'n a wagon. We were lookin' for Mama's [third] brother, Rufe, who worked in a steel mill there. He was married to a lady named Florence, so we used to call 'em Uncle Rufe and Aunt Flor. Get it?"

They reached Rufe's neighborhood by midnight, so confused from their urban ordeal that Lula was unable to find the house. Finally, a passer-by directed them and Aunt Flor put the exhausted family to bed. Rufe had just left to work the graveyard shift at a local mill.

"Next mornin' Rufe comes in," continued Fred, "and says to Aunt Flor, 'Know what I seen last night? The strangest sight—a man, woman and five kids, just a-walkin' with a suitcase.' And Aunt Flor says, 'Well, they're right in there!'"

The encounter was so bizarre that neither Lula nor Rufe was able to recognize a blood relative. Why should they? A young family living from hand to mouth on the road—such things simply were not supposed to be happening. In the months and years ahead, such scenes became common, but the spring of 1933 saw the very first stirrings of what would become a torrential exodus west. Typically, the Maddoxes were ahead of their time.

It had taken them three days to reach Birmingham—slow going. They had only averaged thirty miles a day, even with the occasional ride, and once outside the city they were in completely foreign territory. There would be no more relatives along the way, not even those whose mocking laughter was an anchor to the familiar.

From this experience, which would be the adventure of a lifetime at any age, the Maddox children received a unique education. It helped to shape a common bond and a singularly resilient family character, whose main characteristic was an inexhaustible drive. Always at the head of the column was Lula, holding her family so uncompromisingly in line as to seem almost cruel. She was a tough customer.

"My mother was hardcore," Rose said. "Mama was a very dominant, very determined person. She had this trip west in her mind, and it was exactly what she was going to do. When they made her, they threw away the mold . . . she was not a loving person. In all the time I can remember, I never heard her say 'I love you' to any of us kids."

Outward displays of affection were simply not Lula's style. As Cliff's wife recalled, "I remember Mama Maddox told me one time, 'Gordie, if I like someone, I wouldn't ever let 'em know it.'"

Nevertheless, Lula's absolute authority was tempered with compassion and love, even if she did not express those emotions in so many words, and the children returned her love unconditionally and with unquestioning loyalty. "It's just as simple as that," said Alta. "We never, any of us, ever thought of goin' against what Mama told us to do. I guess if she was still here I'd still be the same way. There was no gettin' around her. She was as good as she was strong, but she didn't let the good come out to other people because she didn't want anybody to know that she wasn't as hard as she acted."

Lula had to be hard. The life her family was forced to live demanded toughness. Fearful of depleting their thirty-five-dollar bankroll, the family took to begging for food. "It wasn't begging—just asking folks if they could spare any food for kids," insisted Rose. At first, Lula and Fred knocked at doors along the way, but as Fred recalled, he soon became the main agent for procuring handouts, usually with little five-year-old Henry accompanying, to present the most persuasive face of want.

"We was starvin' to death," Fred recalled of one particular scavenger hunt. "I seen a farmhouse, way over 'cross a field. I went over there and the lady gave us about thirteen biscuits, some of 'em with sorghum in 'em." He paused, as if still savoring the pressed cane. "While we was eatin' that, it started to rain."

The Maddoxes moved on, and as they did the children took in all the strange new sights through the curious prism of childhood. Gradually, the youngsters achieved a sense of order and understanding. From a world of flukes and uncertainty, they developed an entirely new vision of life off the cuff and on the move. But the journey was not without its terrors. Ten-year-old Don, in particular, remembered the march west as a disturbing ordeal.

"The closer we got to California," he said, "the more I began to hear about the earthquakes out there, and then I didn't want to go on account of them. I was scared."

Don's fears were by no means groundless. On March 10, 1933, just a week before the Maddoxes set forth, the biggest earthquake since San Francisco's 1906 catastrophe had struck California. At Long Beach, the epicenter, the quake measured 6.3 on the Richter scale. Back in Alabama, Lula, of course, would brook no such fears and pressed on. They continued to hitchhike, gaining most of their rides from passing truckers. Once they rode all night on a flat bed, Fred recalled.

"Well, get in," the driver told them, "but you'll have to ride with the cow."

"Come daybreak," Fred recalled with a laugh, "we sees that cow we were ridin' with was a buffalo!"

Finally, with swollen feet, they reached the Alabama state line—seven gaunt, dusty figures who had endured five days of walking, hitchhiking, aching, and pondering. They trudged toward Meridian, Mississippi, first city over the state line. On the outskirts of town they struck up a friendly conversation with a young couple who carried an infant child. This pair, in much the same fix as the Maddoxes, had apparently been out on the road for a while, and the couple was surprised to learn the Maddoxes were not using the best available means of transportation: jumping the freights. "Well, Mama said she didn't know how it was done," explained Fred. "So they said they would show us."

The friendly drifters led the Maddoxes through the railyard. Following a quick rundown on what to watch out for and an offer of sincere wishes for the family's good fortune, the Maddoxes had their ticket west. It was certainly appropriate that the began their boxcar odyssey in Meridian, for the city had been home to Jimmie Rodgers, whose words they had often heard Cliff sing: "When man gets the blues he grabs him a train and rides . . ." The Maddoxes would jump freights the rest of the way out.

From Meridian onward, through the open door of a slow-moving boxcar, the Maddoxes witnessed scenes of desolation unlike anything they had ever encountered. It was the Dust Bowl, where once-fertile field rows now acted as sluices, funneling streams of dust up into the sky as dark, boiling clouds. Watching the colossal clouds block out the sun, literally tasting dust gritty on their teeth, the Maddoxes must have felt a helpless, dull horror. But they trusted that they would pass through this wasteland, as Lula reminded them almost nightly, to a land of milk and honey where gold could be plucked from the trees.

Jumping boxcars was in itself a confusing and often hazardous pursuit. Without a degree of familiarity with the routes and yards along the way it was easy to lose a westward line. Fortunately for the Maddoxes, shortly after leaving Meridian they were discovered by a brakeman who, to the family's surprise, was sympathetic to their plight—and not a little surprised himself at finding a young family of seven aboard a boxcar. Once again, the Maddoxes' knack for enlisting unsolicited aid eased their worries.

"The brakemen were just great to us," Rose recalled, "because at that time there were no families riding the rails. They would help us out, switch us from one train to another and make sure we were going in the right direction. They brought us food, hot coffee, fresh milk, and all such as that. Often times they took us from the boxcars into the caboose, where we could sit. They had benches in there and a pot-belly stove with a fire burning when it was cold. And they made sure the others knew, ahead of time, that there was a family with young kids coming through. The brakemen and conductors would telegraph ahead. When we'd pull into a yard, the brakeman would come and get us and put us on the right train, because, of course, the railroad bulls were bad then, very bad."

"As we came through Shreveport, Louisiana," Fred recalled, "this brakeman who had got to know us kinda, he says 'There's a railroad bull down here, Texas Slim, and he's meaner'n a snake and you ain't gonna get through him. Tell you what—I'm a-gonna lock you in this reefer car and put a sealer on it. When we get out of the yard, this train slows down so another can pass, and I'm a-gonna unlock it.' And he did that very thing.

"So we went through Shreveport, and we could hear that ol' Texas Slim just a-cussin' and shootin' his pistol off. And after the brakeman opened that car up, them hobos started pilin' inside. Their clothes was half tore off from jumpin' barbed wire fences and everything else while Slim was shootin' at 'em. When we pulled out of town, there must have been fifty of us in that boxcar."

Similar scenes were played at every railyard. "You could hear them hobos runnin', hear 'em and see 'em," said Rose, voice rising with excitement at the memory. "With those railroad bulls shootin' at 'em! Of course, they were shootin' over their heads, not at them. They'd swing on at the edge of town and you hear 'em gettin' on, just laughin' at everything they'd run into gettin' away from these bulls!" The seemingly endless parade of bindlestiffs was in sharp contradiction to Lula's dime-novel vision, but none ever molested the family, and both Rose and Fred remembered the hobos with affection and respect.

The Maddoxes often rode straight through for two or three days, laying over occasionally in towns where Charlie and Cal would look for odd jobs. Anything that broke the punishing routine of rocking boxcars was welcome, and whatever Charlie earned helped preserve their thirty-five-dollar nest egg—none of which was spent on the entire journey west. During such layovers, the family stayed in hobo camps, always found a short distance from the railyards. "And there ain't nothin' tastes as good as that hobo stew!" said Rose with a smile.

After three grueling weeks riding the rails, the Maddoxes arrived at the trainyard in Glendale, California, a Los Angeles suburb. Sore, stiff, and exhausted, they tumbled out of a boxcar, huddled and squinting into the bright California sunlight. Word of their desperate journey, passed down the line by their impromptu support network, led members of the Salvation Army there to meet them. Seeing their dark uniforms, Don feared the worst.

"I thought they was goin' to run us in," he said. "But they actually took us in a big black touring car down to the YMCA for the night, gave us some groceries and things."

The Salvation Army put up Lula, Rose, and Henry in a hotel. Don and Fred stayed at the near crowded Y, while Charlie and Cal, for want of better accommodations, spent the night at the local jailhouse. Reunited the next morning, they timidly explored Glendale's prosperous streets. Fred, all fired up by the posh new surroundings, commenced to operate.

"Me and Don, he was about ten, we went over to this restaurant and asked 'em for somethin' to eat," he said. "There was this sorta rich family in there who heard what we was doin', and they seen Mama, Papa, and the kids outside. They made us go get 'em, and we set down in that restaurant and had the finest meal you ever seen. And that man offered Papa a job but Mama said, 'No. We're goin' up to the gold fields in Sonora.'"

Since it was her dream, not manual labor, that Lula sought, the family hit the rails again almost immediately, headed north this time to Bakersfield and points beyond. Upon leaving Glendale, however, they had a scare.

"When we went to the yard to catch the train out," Don said, "we were way out in the middle of the yard when here comes a freight this way and another one was comin' the other way and we got caught in between these two moving freights. We didn't get hurt or anything, but it was a real frightening experience for a bunch of kids." Lula rallied her family and they climbed aboard a northbound train.

"When we got up to Bakersfield, well, there was a restaurant there covered 'bout half a block," said Fred. "It was a Salvation Army deal, and ever'body ate there, 'cause anything on the menu cost one penny. You could get a bowl of oatmeal or glass of milk for one penny. So we stayed there for about seven days!" Even as Charlie and Lula used the time to study up and determine what they would need to strike it rich in Sonora, they realized they were in the heart of yet another Depression-ravaged state, amongst ever growing numbers of unlucky others.

They continued north to Oakland, on the eastern side of San Francisco Bay, arriving at one of the West Coast's saddest and most original answers to the rigors of the Depression: Pipe City. A settlement several hundred strong, Pipe City was the archetypal Dust Bowl refugee community, complete with a government and self-reliant sense of civic pride.

"Well, there was this company that made big culvert pipes," Don explained. "The hobos had made a city there. They lived in the pipes, and they had a city hall and a city council and all of that, made up of transients. There were three tents for the people that ruled the city; one of them was city hall."

"They had all these big cement pipes," added Fred. "Some of 'em big as a house, and they'd hang blankets over the front, make it up like a home. Ever' one of 'em was full. And the head man, he was a high-class hobo. He let us move into his own big pipe."

"The mayor of the city, he was a big fat German with an accent," Don explained, "and he said he could get whatever he wanted—all he had to do was call the newspaper, and he could get anything. So he called and told 'em there was a family stayin' there. They sent a reporter out, and I guess we were in the headlines of the *Oakland Tribune*."

They were page-one news, in fact. "FAMILY ROAMS U.S. FOR WORK," the headline read, with an accompanying photo of the family huddled together, looking weary yet determined. For the *Tribune*, they made great copy—a litmus of misery completely typifying the times. "A hitch-hiking family of seven found shelter at Oakland's 'Pipe City' after a cross country trip from Alabama," read the photo caption (which misspelled their surname as 'Maddux'). "They have 'ridden the rails' in their westward trek and hope to make their home in California."

"On account of that story," said Don, "a lot of curious people came out to see us. Mama, she wasn't too interested in that, and she took us kids out to a park some place to get away from the crowd. But Papa, he stayed and met the people. We got a few contributions out of that and, I guess, some job offers, but they didn't work out."

Lula hated the position she found herself in; very soon she had her fill of accepting handouts and waiting in breadlines. Rose recalled her fuming: "They can tell I was just there the day before!" In keeping with her romanticized notions of life in the Golden West, Lula offered what seemed the obvious solution to their problems: they would pan for gold. So the Maddoxes jumped another freight train, riding 150 miles northeast to the end of the line at Tuolumne. There, in the forested foothills of the Sierra Nevada, lay the region's fabled mother lode.

"That had been her dream, to go to California and pan for gold," said Don. "She didn't realize that most of it had been panned out years before. When we got up there, there was already a lot of transients panning. I don't think anybody was making any money." He laughed mirthlessly and continued: "It had been a lumber town, but it was all closed down due to the Depression. They had some cabins up there that were vacant and the owners let us use one.

"We didn't dig there. We went upstream and panned but there wasn't any gold, just a few flecks. I think after two weeks we had collected eighty-seven cents' worth or something. We were just marking time, to see if we could do anything with the gold fields. Me and Fred, we went out and hunted frogs, dressed 'em, and sold 'em to people for food."

For the kids, settling into life out west was easy. The weeks on the road had primed them, and for the rest of their lives they would continue to operate with a constant forward motion. The same relentless desire that motivated Lula now became a part of her children. She had instilled in them a desire not only to survive but to succeed. One thing that significantly set the Maddoxes apart from the thousands of other displaced Southerners coming into California was that they had arrived by choice—a choice that Lula had been moving them towards for years.

Although hard times were the catalyst for their migration, the Maddoxes were following their own personal star, not striking out in panicked desperation.

Yet in their shack amongst the thick forests of Tuolumne, Lula was stymied. Without the momentum of the road to carry her along and with hopes of easy riches panning gold revealed as hollow, she found herself off balance and at a loss for what to do next. For the first time in her life, Lula faltered.

CHAPTER THREE

Way up in Tuolumne, scratching out a meager existence from frog legs, hope, and eighty seven cents' worth of gold dust, Lula surveyed their circumstances with a gimlet eye. What she saw made her angry. The land of milk and honey proved to be as harsh and rough as every other state they had rolled through. She would not stand to have her family live that way.

The dire circumstances forced Lula to consider giving up her children, just so they could get a decent meal. "Well, we just, . . ." Fred faltered in recounting the memory. "It was so bad that we got to the point where it felt like we was just a-gonna have to put one kid here, another kid there . . ." The family itself started to crumble.

"I had started school up in Tuolumne, and became good friends with a little girl there, who was the daughter of the postmaster," Rose recalled, "and they wanted to adopt me, as a companion for their daughter. Well, back then, you could give your kids away for their betterment. There was no law saying you couldn't."

Lula resolved that Rose would live with the postmaster's family. She announced her decision, by flickering lamplight, in the old shack that the Maddoxes called home. Broken sentences, by way of explanation, to a hushed family feeling lost in a strange black forest two thousand miles from home, did little to reassure. This single act did more damage to the family than any of the troubles already suffered.

Rose continued, sharp in her description of how she felt about the arrangement: "What do you think? I got nice clothes, I got treated like a queen, and me and that little girl, we were the best of friends—until I moved in with 'em. Then we fought just like cats and dogs. We could not get along! I was the meanest, hatefullest thing that had ever been. I did anything I could get away with. I was just tryin' to get back home, is all I was tryin' to do. I was with them about a month, and then they had to give me back to Mama."

Over fifty years later, the story of Rose's separation from the family seemed a very uncomfortable one for Don and Fred to retell, and they hastened past it. For her part, Rose was happy at the time to be back with Lula and Charlie, yet Rose acknowledged that there was some suppressed anger and that the separation was the first seed sewn in what proved to be, decades later, a spectacular showdown between mother and daughter.

In the meantime, Charlie, now on a first-name basis with most of the railmen on the Tuolumne line, began riding freights fifty miles west down to Modesto, a small city at the northern end of the San Joaquin Valley. He spent each week there, working at various orchards and cotton fields, returning to the family every Friday night. Cal, Don, and Fred continued to fish the log-jammed lake, trading their catches for flour, lard, and whatever else they could barter for. The local game warden once caught Cal red-handed with some obviously poached wildlife. Following the resourceful example of his dad, Cal ended up swapping his catch to the warden for household staples.

Finally, Charlie secured a steady job at Talbot's Ranch, a large orchard just outside Modesto. The Maddoxes jumped their last freight and moved on to a whole new way of life as itinerant workers: more commonly known as fruit tramps. "They got us a tent, and we pitched it under a big peach tree," said Fred, "and we stayed right there until all the peaches and ever'thing had been picked. By that time, we had got us a car, a '31 Model A Ford." (Between the remnants of the thirty-five-dollar bankroll, and Charlie's "get-around" knack for obtaining credit, such an acquisition was easier than it seems.)

"Papa got a job on Talbot's Ranch," Rose remembered, "and we went down there, camped in the orchards, and the whole family worked the fruit. Mama discovered that the 'gold of California' was the fruit of the San Joaquin Valley—but she didn't know this until we went to work. So we started following the crops. . . . Up and down the Valley, all over California, down over in the Imperial Valley, and over by Salinas—'The Salad Bowl of the World'—all through there.

"We weren't going to school at the time, just following the crops. We'd stay until the season was over, and when it was pickin' time or cuttin' time somewhere else, we'd move on to there. We went as far as the Imperial Valley, and into Yuma, Arizona. We were living in a tent on a lake in Yuma, and I went to school on the California side, in Winterhaven. I went to school for as long as we stayed, which was about a year, I guess, living on the lake there."

She paused and laughed. "I remember it distinctly, because the school sent me to a dentist who pulled one of my teeth—which I'll never forget! We worked the crops in Winterhaven, and come fall we'd go back into the San Joaquin Valley, pickin' cotton and cuttin' grapes, all of that. And we'd camp out in the fields, in migrant camps, with all the other people who were in the same situation as us."

It was a life of turmoil—blazing sun, hard labor, bad food, canvas tents, human filth strewn carelessly on the earth around them, with very little chance of better times ahead. Scorching days, freezing nights, cooking on the ground, fetching tepid water in a rusty bucket. In their search for water, the homeless crowded around whatever stinking little well or stream that had been sanctioned for their use. Dust storms and thick, low-lying tule fogs were common in the Valley. People awoke with dew on their blankets.

"There was hundreds of 'em," remembered Fred. "Just hundreds in those camps. Sometimes you'd be lucky enough to get under a big shade tree, but if not . . . boy!" Trying as hard as humanly possible to remain civil in spite of privation, the fruit tramps clung doggedly to what few manners and morals that survived under such conditions.

The Depression was a monster no one could tame. As early as 1931, President Hoover had thrown in the towel, announcing, "We have done all that we can do; there is nothing more to be done." His successor, Franklin Delano Roosevelt, despite his ambitious socioeconomic programs, inspired the popular wisecrack, "New Deal? They forgot to cut the deck—that's what we say around here." The prevailing point of view, in the words of an anonymous unemployed laborer, circa 1935, was "We're about down and out and the only good thing I can see is that there's not much farther down we can go."

Yet for the Maddox kids, the privation was merely standard operating procedure. Asked if life had been better in Alabama, Rose scoffed. "What do you mean? It was always hard times as far as I was concerned. We were lucky to get what little cornbread and potatoes that we did."

California, at least, offered abundant fruit crops and a chance of employment in harvesting them. Back in Alabama, desperation and poverty redoubled for Cliff and wife Gordie, who finally resolved to head west and find the family. Even though Charlie and Lula sent occasional letters, their first-born son had no idea where to look for them, but set out regardless.

"We hitchhiked," Gordie recalled. "Took, oh God, a week or more, and Cliff carried his guitar the whole way out. He loved that guitar. We came first to Arizona, stopped there, and worked awhile." Cliff got a job in a restaurant and wrote back to sister Alta in Gadsden, saying, "If you know where Maddoxes are, let us know."

She did. "At that time, Maddoxes had left Modesto and gone to Yuma, to work the lettuce," said Gordie. "We were in Phoenix, so we met them there and all went back to Modesto together."

This was in 1934. Cliff and Gordie, mindful of Lula's distaste for in-laws, didn't wear out their welcome at Talbot's Ranch, but instead moved north to Hayward, where they got work at a Heinz pickling plant, remaining there for the next year. Cliff hooked up with a distant cousin, Kurt Tony, who had earlier come to California seeking his fortune. The pair began playing and singing regularly, and even broadcast from Modesto radio station KTRB for a time. Not long afterward, Alta's marriage (the first of three) fell to pieces, and so she too looked to rejoin her family. Pregnant, a single girl again, she boarded a Greyhound bus and set out alone for points west.

"I was expectin' my first baby when I came out to California," Alta remembered. "When she was ten months old, her father came out here and kidnapped her, took her back to Alabama. I never saw her for years and years. When she was seven years old, I think, he came through, a-goin' to visit some folks in Oregon, and they stopped by for a few minutes."

Though Alta was welcomed back into the family, she had misgivings about the arrangement. "My married life was never around my folks because Mama was very strange about that," Alta said. "She wanted ever'body under her control, and you know in-laws don't like to be controlled. So my married life was never around home."

Just as with Cliff and Gordie, Lula's domineering behavior had remained true to form. Alta's acceptance of this status quo was typical of the family, where married Maddoxes conducted an exasperated on again/off again relationship with the rest of the family, balanced by just enough mutual affection to keep both camps on civil terms.

Now the Maddoxes were established in California, and their lives followed the cycles of the crops and seasons, month following month, stretching soon into years. They endured a mean hand-to-mouth existence, lying flat-out on the dirt most nights, staring at the grimy ragged canvas tent above, moonlight slipping in and over the children's huddled forms. The family's sole luxury was their trusty Model A, which really only got them from one clamorous camp to the next, from one grueling stretch of the bosses' rows to another, then back to the campsite again.

The Maddox children continued to grow and sharpen their wiles, grasping any chance for pleasure or experience, taking on every challenge that confronted them. "When we's livin' in the peach orchard out north of Modesto," Fred recalled, "this other kid kinda got in with us, and he had a bicycle, just ridin' alongside us while we walked, you know. And I wanted to ride a bicycle so bad I couldn't stand it! So this kid come on down to our tent one day, and I got him and Rose and Don to go out and play in the orchard." A slightly devilish light gleams in his eye. "While they was out there, I got his bicycle, jumped on it—I had never even touched one—and I rode it for about a mile, then brought it back.

"Now, he never even knowed I rode it, but I wanted to do it so bad, it just happened. . . . I didn't even have to learn to ride it. We just fell into ever'thing, like later when we put Don on fiddle, 'cause it was what we needed, see? Henry was the same way, when we put him on the mandolin. They both just learned right onstage. See, it just seemed like we had to do it."

From Talbot's Ranch, they followed crops up and down the Valley, though Modesto remained their base of operations. They soon moved on to better accommodations. Rose described their new home: "We lived in a little place called Ingle's Camp. It was a three-room cabin. It had a kitchen, a bathroom, and a bedroom, and that was about the extent of it. It was there on the river, where they had several cabins, plus people camped out in tents, but we were lucky enough to get one of the cabins."

Out in the fields, baby Rose had it easy. "Mama and them was pickin' cotton. 'Course, I never picked cotton. I'd wait till Mama had her sack about half full, and then I'd get on it and let her pull me along. See, I was the only girl, little one, and I was real, real skinny. My legs was like two match sticks stuck up in a bundle of straw, and I always played off the fact that I was too little to do anything, and Mama let me get by with it. She never let me out of her sight, never did. I just did my own little thing, as long as I could get out of workin'!"

Gordie and Cliff moved down to Modesto in 1935. "We lived in an apartment. There was a big living room, and we had the bed in there," said Gordie. "Rose would show up and say, 'Gordie, let's lay on the bed and sing.' And I'd say, 'I don't want to sing,' but she'd yell, 'Come on!' and wouldn't shut up until I'd lay down on the bed and sing with her for a couple of hours. We'd lay there talkin', and then she'd want to sing again. She had a good voice even when she was small, and she was always a little cowgirl, with her hat and six shooter."

Asked what she was singing then, Rose replied, with some irritation, "I don't know! The songs they taught you in school.

"Henry and I started school in Modesto then, but the grade they taught music, they skipped me over; and they didn't know I didn't know music, 'cause I faked it. Them notes didn't mean a darn thing to me, and it wouldn't penetrate my thick skull. To me, they was just old dots down there on paper.

"I had been trying to sing for as long as I can remember. I'd sing to the top of my lungs, and I can still hear Mama sayin', 'Get out of here, Rose, I'm tired of listenin' to you! Go sing to your Daddy for a while!'" She began entering grade-school talent contests, usually taking second or third place. Often Cliff and Cal would bring guitars and back her up.

The Depression eased off the Maddoxes a bit around then, and an important force had entered their lives: radio. At night, they'd tune in powerful stations like XERA and XERB, broadcasting from just over the border in Mexico, and hear Patsy Montana, the Carter Family, and— Rose's personal favorites—the Sons of the Pioneers. (Listening to the Sons always seemed to touch off an enthusiastic yodeling spell in young Rose.) The songs were wedged in between bizarre commercial pitches for live baby chicks by mail, the all-purpose purgative Crazy Water Crystals, Dr. Brinkley's goat-gland treatment for impotence, and genuine wood chips from the Calvary cross. Cal heard a radio advertisement for a fourteen-part mail-order course in guitar playing, which included a small Martin guitar, just like the one Jimmie Rodgers played—all for seven dollars. With Mama's blessing he signed up and, unknowingly, pointed the family toward a new course.

Soon Cliff and Cal began singing and playing around the fire at Ingle's Camp almost every night when the family was not out following a crop elsewhere in the Valley. Rose and Fred sat staring into the flames and listened enraptured to the blue yodels and hymns, both children conjuring up their own fanciful visions. Neither one realized how close they were to reaching out and pulling down the very stuff—fantastic yet tangible stuff—from which their dreams were wrought.

CHAPTER FOUR

By 1937, the Maddoxes had settled into a routine. The family still divided their time between Yuma, Arizona, and other points in the Valley, but Modesto became the first real home they had had since leaving Smith's cotton patch in Boaz four years earlier.

Located at the northern end of the San Joaquin Valley, eighty-five miles east of the coast, downtown Modesto today remains much the same as it was the 1930s: a small, flat, dusty, sleepy city, crisscrossed with wide, sunbaked streets. There is little movement apart from the freight trains that still regularly hurtle through the center of town. Scorched and moribund, Modesto clings to the rapidly disappearing agricultural way of life. It is an isolated farming community, worlds apart from the cosmopolitan tilt of nearby San Francisco. As Alta, who now lives in nearby Ceres, puts it, "Modesto is the sorriest place, to do anything, that there is."

But for the Maddox kids back in the 1930s this town of sixteen thousand souls was the big city and increasingly they became drawn to its charms. Sunday mornings, Rose and Henry would rise at four o'clock to beat the other kids to a parking lot at the California Ballroom, where they collected empty whisky bottles left over from the previous night's dance, in order to turn them in for a penny deposit.

"When we'd get a dime apiece, we would go to the movies," said Rose. "One Sunday, the Sons of the Pioneers were appearing [in person] at the Strand Theater in Modesto, and I absolutely fell in love. I thought they were the greatest thing that had ever been. I was about ten years old, and after that I did anything I could in the line of singing. I was bound and determined that that was what I was going to do. It was my dream after I saw them. I thought if I could sing like that, I would never quit." Small wonder, as the Sons were then at their artistic peak, with a lineup that included a young Roy Rogers. Their soaring, intricate trio and quartet harmonies were the hottest thing going in western music at the time.

The Maddox children were starting to hammer out plans of their own. "By '37, we had got an uptown kinda house," said Fred. "We was payin' twenty-five or thirty dollars a month, but travelin' around the way we did, I stayed in the sixth grade for four years! When we settled in Modesto finally, by the time school let out, I was sixteen. Then you could quit school, and I had to quit and go to work. I was a newspaper boy, peddled the *Modesto Bee*. It was better'n nothin' at all. Made a penny on each paper I sold. It was pretty good. Didn't have no troubles, no worries. It seemed like you didn't care. You knowed you was gonna eat somethin'.

"About November of that year, it was colder'n the dickens, and me and Mama and Cliff and Cal went down by Tipton, pickin' cotton. Rose and Don and Henry and Papa stayed in Modesto. Just before we left there, I had gone to a rodeo and seen Logan Laam & the Happy Hayseeds, the only hillbilly band I'd ever seen, except for Cliff and Cal. This was a band out of Stockton, and I heard they got paid one hundred dollars for doin' it, and I thought, My God! I thought about that for days.

"So we get down there, east of Fresno, pickin' cotton, and I jus' couldn't do it. When I got out in that field, all I could do was think, Boy, if I wasn't here, what I could be doin'. . . . . Mama and Cliff and Cal was way ahead of me. Each had about a half a sack of cotton, and I had about ten pound in mine. I jus' sat down on that thing, and they all said, 'What are you doin'?' And I said, 'I'm a-thinkin'.' 'Well, what are you thinkin'?' I said, 'I'm a-thinkin' we should go into the music business!'"

Fred recounted this epiphany with a mischievous half-cracked leer, for he had not forgotten the lunacy of his announcement those many years ago. At the time, Fred (then eighteen) neither sang nor played, and he had little recollection of seeing Foncy perform back in Boaz. His only exposure to music, prior to the Happy Hayseeds, was as it had been presented to him, something purely social: family fun and games.

But he owned a jew's harp, and he could talk his way into (and out of) any imaginable situation, so naturally he figured he had it made. Cliff and Kurt Tony, after all, had already broadcast out of KTRB. From Fred's viewpoint, entering the music business was a simple, straightforward proposition. To anyone else with so little musical experience it would have been absurd.

"So I told 'em I'd be the manager and ever'thing, and they said, 'Okay. Let's do it.' Just took the tent down, got in that Model A, and left, right then."

What a drive up Highway 99 that must have been: dust boiling up behind the Ford, and conjuring up for Lula the outlines of a whole new dream. Just picture them: four pathetic, filthy, desperate field hands, rolling through the Valley's endless expanse—or were they four chosen native voices, called from the ranks of the Okie diaspora to translate that life into music? The beauty of the Maddoxes is that they were both.

Upon their return to Modesto, Fred called a family meeting. They dreamt up a repertoire and a name. Tellingly, Fred initially dubbed them the Alabama Outlaws. By way of rehearsal, he fast-talked them onto the air, as guests on radio shows at Stockton's KGDM (possibly with the Happy Hayseeds) and also in either Turlock or Merced. Encouraged by those first radio appearances, Fred next began scouting a suitable sponsor for a regular slot on radio—the best way for a hillbilly band to get exposure. He eventually settled on Rice's Furniture Store in Modesto, even though he had never set foot in the place. "It just looked so prosperous," he said. "One of those stores you look at and say, 'I want to trade there.'"

Fred had come in straight from the field, looking for all the world exactly like the typical transient Okie whom merchants all over the West Coast were refusing to serve. Fred Maddox, though, possessed a singularly persuasive, charming line of talk. With folksy repartee, a clockwork sense of timing, and a disarmingly exaggerated drawl, this sly, seeming simpleton knew how to charm and persuade.

"I went in there and talked to Mr. Rice. I must've talked for twenty or thirty minutes, and he never said a word—but I knew I wasn't going back to that cotton patch! Finally he said, 'Tell you what I'll do: I'll put you on the radio, but you have got to have a girl singer and you have got to do the talking. Just to listen to your voice is worth a million dollars.' And I said okay, although I'd never even seen a microphone, except at the Happy Hayseeds.

"So I told him we had the best girl singer there was. I didn't know that we had one for sure, but I knew that Rose could sing louder'n the dickens. And I told Mr. Rice that I wanted a bass fiddle. I'd seen 'em playin' one at the rodeo, and I really wanted it. So he ordered one for me, ten dollars down and ten dollars a month. When it came in, Cliff and Cal strung it and tuned it for me. The first time I played it was on the radio, and I still play it the way I did then."

Jim Rice arranged for the Maddox Brothers & Rose (as they now billed themselves) to broadcast over Modesto's KTRB from 6:30 to 7:00 every weekday morning. Fred, Cliff, Cal, and Rose took to the air, a quartet of ragtag fruit tramps with only a shred of experience in performing among them. In their first week on the air, the Maddox Brothers & Rose received over one thousand fan letters. And Jim Rice's furniture was selling at a healthy clip.

For novices, the Maddoxes took to their new trade with a high degree of professionalism. "Bill Bates, the owner of KTRB, thought they were great, and if anybody said anything bad about them, boy, he'd rake 'em over the coals," recalled Alta. "He'd say, 'I've had groups on my radio station that come up in the morning looking like they've just crawled out of bed—they're still wearing their pajamas and their hair isn't combed. But the Maddoxes come in here and look just like they're going onstage, and they act just like they're onstage when they are in the studio.'"

As Rose recalled it, the switch from riding on Mama's cotton sack to singing on the radio at age eleven was simple, nothing to get worked up about: "I can't really remember the first show. We just went in and hit it. I was doin' songs like Elton Britt's 'The Little Girl Dressed in Blue' and Patsy Montana's 'I Want to Be a Cowboy's Sweetheart,' things like that. I was yodelin' my head off!"

Charlie was quietly proud of his children; this was ample justification at last for leaving Alabama. For her part, Lula had found the business into which she would throw herself for the rest of her life, with amazing results. Fourteen-year-old Don, though, who would not join the band for another three years, was hardly confident about their future.

"I don't know," said Don. "I was kinda introverted, and I was kinda embarrassed because I didn't think they were that good. Actually, during the whole deal, I didn't think the whole band was that great, but it was a success, and you can't argue with success."

The family received no payment from either KTRB or Rice, and they soon realized that the radio exposure they got would pay off only through personal appearances. For a time they perfected their material in the KTRB studio (Lula discouraged rehearsals), while continuing to work other jobs. Initially, they used "Oh, Susannah" as their theme song, with Rose singing lead, the boys adding the harmony, Cliff on guitar, Cal on rhythm and harmonica (worn on a yoke, same as bluesmen of the day), and Fred on his brand-new stand-up bass. Besides performing the songs of Elton Britt and Patsy Montana, they also covered Sons of the Pioneers songs, sacred and gospel selections, and as Fred put it, "strictly country stuff."

"We did lots of yodelin' stuff," said Rose. "Fred would ad-lib all the commercials. He could read, but he was very, very slow at it. Or I would read the commercials and Fred would ad-lib behind me. The sponsor liked it okay, because all they cared about was whether or not we was sellin' their furniture, and we was."

Hillbilly music in California during the 1930s wasn't exactly a meal ticket. Only a handful of artists attempted to earn a living from it, and most of these were western entertainers based in Los Angeles. There, the top acts were the Sons of the Pioneers, who at that time broadcast over KFI; followed by Stuart Hamblen's Cavalcade of Stars (featuring Spade

Cooley, Wesley Tuttle, novelty virtuoso Herman the Hermit, and his son, Cliffie Stone); and, before the group splintered in 1933, Zeke Manners's popular Beverly Hillbillies (featuring Elton Britt, who later scored the first certified gold record by a country artist for 1942's "There's a Star-Spangled Banner Waving Somewhere"). Both of the latter groups broadcast over KFWB (then located in Warner Brothers' Sunset Boulevard studio) from a large soundstage that regularly filled to capacity with fans.

Other acts, like Sheriff Loyal Underwood & the Arizona Wranglers and Jimmy LeFevre & His Saddle Pals, helped fill Southern California's airwaves with western and hillbilly music seven days a week. In general, however, country musicians had to hustle to make a buck, for in the late 1930s most country music played in California was heard on radio or in the movies that featured singing cowboys like Gene Autry, Roy Rogers, Tex Ritter, and later, Jimmy Wakely and Eddie Dean. Although musically rich, California's heyday of sold-out "dance jobs" for country bands was still several years away and would not arrive until the Second World War, when the swing-shift audiences and western swing bands collided with spectacular box-office results, setting the stage for a postwar explosion of country music talent and activity throughout the state.

But in the San Joaquin Valley of 1937, Logan Laam's one-hundred-dollar rodeo gig was the prestigious exception, rather than the general rule of the local circuit. (The stringband called Laam's Happy Hayseeds was one of the West Coast's earliest established professional country music acts. Originally based in John Day, Oregon, the family group moved to Stockton in the 1920s, recording four songs for Victor during that period.) Apart from beer joints and saloons, there was only a handful of available venues. Most performers earned their money from tips, and the best circuit for this was to "follow the rodeos."

"Weekends, there was usually a rodeo near by, and we'd go into the town where it was being held, pick out a bar, go in, and ask the owner if we could set up and play for tips," Rose explained. "Well, that was free entertainment for them, so of course they said yes. Every bar in town had somebody playin' in it. The towns were loaded with cowboys and people there for the rodeo."

In those days, rodeos and "Frontier Days" fairs were major social events all across the Golden State. The handsome program booklet from Bakersfield's 1937 three-day Frontier Days festival at the Kern County Fairgrounds gives some idea of the money involved, the scale, and the drawing power of such events. Filled with historic photos of Kern County pioneers (and even lurid tales of the notorious Valley bandit Joaquin Murietta, whose career was cut short by decapitation), the program outlines an impressive schedule of events, including the Mammoth Western Parade, a Chuck Wagon Race, an Indian Pony Race, Wild Cow Milking, the Whiskerino Contest, the Judging of Silver Mounted Equipment, and the Bakersfield Cowgirl Banquet, just to name a few highlights. The Maddox Brothers & Rose were part of the spectacle.

Lula would take Cal, Cliff, Fred, and Rose in the Model A to wherever the nearest rodeo was, secure a barkeep's consent to perform, and drive (always with Cal at the wheel) to the edge of town, where they would pitch their tent and await dusk. The fiesta that had been, by day, in the hands of merchants and rodeo entrants was, by night, their exclusive territory.

Going hand in hand with any rodeo, of course, was some very high-spirited celebrating after the formal events were completed. The celebration usually took place in a jammed, smoke-filled beer joint, filled with the shouts of thirsty cowboys and farmhands, most of whom had been drinking since early afternoon. In front of that clamorous mob stood the Maddox Brothers & Rose, unshaken by the riot, running through their songs and responding to the din and cowboy yells blow for blow. And the focal point was Rose Maddox, all of twelve years old, singing at the top of her lungs for this mob of rowdies.

The modus operandi of the Maddox Brothers & Rose was quickly established. Lula was in charge. She would see to it that they had a bar to play in, supervise their musical selections, and get them out of town early enough to make their 6:30 A.M. broadcast on KTRB. This often meant an all-night drive back to Modesto. They followed rodeos as far south as Bakersfield and north to Susanville, three hundred miles of rugged road, much of it mountainous—playing for tips alone.

"It was better'n pickin' cotton, and we was eatin' better," Rose said. "And Mama was there the whole time—she was as strict with the boys as she was with me."

It was in Susanville, shortly after they began on KTRB, that the Maddoxes made the acquaintance of Jack and Woody Guthrie, a couple of singing Okie cousins who had also broadcast over Los Angeles radio station KFVD. The Guthries were working the bar across the street from the Maddoxes, and the Maddox boys (who as Rose recalled it probably had not heard any of the Guthries' broadcasts) listened and liked what they heard. The Guthries' sardonic song lyrics perfectly suited the Maddoxes' wise-guy style, particularly the two songs that eventually entered the Maddox repertoire, "If You Ain't Got the Do-Re-Mi" and "The Philadelphia Lawyer," which the Guthries originally titled the "The Dust Bowl Blues" and "Reno Blues," respectively.

Like Woody Guthrie (but without his portent and politics), the Maddoxes dealt in folk music, both traditional and contemporary. They created a unique style that not only preserved the symbols and traditions of the Old South but also looked eagerly to the future. They offered the music of home for people who no longer had a home. There was no commercial guile or social pandering involved. When the Maddox Brothers & Rose played, their music was a personal expression. Though crudely tailored for a mass audience, Maddox music was made the only way the Maddoxes ever heard music—as fun and games, pure and simple. In so doing, they stumbled into the hearts of displaced Okies and Southerners across the West.

At the center of this rapid metamorphosis—from fruit tramps to radio stars, from no-account hillbilly band to closely attended song stylists— was a twelve-year-old girl, protected by her mother and four big brothers. Rose had grown up on the road, and she was now seeing a whole new world, the wild side of life.

CHAPTER FIVE

The entire family became caught up in the new career Fred had staked out for them. By 1938, all earnings—even Charlie's, Alta's, and Gordie's—went into a common band-fund, carefully managed by Lula. Increasingly, the lion's share of earnings was spent not only on maintaining their Ford but also on appropriate stagewear. Lula felt it was important that, as bona fide professional musicians, the Maddoxes look the part. Following the leads of Patsy Montana, Gene Autry, and the Sons of the Pioneers, the Maddoxes were soon sporting the finest western wear Modesto offered, most of it purchased at Hub Clothiers downtown. Rose's cowgirl outfit typically consisted of three-quarter-length fringed skirt, worn with belt and suspenders, matching vest, scarf, hat, and boots. With her hat at a tilt, fringe shimmying as she swayed in time to the music, young Rose struck quite a pose. Her brothers wore cowboy hats, gaudy satin cowboy shirts with bandanna ties, new boots, and new jeans with three-inch rolled cuffs. Cliff was given to affecting an ascot, which Fred and Cal also took up, while Don, when he later joined the band, wore a slouch hat pushed over his face at a gangster's angle, with a scowl and dangling cigarette to match. Cliff, Cal, and Fred all cultivated long, full sideburns.

Rose was the only one in the band still attending school. She staunchly maintains that she suffered no effects, good or ill, from her newfound celebrity. Indeed, she seems to take for granted the entire chain of unlikely events that brought her into the music business, as if there were no other imaginable turn her life could have taken.

"I never was conceited, never had the big head," she maintained. "I was just a kid, and it was something I was told to do. Mama said, 'You're goin' to sing with us,' and I did it—what's to get a big head about?"

As a result of their success, minor as it was thus far, the family's self-esteem and sense of belonging was strongly enhanced. It was as if a great logic had been shown them: Lula's wild vision of a rags-to-riches life out west now appeared to be just over the horizon, as she had always insisted.

Charlie was relieved that his wife had found an outlet for the fierce, indomitable will that had already driven them two thousand miles from home. Both Gordie and Alta shared this relief, too. Lula rode herd on all kinfolk, but the band now gave her an entirely different focal point and a new set of rules to maintain.

Only Cliff felt at odds with the direction their lives had taken. Between Fred's self-appointment as manager and Mama's indisputable power over all, he felt that his rights as first-born (not to mention his musical experience and his being the first to broadcast on KTRB) had been inconsiderately overlooked. Still, he stuck loyally with the family, helping both Cal and Fred sharpen their skills and teaching them all he knew.

For their part, Fred and Cal made progress by leaps and bounds, experimenting with the percussive effects Fred's slap bass style produced and always searching for fresh material, new songs they could adapt to their style. They constantly pored over KTRB's library of old 78s, listening for and grabbing any songs that suited them.

The Maddox Brothers & Rose had tapped into a waiting radio audience. Shortly into the new year, as fan mail increased, KTRB added another daily broadcast by them, airing at 6:30 P.M. They were now scheduled at both prime hours for rural listeners. Fred began making it a point to announce their upcoming personal appearances as far ahead as possible. Although they had few advance bookings per se, he announced what towns they planned to appear in, and listeners knew they would be there. Soon they were also broadcasting regularly over Stockton's KGDM, where they had first hit the airwaves as the Alabama Outlaws just a few months earlier.

"We got mail, oh, a lot of mail, and people would usually call into the station, too, all day after the show," said Fred. "That was the main thing: if you didn't get no mail, you didn't stay on the radio very long, because your sponsor was in it only for the publicity. And when we weren't on the radio, me and Mama and Cal would be out lookin' for work—huntin' for it—and doin' pretty good." He laughed at the memory. "I was the booker, manager, and floor sweeper! Mama was really the boss, but she was a silent partner type of a deal.

"See, it's hard for brothers and sisters to work together, and since I was younger'n Cal and Cliff, they figured, 'Why should he boss me around?' But they couldn't handle the situation like I could, so I'd just do it through Mama. I'd tell her what we should do and she'd tell them, with no problems. If she hadn't've been there, we probably wouldn't have been together for any time at all."

Cal began writing songs tailored to their new western style. Even when they covered Sons of the Pioneers songs, it was with a jumped-up feel that really transformed them. With Fred's buzzing slap bass, Cal's demented, high-pitched chuckle and steady rhythm guitar, and Rose's clear, pealing vocals, they really shook up whatever material they chose. Their song list covered a lot of territory; it explored the blues with "I'm Talkin' 'Bout You," and also verged into proto-rockabilly territory on songs like "Small Town Mama" and their favorite, "Sally, Let Your Bangs Hang Down," learned from an old Clayton McMichen–Riley Puckett number in the KTRB collection that might otherwise have slipped into obscurity.

Apart from the KTRB library, the Maddoxes drew a great deal of material from songs they heard on other radio shows, such as Chicago's WLS "National Barn Dance." One of their favorites gleaned from radio was Wiley Walker and Gene Sullivan's "I Want to Live and Love," which, at Cliff's suggestion, later became the theme with which the Maddoxes would open and close each radio show. Though Cal continued writing songs, the variety of styles the band specialized in required as many different sources for songs as could be found. When they added to this musical program a solid helping of sacred and popular romantic songs, they had a recipe for success in Southern California, circa 1938.

While Western-style songs dominated their late 1930s repertoire, the Maddoxes' characteristic hillbilly boogie approach was unmistakably taking shape on their earliest radio programs, from 1939 and 1940 (which were recorded on radio transcription discs for later broadcast). "I'm Talkin' 'Bout You," with its call-and-response chorus and "dirty blues" verses, while hardly atypical for country performers of the day, was a clear signal of their affinity for black-oriented material. As the band matured, boogie was to become a staple ingredient, one that Rose insisted was key to their style from the beginning. While some of this bluesy influence can no doubt be traced back to Foncy, Cliff was hardly a conduit for it. He remained true to traditional song and, while enamored of Rodgers-style blue yodels, Cliff actively resisted Cal and Fred's desire to boogie. Like the Delmore Brothers, who would popularize country boogie in the late 1940s, the Maddoxes found the eight-beats-to-the-bar boogie rhythm was a natural style for them; they began to incorporate elements of it into their brand of country music, years before its postwar rise to prominence.

Success did not come without hard work, and the family kept pushing forward. In a sense, the Maddox Brothers & Rose never really left the road. After their trip west in 1933, travel had become a way of life. Home was only a secondary base of operations. Being back in Modesto meant the KTRB studio, going through dedications and greeting fans, which left little time for relaxing afternoons with Papa or for visits with Gordie and Alta.

Now broadcasting twice a day on KTRB and twice weekly over KGDM in Stockton, they were also making as many live appearances as possible. Between radio and saloon dates, they averaged more than fifteen shows a week. They had established themselves as a dependable act all over the San Joaquin Valley. Now they needed an extra boost, just a slight advantage to break out of the local circuit. Though the band had appeared as far north as Susanville, they were hard pressed to expand their draw outside of the Valley, even with the power of radio to advertise such appearances. True to Maddox form, that chance soon turned up.

The state of California celebrated its centennial in 1939, and accordingly the Sacramento State Fair that year was the most elaborate ever mounted. Among its numerous events was a hillbilly band competition, held to determine the best group in the state.

"Some lady down in Stockton, a fan of the band, told us about this contest," Fred recalled. "She said, 'I'll get you into it,' and she got us the entry form. So we filled it out, got on the contest—found out there was fifteen other bands on it—we didn't even know there was that many bands in the whole country, let alone the state!"

They strapped Fred's bass fiddle atop the Model A, packed up their best duds, and drove to Sacramento to face the competition. Years later, Fred and Rose spoke of it as a trifle, claiming they were not at all nervous, but they must have known—sizing up the other bands—how important it was to win, to prove they were best in the West. Lula must have been fairly shaking with anticipation as she sent her brood out like gladiators into the arena.

The Maddoxes took the stage and tore through "Sally, Let Your Bangs Hang Down," captivating the crowd and the judges alike with the song's risqué lyrics and rocking rhythm. Set off with Cliff's guitar runs, Fred's dancing slap rhythms, and the pure harmonies of Cal and Rose on the chorus, the song was bound to be a winner. Between the music and the energetic clowning of the youngsters, none of the other fifteen entrants stood a chance. The Maddox Brothers & Rose officially became California's best hillbilly band.

As their prize, the band was awarded a one-year contract on Sacramento radio station KFBK, part of the McClatchy Broadcast Network, which reached all of California (including KFWB in Hollywood), Oregon, Washington, and parts of Nevada and Arizona. A one-year sponsorship by Anacin pain reliever made this possible, giving the act the credibility and exposure necessary to expand their audience.

The family was elated and prepared to relocate to Sacramento, although Charlie, Alta, Cliff, and Gordie would stay in Modesto. Since the Maddox Brothers & Rose would continue to broadcast on both KGDM in Stockton and KFBK, they were able to work-in occasional visits with the rest of the family—as their schedule allowed. Performing now took complete priority over domestic family life.

"When we started on KFBK after we had won the contest and started playin' around up there, that's when we felt like we were going to be a success, that things were working out for us," Rose said of the summer of 1939. "We lived out at Del Paso Heights in North Sacramento, Mama and us kids. Papa was working down in Modesto, so he and Alta stayed there.

"We played a lot of places around the Sacramento area, Marysville, Yuba, all those little towns. They'd charge twenty-five cents to get in for men, and ladies were free. We'd usually get 50 or 60 percent of the door, something like that, which didn't amount to a lot, but back then, it was a lot! We played at dance halls, just the three of us—Cal, Fred, and myself—just guitar, harmonica, and bass.

"Don was just learnin' to play the fiddle then, even though he was older than me. He would come out, stand in the background, and he'd play till our first intermission, of which we'd only take a couple a night, and then he'd go out to the car and sleep. Of course, I had to stay onstage and sing all night."

Lula had realized it was necessary to augment the act's sound, and it was she who appointed Don as fiddler. Resentful and embarrassed at having to play onstage while he was still learning, he would often perform with his back to the audience for an entire set.

"Well, they said they needed a fiddle player," he recalled. "Got a fiddle someplace and said, 'Here, learn to play.' I was self-taught, and I don't really like to play the fiddle. . . . I just do it when I have to." In time, he would develop a confident "Don Juan" stage persona and a screeching "mule" fiddle to boot, which would become an integral part of their stage show.

When Cliff was not working elsewhere in the Valley (usually with popular Modesto western swing band Al Brown & his Alabamans), he would join his siblings on the bandstand, but he was not often available. So the Maddoxes began experimenting with several sidemen, trying first an accordion player ("Art somebody or other," who was pretty good, according to Rose) and then a guitarist. Seeking a fuller sound and never considering adding a drummer (a player then relegated, by and large, to the sphere of jazz and swing), Rose took up her own bass fiddle, after seeing Modesto's leading country band, Arky & His Hillbillies, in which Arky's daughter Juanita Stark played bass.

The two young women became friendly, and Juanita not only taught Rose, she also helped Fred refine his technique. Roy Nichols, who played guitar with Maddox Brothers & Rose in the late 1940s, recalled that "Rose played great bass; she didn't slap it like Fred, but she could play the chords real nice. Fred'll tell you himself that he don't know no chords. He just goes up and down, slappin' it. Fred, when he was singin', she was playin'. He'd usually hold it in his hand, and then just slap it durin' the breaks."

With the steady work afforded by the McClatchy contract, the Maddoxes honed their act, sharpening not only their sense of timing and delivery, but also their uniquely relaxed approach to broadcasting. The Maddox Brothers & Rose were formulating their famous "combination show and dance," in which the bandstand became a forum of almost theatrical entertainment. Fred's natural proclivity for ad-lib wise-cracking developed into stinging banter with Rose and Cal, and his casual drawl (which had landed them on KTRB in the first place) soon became widely imitated by other Valley announcers. Indeed, traveling the San Joaquin Valley today, you can stop at virtually any gas station or cafe and find numerous elderly fans of the Maddoxes who are able to recreate, word-for-word, Fred's stock introductions ("Give us a gre't big smile, will ya?").

For years, most commercial hillbilly bands featured a comedian, generally a baggy-pants clown who played the bass. He was the "Toby" character of medicine-show tradition, who lampooned the backwardness of rural life. Fred recalled that Logan Laam's bass man was typical of the type: "Like if they asked him what time it was, he'd pull out an alarm clock on a watch chain." In marked contrast, Fred played the role of wise guy rather than buffoon. When the entire band joined in with a barrage of repartee, hollering, pantomime, and magic tricks, it really set them apart from the stock hayseed gags of the barefoot Beverly Hillbillies in L.A. or Roy Acuff's Smoky Mountain Boys in Nashville.

Life was good for the Maddox family in 1940. "We got rid of our tent and got two houses, one in Sacramento and one in Modesto," said Fred, laughing at the memory. "That's a good 'un—got rid of our tent and got two houses, one in each town!"

The division was Lula's idea. It allowed her to concentrate on ruling the band, personally and professionally, without the distractions and petty annoyances that other family members might bring on. Also, because of her obsessive devotion to the band, she and Charlie were drifting farther and farther apart. The arrangement was a relief for Charlie, Alta (who had just remarried), and Gordie. It enabled them to enjoy the family band's success with fewer of the irritations that so often accompanied Lula's ways.

Keep in mind this family's origins in the parched sod of Alabama's back hills, where the responsibility of raising a family had to be viewed along the lines of basic survival, a stark, almost tribal existence. Early on, Lula adopted the authoritarian approach that typified her every action, partly out of maternal instinct and partly perhaps out of an innate need to be dominant. This same background also influenced the children's stoic, faithful, and unquestioning loyalty to her. Even with that loyalty and obedience, conflicts still developed from time to time, and almost all of them were related to their newfound popularity as entertainers.

CHAPTER SIX

With war breaking out in Europe, America went routinely about business in hopes that direct military involvement would remain unnecessary. For the Maddox Brothers & Rose, 1941 saw a full schedule of radio work and constant travel to gigs up and down the state. That year also found them realizing what well-known, if not downright famous, figures they had become throughout California.

One particular fan, who attended every appearance the group made in the remote Marysville-Yuba City area, zeroed in on Rose. This was Enoch Byford "E. B." Hale, a diehard supporter who never missed an opportunity, at the many dances he attended, to greet the family—especially Rose—and pass the time of night, inevitably working in the request for a date with the yodeling cowgirl. She was fourteen when they first met; he was twenty-one.

Hale somehow managed to avoid Lula's wrath and became accepted as a tolerable presence, partially because of the regularity with which he would turn up. He came from the small town of Wheatland, California, and he found the sight and sound of spunky young Rose as exotic and mesmerizing as that of any Hollywood screen siren. One night in Sacramento, Hale's persistence paid off.

Fred actually managed to persuade Lula to allow him and a girl friend to accompany Hale and Rose on a double date at the skating rink.

"I didn't really know the man, except to see him around the places where we played," Rose said. "I went out with him that one time, when we was on KFBK. We went skatin' with Fred and his girlfriend. Just went to the rink and that was it. At that time, Mama wasn't as possessive on me like she became later, and Fred had talked her into it. Of course, he was right there with me. Mama was always strict, but she would let me go out at night and stuff."

The hectic Maddox schedule left little time for Hale to establish any serious hold as a suitor. When the McClatchy contract expired, it was immediately renewed, and the Maddoxes enjoyed constantly expanding circles of popularity throughout 1941. Even then, Rose's voice had the command and authority which lies at the core of her talent, as radio transcription recordings from the period testify. There is an air of carefree exuberance in her voice—a combination of innocence and determination—that is very affecting. Rose certainly must have won the hearts of every man within earshot. Yet as long as the four big brothers looked after her, her life was strictly business. Nothing could come between the Maddoxes' and their career—except the Selective Service.

Immediately after the Japanese sneak attack on Pearl Harbor on December 7, 1941, all the Maddox boys registered for the draft. Early in 1942, both Fred and Cal were called up by the army. Fred became a mess sergeant. Stationed in the Pacific, he organized his own hillbilly band, the Khaki Mountaineers, and somehow managed to lug a bass fiddle from atoll to atoll, honing his slap style to a fine art in the process. Cal was sent to Australia where, as he later joked, he had "sold hops to the kangaroos." Don followed them into the military the next year and wound up stationed in India. Cliff was exempt because of rheumatic fever, and Henry was still too young to serve.

The family band was in tatters; fortunately, Don's onstage training had paid off. He and Cliff, with Rose playing bass, began to work club dates, but the radio programs were put on hold. Cliff was by far the best musician in the family, and it was a shame the McClatchy network agreed to let them go. But without Fred—the glue that held Maddox Brothers & Rose together on the air—the remaining trio simply did not feel up to the task.

"We were in Sacramento when Fred and Cal got drafted, and I hadn't really gotten into the band," said Don. "I'd sing on the radio once in a while, play the fiddle a little bit. After they got drafted was when I really got into it. And the owner of a club we had played in Salinas came over one day after they were gone, and said he needed a band there at the Rodeo Club. I guess that's when I really started to play the fiddle, because we didn't have any other lead instruments at the time—just guitar, fiddle, and bass. We just played at that particular spot, because we had gotten very popular there."

Even prior to the war, the Maddox Brothers & Rose worked occasional weekends at the Rodeo Club, always filled with servicemen from nearby Fort Ord. They would take the stage early Friday night and remain there until closing time. "We'd play for hours at a stretch," Fred recalled of their prewar appearances there. "If one of us had to go to the rest room or break for somethin' to eat, why, he'd just get off and go, then fight his way back to the bandstand." They were still playing for tips at the Rodeo Club, so the longer they played, the better their take. It was one of their most grueling gigs, and they worked it regularly.

Among the noisy herd of servicemen was none other than E. B. Hale. Having enlisted, he was now stationed at Fort Ord. "I really liked E. B.," Don said. "To me, he seemed like a nice guy. He'd laugh at all my jokes, and that's the important part, if they laugh at all my jokes! We were just friends at the time, and all of us liked him, except Rose. I don't think she liked him as well as the rest of us, but she was the one he was after."

It was at the Rodeo Club that Hale began proposing marriage to Rose. She wanted nothing to do with him and made this quite clear to all who would listen. Lula, however, saw the matter differently. She saw E. B. Hale's marriage proposal as a way to maintain her hold over the family band. She knew, with Cal and Fred out of the picture, that Cliff wanted control of the band and also that his wife, Gordie, herself a fine singer, could only bring trouble to the established order. Lula also realized that

Don, with neither experience nor passion for the music, would be no help; Henry, still a child, was too young to back his mother.

Rather than deal with an in-law that threatened her authority, Lula instead opted to take one of her choosing, one with a distinct and demanding career of his own, enabling her still to call the shots in Rose's career. For the second time in Rose's young life, acting in what she believed to be the family's interests (as in Tuolumne), Lula turned her daughter's life upside-down and thrust her into a desperately unhappy situation.

Hale had had the foresight to propose in Lula's presence, and only a few weeks passed before the final decision was rendered. "So after the boys had gone into the service, Mama come to me one day and said, 'The boys ain't here to look after you. I think you should marry him,'" Rose recalled. "I just set down and wrote E. B. a letter, saying that I would marry him."

Speaking of the marriage nearly fifty years later, Rose seemed as unsure about her decision as she was then. "I'd never been with a boy in my life. I didn't even know what you did to make babies—I thought you could have babies from kissin'!" She laughed, incredulous at her innocence. "I didn't know what men and women did until the night before I got married. Mama and Alta sat me down and told me these things, and I about died. I could not believe that stuff like that went on. I just about died, and I was ready to back out, but Mama said, 'No. You're a-gonna marry him.'"

"I guess Rose thought she wanted to be married," said Don, "but once she got married, she really did not want to be, not to him anyway. I think the reason Mama talked her into it was that she felt Rose, who was sixteen, would start gettin' biological urges, and she felt that she should get married for that reason, so that she wouldn't do anything stupid like a lot of us do. And E. B. was a nice guy. I'm sure he loved her and all that jazz, but I don't think Rose loved him. That was the main problem."

Rose confirms it: "There was love on his part, but there never was on mine, because, like I said, I didn't really know him."

In Rose's collection of photographs, there is one showing her wearing a print blouse and pleated skirt, clutching a small purse and standing arm-in-arm with E. B. Hale. Her eyes are swollen with tears, there is a sad, forced smile on her face, and she appears ready to turn tail and head for the hills. Her handwritten notation reads: "June 14, 1942, 2:00 P.M., Reno, Nevada. Sgt. E. B. Hale and Rose Maddox just before marriage." E. B. is beaming and holds the license in his left hand, like a prize.

She had driven up to Reno with E. B., Lula, and Don. In Modesto, Charlie was unaware of what was happening, which indicates just how far removed from Lula's sphere of operation he was. "I went with them to Reno," Don recalled. "Me and Mama took 'em to get married. Well, they came out of the courthouse, and for lack of anything better to say, I asked Rose, 'How does it feel to be Mrs. E. B. Hale?' And she said, 'I don't like it!' and she started cryin'. I guess E. B. was really embarrassed at that."

Rose cried all that afternoon as she and E. B. drove a hundred miles west to Roseville, on the outskirts of Sacramento, to spend what she describes as "a very unpleasant night. Yes, he was very nice and understanding, but things just did not work out."

Don also said that personal hygiene accounted for at least one problem the newlyweds had: "Rose didn't want to sleep with E. B. because his feet smelled, and she used to try and get him to wash his feet. He'd go, 'Well, goddamnit, if I've got to wash my feet, I may as well take a bath.'"

Rose and E. B. moved to the Presidio at Monterey, living in a furnished house provided by the army. For Rose, marriage was shaping up as a thoroughly miserable experience. The couple argued often, and E. B. spent most evenings out drinking with his pals, which further strained relations. Just sixteen, she felt isolated and cut off from her family, now splintered into several different camps, with her brothers halfway around the world.

Then she heard the government was offering free land in Alaska to anyone who would homestead it. With the band's future in doubt and her natural pioneer's inclination, Rose wanted nothing more than to take advantage of the offer. E. B. would have no part of the scheme. It was a rocky start and things didn't improve.

Before very long any trust between the couple completely dissolved. "Well, before she was married," said Don, "Rose had kept a diary of her personal life, and of course, a fourteen-, fifteen-year-old girl will put all of her secret thoughts and yearnings into her diary, and of course, no one else should see that. E. B. took that away and read it, and he probably read a lot of things that he shouldn't know, and didn't want to know, and that probably drove a wedge between them. After that they didn't seem to get along very well."

Eleven months after the wedding, Rose learned that she was pregnant. When she told her husband, he looked her in the eye and said: "It ain't mine."

Rose is still at a loss to understand his denial. "This is the stupidest thing you ever heard in your life! There was a guy next door, he lived there with his wife, and he came over one morning after E. B. had gone down for his duty, and this fellow asked if he could borrow a cup of sugar. I told him yes and gave it to him. I didn't know him except to see him and his wife. I had told E. B. about it and he didn't say nothin'. Then I found out I was pregnant and he says, 'It ain't mine—it's the guy next door's, the one who came over and got the cup of sugar from you.'"

In a situation right out of a country blues, they played out the final scene. "He said, 'It ain't mine—you can go ahead and move back home.' So I did what I was told to do, and I spent my whole pregnancy time at Mama's. And I never seen him in that whole time. He'd call once in a while, but that was it."

On December 10, 1943, eighteen months after the wedding, Rose entered MacPheeter's Hospital in Modesto and gave birth to her only child, a son she called Donald Douglas Byford Hale (named after airplane mogul Donald Douglas, an updated version of Lula's tradition of naming her sons after automobiles).

"The night Donnie was born, Mama called E. B. and he wasn't there—he was out drinkin', so she left word for him to call. He called later. He was drunk, and she told him I'd had the baby. He didn't care because he had got mugged that night."

As Lula lay the phone down, what was she thinking? Her scheme had failed, and it left Rose a spurned woman, rearing a child whose father flatly denied any paternal responsibility. Rose felt betrayed and wanted nothing further to do with the man.

"He did come over one night when I was still in the hospital. He seen me and Donnie. I don't really remember that—I couldn't have cared less. And then after I got out of the hospital, he came over a couple of times and wanted me to take him back. I said, 'No. If you can't stand by me when I need you, forget it.' And that was the end of it. We remained friends, and I didn't divorce him for several years because I needed the money every month, and he couldn't get out of paying it, because he was in the military and they took it out of his paycheck every month. That's the reason we stayed married."

Rose seemed uncomfortable as she related this story. "He would come around once in a while, for a few years, after Donnie was born and I was back in the music business. Of course, Donnie didn't know him and would run to me a-bawlin' because it was some strange man wantin' to hug him. I'd explain to him that it was his dad, but E. B. would just stay a while, then leave."

The experience left Rose numb and confused. None of her discontent was directed at Lula or Donnie; they were family. The only real effect it had was on her affections for men: love, sex and marriage became something to forget, ignore, and avoid. She turned instead to music. Before Donnie was six months old, he was already being bundled into the Ford and driven up and down California to various auditions. Rose heard that Roy Acuff was in Hollywood, shooting a motion picture, and that he needed a girl singer.

"I called the studio, and they referred me to where he was staying, a motel out on Ventura Boulevard," Rose said. "And I asked him if I could come down and audition. Donnie was maybe six months old at the time, if that old, maybe four months, and Acuff said, 'Sure, come on down.' So I came down and Mama kept Donnie out in the car while I went in and auditioned. We sang all afternoon, but he finally said he was sorry, that he had Rachel [Veach] with him, a girl singer and she's good, and there was no need for another."

Why Acuff agreed to have Rose come all the way to Los Angeles for an unnecessary audition is an interesting question. He was probably interested in seeing what kind of hillbilly talent there was in California. At any rate, it was an honor to be received by a major national star like Acuff. Whatever his motivations were, it didn't amount to anything as far as Rose was concerned. She was able to get occasional work with Arky & His Hillbillies, playing bass and singing a song or two. She sang a little more and also played bass for Dave Stogner, who led a popular western swing band out of Fresno.

Rose would appear there on Saturday nights at the Big Barn, a popular night spot in the central Valley city. Stogner was a pivotal figure in San Joaquin Valley country music; his band played a rough, hillbilly swing that relied on the rhythm section and simple melodies, without the emphasis on free-form, jazzy soloing, or the saxophone and trumpets that Bob Wills used so effectively. By the mid-fifties, Stogner even broadcast his own weekly television show from the Big Barn, welcoming guest artists like Ferlin Husky and Ernest Tubb. But in the mid-1940s, he could only do so much for Rose.

Still, these jobs were far from steady, and Rose aggressively pursued any lead that she heard of. With a musicians union strike that halted all recording between August 1942 and October 1943, activity in the country field was stagnant; only those Los Angeles-based performers able to break into movies, or who could continue working the radio jobs they already had, enjoyed commercial success. Most of these were smooth western entertainers like Jimmy Wakely and Eddie Dean, or long established broadcast stars like Stuart Hamblen, who had been a powerful force on Southern California radio since 1929.

The Santa Monica Pier swing-shift dances, organized by Hollywood disk jockey and promoter Bert "Foreman" Phillips, were phenomenally successful, drawing thousands of defense workers. Though these marathon affairs employed as many different bands as were available (in the process bringing Spade Cooley to the fore), Rose, now seeking work as a single, had little hopes of landing steady work through Phillips. One of the prime motivating forces in California country music, Phillips was promoting concurrent events in up to seven different ballrooms. After the phenomenal success of the swing-shift dances, Phillips continued promoting dances all over Southern California. Before his retirement in the early 1950s, he had his own television program that was carried by KTLA—a live, three-hour show that aired five days a week. For Rose, however, as a girl singer looking for work in the male-dominated country field of World War II–era Los Angeles, there was precious little need for her.

On discovering that Bob Wills, who relocated to the San Fernando Valley in late 1943, was looking to hire a girl singer, Rose put her energies almost full time into trying to land that job. Rose, Lula, and Donnie followed the Texas Playboys all over the state, trying to set up an audition. Although Rose discussed the matter with Wills on several occasions, nothing ever came of it because of Lula's overbearing presence. Wills appreciated Rose's talent and personal charm but would have nothing to do with a package that included her watchdog mama.

"And I was so stupid at the time," said Rose, "that it wasn't until years later that I figured out why." After investing so much time and energy into chasing Wills, the last time she met with him Rose got so mad that she blew up and shouted, "When my brothers get back from the service, we're goin' to start up again and put you out of business!" In the years that followed, Wills often retold this story, invariably ending with the remark: "And you know something? They damn near did, too."

CHAPTER SEVEN

For Rose, the remainder of the war dragged on interminably, blur-ring into a dreary succession of hot, still afternoons. They were all the same. With Donnie down for his nap, there she sat. Houseflies, shining blue and green, floated in lazy spirals around her. The silence, broken only by the flies' sputtering buzz and the freight trains rolling through town, hung all round her. The situation was maddening.

Although she loved Donnie a great deal, her failed marriage and the dull routine of motherhood created a feverish urge to return to singing full time. The abortive meetings with Acuff and Wills had only compounded her frustrations. Simply playing bass for Arky Stark or Dave Stogner, despite the occasional vocal turns she con-tributed, left her yearning more and more for the spotlight.

Lula knew what Rose needed and laid plans, making sure Henry rarely put down the mandolin she thrust upon him shortly after his brothers shipped out. Though he received some instruction from Cliff, his playing (like Don's and Fred's) was primarily self-taught, and Lula saw to it that he would be proficient enough to keep up with his brothers when they returned. All three sent home most of their pay the entire time they served overseas, and Mama salted the money away for use upon their return. There was no question about reforming the band.

Victory over Japan finally came in August 1945, and Cal and Fred were each discharged just in time for the holidays. "I got out of the service on November 30th of '45," Fred recalled. "Cal got back just before Christmas, and Don [who had been drafted in 1943] didn't get back until January or February."

With the exception of Don, the entire family gathered for the holidays, and Modesto was never a better place for the Maddoxes than it was that Christmas, filled with tales from afar, gifts, laughter, and, most importantly, plans. Fred and Cal wasted no time in appraising Henry's new-found musical skills.

"Henry had started playin' by that time, on the mandolin," said Fred. "He'd took it on his own, learned it on his own, and so we went back to work. Cal had the harmonica, using the yoke on his neck, and we used Henry as lead, on the mandolin." Favorably impressed, Cal and Fred began making calls to radio stations and sponsors, assembling song programs, and preparing to prove themselves, once again, to be California's best hillbilly band.

In almost no time at all, they were back on the air. On December 29, 1945, the Maddox Brothers & Rose returned to the studio at KGDM in Stockton, with seventeen-year-old Henry on mandolin. Surviving transcription recordings of that December 29th broadcast reveal the band already greatly altered in their approach. (Arhoolie Records issued this postwar performance, along with a 1940 KFBK show, on Arhoolie LP 5028 and CD 447.) With the addition of the mandolin, and with more concentrated leadership from Cal and Fred, the band displayed a tougher attitude, with a more pronounced Southern hillbilly style.

This harder sound was a direct result of the Maddoxes' own forceful personalities. The band never rehearsed; they simply played. Who they were and what they felt spilled out spontaneously in their music. Such a guileless approach allowed them total self-expression, and their close-knit kinship made rehearsals redundant.

"We just figured out the key we'd play stuff in," Fred explained. "That's all we did. Cal made the program out, I'd have Rose to do all the dedications, and I'd do all the announcin'."

They simply decided what they would do, settled in, and did it. So it was with their return to radio. When they settled on Wiley & Gene's "I Want to Live and Love" as their theme song, that was it for the next ten years.

Though the Maddoxes picked up the vast majority of their material from outside sources, they felt it was absolutely imperative to rework each number into their personal style. They did exactly that, developing over the next few years a set of standard arrangements upon which they would construct new versions of familiar songs. The Maddox Brothers & Rose created their own distinct interpretations of current hillbilly hits, particularly those of Hank Williams. In their wild spontaneity, the Maddoxes' versions of Williams songs verged on staged chaos, and yet their renditions maintained a hardscrabble realism that made an emotional impact.

The Maddoxes were in fine form from the moment they returned to KGDM. They kicked off their reunion show with a rapid-fire "I Want to Live and Love," Henry's mandolin taking a simple, steady lead, and Fred's slap bass sounding much more forceful than on their prewar KFBK shows. Most prominent of all in the musical mix was Cal's rhythm and harmonica.

During the opening number's bridge, Fred stepped to the microphone, sounding much older and more worldly than he had before shipping out, even if the patter still sounded mighty familiar. "Yes, sir an' howdy, folks, how are ya'll this afternoon? Give us a gre't big smile, will you? Thanks a million, folks. This is the Maddox Brothers & Rose. We'll be with you for a while this afternoon, and we hope you like it. Come in, boys," he called out to his brothers, leading back into the song with a sibilant "oh, yasss."

When the song ended, Fred returned to the mike: "Yes sir, folks, the gang's all here this afternoon, and they're lookin' real good. Henry's a-lookin' good, and Rose is lookin' real sweet. She's got on a new suit."

"Thank you, Fred," she replied, bashfully. "Santy Claus brought me this."

"He did?! Well, how did he get it down the chimney without gettin' it all black?" He continued without the slightest pause. "Well, Rose, yo're sure lookin' good, with your ruby red lips and big buck teeth—I mean, yo're big white teeth a-shinin'!"

"Why don't you tell me that at home, Fred?" she coyly asked. "Well, Rose, it's like this: I got another'n you don't know nothin' about. Only trouble is, she's jus' a small town mama."

With that, Fred immediately began slapping the bass as the boys picked up the intro. Fred took the lead vocal, singing, "She's jus' a small town mama, an' when you take her out, she'll drink yo're beer an' whisky, and then begin to shout."

As the transcription recordings show, the Maddoxes were starting to reach beyond the simple western fantasy that dominated California's prewar folksong offerings and increasingly placed greater emphasis on rhythm-and-blues–tinged heat. It was almost as if Fred and Cal's time overseas had rekindled a lost sense of home and a musical feel peculiar to their Alabama origins. Yet at the same time they were caught up in a desire to push beyond traditional hillbilly styles. Having recognized the need to devise a more modern entertainment, they soon found the conventions of hillbilly stringband music a bit too constrictive. The Maddoxes began working out a groove-oriented, anarchic boogie completely different from the work of any other artist of the day, and the application of Rose's dynamic, roadhouse femininity and clear, driving vocals evoked an entirely different set of audience responses. And audience response was everything.

"After Don got back, we started playin' dances, and people just couldn't hear you," Fred recalled. "We just had one little ol' amplifier you sang through, and the crowds started to get . . . restless. We heard about Bob Wills bein' electrified, so we started doin' ours that way. Got pickups for all the guitars and fiddle and mandolin, had to buy amplifiers, of course."

The result was electrifying in more ways than one. "It made us feel it more, because we could really hear it," Fred maintained, "and we could feel what we was doin' then, and the people could feel it a lot more, see?

"And we were known as the loudest band in the country. The louder you get, and the more power you put behind it, it puts it in the people's feet and in their bodies, see? That's what we did—put it in the people's feet and in their bodies and it made us feel it when we played, and it made us do a show."

When Fred spoke of the days following the war, his voice assumed a tone of pride, and his whole attitude and carriage reflected the strength he had felt back in the old days. This new style of Maddox music was something he and Cal fought for.

"Well, when we came back, Cliff thought that we should keep the old beat, 'the ol' hillbilly beat,' we called it. And I said, 'You've got to have somethin' that they can dance to, somethin' to make 'em feel it.' Me and Cal was already a-doin' it, but Cliff, he was older and set in his ways, so me and Cal just said, 'We have got to have that beat!' And we got it, and stuck to it. People just couldn't stand still—they had to dance to it."

There was nothing new to their approach, just as there was nothing new in their argument with Cliff. It was the same old sibling rivalry—only now, country music had caught up with the Maddoxes, and the postwar trend away from traditional folksongs and into neon-lit celebration provided ample justification for modernizing the music. It was something Fred and Cal had been pushing for ever since they began performing in the late 1930s.

Early in 1946, with Don back home and working regularly on all their radio shows and personal appearances, the brothers realized it was necessary to augment their sound even further if they were to compete against Spade "King of Western Swing" Cooley, and Bob Wills & His Texas Playboys. (At the time, the two bandleaders were locked in a fierce struggle for dominance of California's dance halls. Cooley ultimately, if only briefly, won; Wills conceded and went back to Tulsa.) Cal and Fred wanted to go to a six-man lineup, which would allow them to forego the union fee they erroneously believed was required on any date worked with fewer personnel. While such a minimum was enforced for theater and auditorium engagements, other performances were not covered. The Maddoxes were so leery of union involvement that they did not bother to check the rules. In their view, the less contact made with the union, the better; in fact, prior to their becoming union members, several of their prewar dances had been picketed. So Fred set about hunting up some sidemen to bolster their numbers and their sound.

At the time Cliff was working steadily with Al Brown & his Alabamans, playing the California Ballroom (where Rose and Henry had scavenged empty bottles for return deposits ten years earlier), and broadcasting over KTRB. As it happened, Brown's fiddler had a son who was getting pretty good on the steel guitar. Both his father and Cliff mentioned this fact to Fred several times. After finally meeting the lanky seventeen year old, Fred hired him on the spot, even though he was still underage and would have to sneak into the clubs by the back door. The kid's name was Bud Duncan.

Duncan's background was similar to the Maddoxes. A recent arrival to California from Missouri, he had graduated from following the crops ("If it didn't move," Duncan later wrote, "we picked it") to working with Logan Laam in at Stockton's KGDM, receiving fifty cents a broadcast. Duncan's steel playing soon became one of the most important and distinctive aspects of the Maddoxes' music. Duncan was already developing his own twist on the San Joaquin Valley's raw hillbilly sound. Despite his self-effacing claim that "I literally learned how to play the steel guitar on the bandstand while playing with the Maddox Brothers & Rose," Duncan's frolicsome, fluid steel had an evocative flair that helped smooth over many rough spots in the brothers' playing.

The brothers, after all, were still rudimentary musicians. Though able to create a remarkably intricate series of percussive effects, Fred nevertheless could not tune his instrument, never played chords, and could only do songs within a limited range of keys. One night in Sacramento, as the Maddoxes were leaving the stage for an intermission, a young man who had been staring intently at Fred asked for a word with him: "Excuse me, Mr. Maddox. I'm a music student here at the university and . . ."—he paused, as Fred looked down at him from the bandstand, perspiration dripping from his satin cowboy shirt—"You don't really know how to play that bass fiddle, do you?" Fred, not missing a beat, shot back, "Well, I got the job, don't I?"

Immediately after taking on Bud Duncan, Fred also began scouting the area for a lead guitarist who could match their unorthodox style. One afternoon at the Musician's Union Hall in Modesto, Fred saw a young man fooling around with a guitar. This was Jimmy Winkle, whom Fred had previously seen sitting in with Al Brown's band. Fred liked what he heard and offered Winkle the job. But the young picker was much in demand; he also sat in regularly with Arky Stark and had just been offered a job with the Sagebrush Serenaders, the Valley's leading western swing band after Dave Stogner's outfit. Winkle naturally hesitated.

"I mentioned to the union secretary that I was going to be playing with the Sagebrush Serenaders," he recalls, "and that the Maddox Brothers & Rose wanted me to go with them, too, and he said, 'Well, they'd be a much better deal—the Maddox Brothers & Rose are gonna go places.' So I joined them."

Both Duncan and Winkle, soon known to Maddox fans as "the two hired hands," joined the Maddoxes in April 1946. The band began working dances with a redoubled effort. "The first place I played with them was at the California Ballroom in Modesto," Winkle says. "Soon we were real busy, around Salinas, Sacramento, Pittsburgh, up to Grass Valley. We got up to Reno; we didn't have to go far to play. When I started with them it was just one night a week, then two nights, then five and pretty soon it got up to where we were working seven nights a week. I went down from 170 pounds to 130!"

Winkle's r&b-style guitar runs, in tandem with Cal's muscular rhythm guitar, began to push to the forefront of the Maddox sound. While Winkle and Cal developed a distinctive boogie style from these bluesy runs, Duncan balanced their sound with a more traditional yet imaginative playing on steel that kept them firmly in the realm of hillbilly music.

Drawing on the band fund, Fred managed to obtain two brand new '46 Chevrolets through a black marketeer in Grass Valley. ("I had to pay five hundred dollars under the table, to get one!") Once they were riding in style, Lula turned her attention to the band's look, which was in need of an update as well. The Maddoxes needed new finery to match the wild, new music they were playing. And a performer's look was important. After all, people crowded around the bandstand when Bob Wills played, not only for the music but also to marvel at his handmade boots, which were rumored to have cost two hundred dollars.

"We had seen the western movies, and we wanted somethin' like that," said Fred. "We met Roy Rogers in Modesto. We were eatin' at the same place and we had breakfast with him. He told us that his clothes were made by Nathan Turk, down in Van Nuys.

"We wanted a certain type, with bell bottom trousers and Eisenhower jackets. At the time, Gene Autry and them [singing cowboys] was the only ones who used Turk's uniforms. Then, we went a little beyond that, got kinda outstanding on it, to where you could really see us!"

Nathan Turk originated the extravagant rodeo stagewear which soon became synonymous with country music. His more famous competitor Nudie (whose first shop, at Victory and Vineland in North Hollywood, would not open for another four years) rose to national prominence after wooing Roy Rogers, Dale Evans, and Gene Autry away from Turk in 1950; subsequently, Little Jimmy Dickens, Cowboy Copas, and Hank Williams made Nudie costumes de rigueur in Nashville. But Turk was the first to explore the garish outer limits of western costuming—a style in which he excelled. Rose, for her part, stuck with Turk until his retirement in the late 1950s. ("I never did like Nudie's stuff," she said. "He always made those 'high-water pants.'") With the Maddoxes, Turk outdid himself.

"We heard about Turk," Rose recalled, "that he was the tailor who made all the costumes for the western stars, so we went down there and had some made. He designed them himself, and they were absolutely fantastic. The boys didn't like straight-legged pants. They wanted bell bottoms like sailors had, and they looked great. Nobody else but the navy had 'em! And we had the short jackets like Eisenhower wore; that's where we came up with the idea. We had some made with the longer jackets, but most of 'em was short. The shirts was all embroidered satin, to match the suits, so that in hot weather you could take the jacket off and still have the shirt with matching embroidery and rhinestones, ever'thing to match the trousers. The suits was all made of wool gabardine, a heavy material that stayed looking good, and the shirts were all heavy satin, not this flimsy stuff, and the inside was lined. But we had to take them to a special cleaners and have 'em hand cleaned, otherwise they'd run 'em through a machine and ruin ever'thing."

Regular visits to the dry cleaners soon became an important aspect of between-dance road scheduling. "We never had 'em cleaned on the road," says Rose. "There was a cleaner out below where Turk was, in Sherman Oaks, who did that kind of stuff, and we always took 'em back there. We always had enough of 'em so that we could last on the road, until we got back to have 'em cleaned. We were making money from playing all these dances, and we had several outfits made up. We were wearing those before we ever started recording.

"Turk was a great person. I just thought the world of him, and he did of us, too. He was very genuinely sincere about his like for us. He and his son-in-law did all the stuff. Of course, the embroidery was all done by machine, and he did have some people working for him; they'd do the basics and he'd go from there."

(One of those unnamed apprentices was Manuel Cuevas, who later married Nudie Cohn's daughter and who now continues the tradition of opulent western stagewear from Nashville, costuming the likes of Marty Stuart and Dwight Yoakam. Now known by his first name, Manuel got his start sewing grape leaves onto Maddox Brothers costumes.)

With flashy new costumes and talented young sidemen, the Maddoxes' bookings were on the increase. They worked the Valley constantly, broadcasting on both KTRB and KGDM, and later that year added shows out of KDRU in Dinuba. For Henry this was invaluable experience, and his mandolin playing soon reflected Winkle's influence. The whole family knew they were getting better, building greater momentum with every dance and radio show played. They knew it was time to push their career forward, that it was time to make records.

Following the war, jukeboxes became an important gauge of an artist's popularity. The jukebox's prominence soon reached such a level that James Petrillo, national president of the musician's union, fearing they would kill off night club work altogether, instituted a nation-wide strike in 1948 that lasted until arrangements were made for royalties from jukebox play to be paid to the union. For their part, the Maddoxes realized that without a record playing in the juke joints all the radio fan mail they received daily was meaningless.

In 1946, the recording industry was a commercial frontier of vast promise for both the Maddoxes and whoever would be lucky enough to record them. The war, the recording ban of 1942–43, the subsequent unavailability of shellac to produce discs, and the scores of artists whose careers were disrupted resulted in a fallow period that restricted most record industry activity. It also created a climate in which small, independent labels stood a better competitive chance than had existed prior to 1942. Though the major companies—RCA Victor, Columbia, and Decca—were still the rulers, new West Coast outfits like Capitol (founded 1942), Specialty (1944), Aladdin (1945), Modern (1945) Gilt Edge (1944) and 4 Star (1945) were able to get a running start, with dreams of becoming a force to rival the "Big Three." Even though radio was still the biggest popular force, recorded music was experiencing an explosive renaissance, both artistically and financially. Of all the West Coast independents, only Capitol eventually came to rival the Big Three and join them as one of the "majors," but the 4 Star story typifies the potential and thrill of the postwar record business.

The label was founded in July 1945 by Richard A. "Dick" Nelson as a sister to Nelson's Gilt Edge Records, which was already off and running thanks to Nashville r&b pianist Cecil Gant's "I Wonder," a smash hit covered by Louis Armstrong, among numerous others. When Bill McCall, a flinty Texas hustler who had most recently (and unsuccessfully) plied the trade of get-rich-quick miner in Nevada, bought into the company for $5000 in 1946, it was on the verge of going into receivership. Don Pierce, who later became co-owner of Starday Records, was an A&R man and salesman at 4 Star Records in 1946, and he described how the label evolved: "It started in WW2, really. They had a race record [i.e., a record by a black artist] by Cecil Gant, called 'I Wonder.' It was a big hit, and they had a hard time producing enough records, because during the war, supplies were extremely low.

"That's what really kicked off 4 Star, and after I got out of the army in '46, I got acquainted with Bill McCall and Dick Nelson, and became involved with 4 Star, which was an outgrowth of that start [with Gilt Edge and Cecil Gant]. By then, they were already trying to do the pop field, with Al Donohough and Ted Fiorito, 'the Idol of Sophisticated Society,' which was a disaster, but they were having some success with T. Texas Tyler in the western field.

"They weren't particularly interested in the country & western field," Pierce said of Nelson and McCall, "but they couldn't ignore the success of Tyler. He had come on board when they were trying to be a potential major label. They had tried to do it all, and with no success whatsoever until, and except for, T. Texas Tyler."

Reluctantly and quite accidentally, 4 Star fell into the field of hillbilly music, which would eventually become a major portion of the record market. The label's skeptical outlook was shared by most other companies, whose greatest successes were dominated by pop and swing artists, followed by race records. Hillbilly and folk releases (as they were categorized by *Billboard* magazine until June 1949) trailed behind. Few artists enjoyed the consistent sales of a Roy Acuff, and in the late summer of 1946 4 Star was struggling, looking for another artist who could duplicate the solid sales of Tyler's "Filipino Baby" (#5 on the *Billboard* charts) or perhaps match the success of earlier best-sellers like Al Dexter's "Pistol Packin' Mama," Ernest Tubb's "Walking the Floor over You," or Ted Daffan's "Born to Lose."

"You've got to figure it this way," Pierce explained. "It was before the majors had gone into Nashville, it was before the Jim Beck Studio in Dallas got going. It was shortly after the war, and you had the influx of the Okies and Arkies, the Dust Bowl people. Spade Cooley had his all-night swing-shift dances, and Bob Wills was very popular. Of course, he was popular before and during the war, so he was the leader, and many acts followed him, including T. Texas Tyler. He had got a radio show in Pasadena, California, and had become extremely popular through his recordings of 'Remember Me' and 'Deck of Cards,' and I believe that is what brought the Maddox Brothers & Rose to us."

CHAPTER EIGHT

"We decided that we wanted a recording contract," said Rose. "We wanted to record. So Mama and I took one of these big [sixteen-inch acetate disc] transcriptions of songs that we had KTRB record for us, and we went to Hollywood to make the rounds. We had two days to do it in, before we all had to go back to work. We went to all the companies, and nobody was in that could listen to the stuff and do it."

Capitol Records—the fledgling outfit founded in April 1942 by singer-songwriter Johnny Mercer, music store owner Glenn Wallichs, and Paramount Pictures executive producer and songwriter George "Buddy" DeSylva—was a freewheeling operation unafraid to experiment with every different type of music being performed around Hollywood. Located above Wallichs's Music City store at the corner of Sunset and Vine, Capitol had scored in the pop and jazz fields with the likes of Ella Mae Morse, Jo Stafford, Nat Cole, and Stan Kenton and, following the war, was just starting to build up its hillbilly/folk roster.

One of the label's very first signings had been cowboy singer Tex Ritter, whose debut single, "Jingle, Jangle, Jingle" (1942), sold well right out of the gate. In 1946, Capitol's second folk acquisition was

Wesley Tuttle, a smooth Western-style entertainer who wore a prosthetic latex glove onstage to hide the results of a childhood accident at his father's Pacoima butcher shop. (He lost three fingers in a meat grinder; as a rather historic result, Leo Fender constructed the first lefthanded electric guitar for him in 1938.) Tuttle had substantial sales with "Detour" and its follow up "With Tears in My Eyes." Tuttle also brought Capitol a shrewd operator named Cliffie Stone. Tuttle had first met the portly young bassist on the playing fields of Burbank High School in 1932, and the pair subsequently worked together on Stuart Hamblen's "Cavalcade of Stars" and "Cowboy Church" radio programs.

An adept musician with an ear for talent, Stone soon became right-hand man and talent broker for Capitol A&R chief Lee Gillette. Also a hillbilly disc jockey for several Hollywood stations, Stone was well aware of the Maddox Brothers & Rose's popularity, and the day Rose and Lula appeared in his office he wanted nothing more than for Capitol to sign them.

"Cliffie wanted us real, real bad," recalled Rose, "but Lee Gillette, who had the final say, was sick in bed at home, and they wouldn't even let Cliffie through to talk to him on the phone." This was one occasion when a little patience and some of the fabled Smith presentiment would have served Lula well; if she and Rose had only waited for Gillette to return to work, the name, career, and bank balance of the Maddox Brothers & Rose would have been much more prominent. But she was too headstrong to wait for Gillette. Rose and Lula stood at Sunset and Vine, and pondered their next move. It was a brief conference.

"When we came out of Capitol, we were already on our second day [of looking for labels]," Rose said, "and I told Mama, 'Let's go to 4 Star,' because T. Texas Tyler was goin' great on 4 Star. He was the biggest thing around. 4 Star was located in Pasadena, in a big warehouse that they had their offices in, did their pressing, and everything else there.

"They listened to the transcription and thought it was just great, but Bill McCall said, 'We want you, but we don't want the boys.' So we called Fred and told him what they had said, and he says, 'Tell him they can't have her without us!' We told him [McCall], and in order to get me they took the whole group, which they was never sorry of."

4 Star head Bill McCall, a notoriously tight-fisted businessman, naturally wanted to sign the star vocalist as a single; it was the less expensive way to go. Unable to get around the family, he arranged for them to return to Pasadena and finalize the deal. Don Pierce had been out of the office when Rose and Lula first dropped in, but he was at his desk when the entire group returned. McCall had neglected to mention their initial visit, and they made quite an entrance.

"I recall very vividly when they came into our place on Larchmont Avenue," said Pierce. "They all had their uniforms on, and they had no appointment. You have to have a lot of ego to be successful in that business. Lord knows, they were dealt a good share of it, and I don't mean that in a disrespectful way.

"They came in and said, 'We've noticed that T. Texas Tyler is on every jukebox and radio station in the San Joaquin Valley, where we work, so we have selected you to record us.' Now, that's pretty strong! And I said, 'Who the hell are you?' I'd never heard of 'em. It was Mom, Fred, and Rose doing the talking. They were the spearheads, and they were really rather impressive, because you got the feeling that nobody could hardly stop these people. They were irrepressible."

The Maddoxes were so eager to record, and so accustomed to doing studio work for free (even the McClatchy contract had paid only a nominal fifteen dollars a week), that they never questioned the niggardly terms McCall offered them.

"They didn't have the money, they said, to put out any big money for an advance," Rose explained, "and we signed to a seven-year contract. It was union rules that they had to pay us when we'd record, so when we did record, they would pay us—and then we always gave the checks back to them. The deal was that they would get us known all over the United States by sending our records to every radio station in the country, and they did keep their part of the deal, but we never got any money from 4 Star, never got any royalties, even though we were supposed to. They kept two sets of books, just like most of 'em did back then, and according to them we just weren't selling."

In an era when song publishing rights were often pirated through fine print and royalty rates were so low they were reckoned in fractions of a penny, Bill McCall exemplified the cunning, exploitive nature of the post-war record man. In fact, he went above and beyond the prevailing level of chicanery and routinely fleeced every artist under contract to him.

(One of the rare instances that McCall did pay an artist, so the story goes, was when he was threatened at gunpoint in his office by Slim Willet. Willet's "Don't Let the Stars Get in Your Eyes," after being refused by almost every label and publisher in the country for its odd Cajun-based structure and use of meter, became a hit on 4 Star and was quickly covered by Skeets McDonald on Capitol and Perry Como on RCA, whose version crashed into the pop Top Ten. It was the biggest hit ever introduced on 4 Star, so there was a lot of royalty money at stake. In this case, Willet's 250 gun-toting pounds convinced McCall to make good. Willet, a flamboyant entertainer known to drop and roll around on the stage, returned in triumph to hometown San Antonio, where he cheerfully held forth in a office decorated with framed letters of rejection for "Don't Let the Stars" from dozens of record and publishing companies. There, Willet also emceed a weekend hillbilly package revue that featured Riley Crabtree and Jackie Lee Waukeen Cochran, and, with the song's proceeds, bought the city's only ice cream factory.)

McCall had no intention whatsoever of honoring his royalty agreement with the Maddoxes. He not only made them return the checks 4 Star issued but also pocketed the family's portion of retail sales. But McCall did supply the family with unlimited quantities of their records to sell at personal appearances. This arrangement was a shrewd psychological ploy, enabling the family to earn at least a little from their records and maintain their enthusiasm for recording.

For the Maddoxes, the increased popularity and gate receipts they enjoyed after their records were available made McCall's terms easier to swallow. "Well, it was all right with us at the time," Fred said, "but then we felt that we should be paid and given royalties, as much as we was doin' for them. But I found out later we had a better deal with them than we got with anybody—because we got the publicity, that was really terrific."

After signing with 4 Star, the Maddox Brothers & Rose cut two uncharacteristically low-key songs for their first single, "Careless Driver" and "The Midnight Train." "Careless Driver" was not a particularly memorable debut, although Rose was in fine, throbbing voice, and the two hired hands played a lovely, unison break. If not for the unmistakable backhills folk harmonies and Henry's crude, trilling mandolin, the record would have sounded more like a Tin Pan Alley ballad than the stuff that thrilled Okies all over the state. The family paid Winkle and Duncan out of their own pocket for the session, then returned to the Valley and waited for the record to come out. It was issued in the fall of 1947. On the record's label, Rose was billed as "The Sweetheart of Cowboy Swing."

"We did that record, had a little bit of business with that, mostly because of the following they had established up and down the Valley," said Pierce. "It was very shortly after that they recorded 'Whoa, Sailor,' and that was a very, very big thing all up and down the coast."

Hank Thompson, fresh out the service and still wearing braces on his teeth, had just recorded his song "Whoa, Sailor" in Dallas, Texas, for the Globe label. When a copy of the record came to KTRB and the Maddoxes' attention, they decided to record the song immediately. As Thompson himself points out, "Hell, there wasn't a lot of songs that girls could sing, so when 'Whoa, Sailor' came along, it had a deal where a girl could sing it. There just weren't many songs a girl could sing that really had some punch to it, and that one did."

Released in early 1948, the Maddoxes' 4 Star "Whoa, Sailor" was the first accurate representation, on record, of what they were about: loud, rude, and very funny. Fred took his first turn as a lead singer on record, sharing the duties with Rose. The two alternated verses as they told the tale of a lonely sailor who, "back from overseas, wher' ther' are no girls or rye," tries to chat with a young lady of questionable morals. The arrangement and playing were equal parts honky-tonk and primitive western swing (or "Hillbilly Swing," as Don Pierce fittingly dubbed it) and the record raced along, a delight from start to finish.

It was the ideal vehicle for the group, and it perfectly captured the nutty, freewheeling atmosphere they had perfected on radio. When Fred sang about stepping "into a cabaret to get myself a beer," Cal leaned into the microphone and delivered a piercing hiccup. Throughout the record, Cal chimed in with sardonic *uh-huh*'s and a running commentary above the singers: "Ah, they all say that!" and "Oh, you pore boy!" When Fred yelled, "Quit your beefin'!" Cal snarled back, "Who's beefin?", then unleashed his famous cackle, a memorably maniacal laugh that the Surfaris would later borrow to open "Wipe-Out."

"Rose had a great, great feeling in that song," said Cliffie Stone, "kind of like she really was a streetwalker on some San Diego corner, singing 'Whoa, sailor!' . . . I mean, that's really where a hit record is at: the impression, the emotion that you get when you hear it. That's where it's at, you know. It is nothing but that."

Stone remained one of the Maddoxes' biggest fans, following their career closely throughout the years and stepping in to help at several crucial points. "They were innovative, creative, original, and thoroughly traditional. They came up with stuff that nobody else had ever heard. 'Whoa, Sailor' had been recorded by Hank Thompson in Texas, but they picked up on it some way, and their version was the first I ever heard. And 'Honky Tonkin'.' She had the first [cover] record of 'Honky Tonkin'.' They were right onto what was happening."

Nashville disc jockey Hugh Cherry, a close friend of Hank Williams, agreed that the Maddoxes' "Honky Tonkin'" (Williams's original was released in May 1947 on the Sterling label) was the leading version of the Williams song on the West Coast in terms of programming and popularity. Rose learned it one afternoon from a jukebox at a Riverbank, California, drive-in during the spring of 1948. She copied down the lyrics while waiting for her hamburger, and the Maddoxes cut the record as soon as possible. (It was on this record's label that 4 Star billed Rose for the first time as "The Sweetheart of Hillbilly Swing," a subtle though not insignificant change of title for a West Coast artist to adopt; by this time 4 Star had also begun printing the act's "Most Colorful Hillbilly Band in America" moniker on record labels as well.)

Meanwhile, the Maddoxes' mischievous approach to hillbilly music and performance was becoming a more focused and sharply defined show. Each brother created an onstage persona, defined and announced by Fred. Cal, always known as the "Laughing Cowboy," was now joined by "Don Juan and his Mule Fiddle," "Friendly Henry, the Working Girl's Friend," and "last but not least, ther' is Rose, the Sweetheart of Hillbilly Swing." The "Two Hired Hands" were known as "Honky-Tonkin' Duncan" (or "Smiley") and "Jimmy with the Light Brown Hair."

Onstage, Rose, Fred, and Don were the front line, with the hired hands at the far left and right. Cal and Henry, behind the front line, would dart to and from the microphone with an almost choreographed fluidity. Rose was the focal point for audience and musicians alike, tapping out time with her boots and signaling each song's close with a distinctive salute. Each time she waved her upraised fist in a circular motion to signal a number's windup, she left no questions as to who led the band. By all accounts, it was an engrossing, kaleidoscopic visual presentation, one that smoothed over numerous technical rough spots in the band's music.

"I've always said there wasn't a musician in the bunch including myself," Jimmy Winkle said, "but we sure enjoyed ourselves. . . . They were a lot of fun to work with, so doggone corny, you know—old slapstick comedy and ever'thing. One time we decided to get some old ragged bib overalls, and during intermission we'd put those on, go out onstage and horse around, cut up and what not. Don Juan had a big old quarter cigar, about a foot long and two inches through, and he had a cigarette lighter that he'd keep tryin' to light it with, but the thing wouldn't light. So I had a great big box of kitchen matches in my hip pocket. I'd take one of them, strike one, light his cigarette lighter, and then he'd light that big ol' cigar off of it. It was crazy things like that. Just corn."

The inherent strength of the Maddox Brothers & Rose, their secret weapon, was a natural sense of comic timing. With Fred in command, hokum never played so well. One hand on his hip, the other draped around his bass fiddle, he would stare into the crowd and drawl, "I'm not feelin' too good tonight, folks. The hotel I stayed in last night, I couldn't get any sleep a-tall. The ol' faucet was a-drippin' in my bathtub, jus' drip,

drip, drip . . . finally, I called up the manager and said, 'I can't sleep, I got a leak in my bathtub.' He said, 'Well, go ahead—yo're payin' for it!'"

Fred would leer, deliver a swift kick to the backside of his bass fiddle and continue, "Started to check out this mornin', said, 'How much do I owe you?' He said, 'Fifty dollars.' I said, 'Fifty dollars! For that little ol' room?'

"'That included your meal.'

"'I didn't eat no meal!'

"He said, 'Well, it was there for you, if you didn't git it, I don't care!'

"So I give him ten dollars and said, 'I'm chargin' you forty dollars for makin' love to my wife . . .'

"He said, 'I didn't make love to your wife!'

"'Well, it was there for you—if you didn't git it, I don't care!'"

Apart from the boogie numbers on which he usually took the vocal, Fred's specialty was comic songs like the old "Quit Kickin' My Dog Around," "Small Town Mama," "Red Silk Stockings and Green Perfume," and "Shimmy Shakin' Daddy." The latter was one of Fred's best 4 Star efforts; he had learned it from labelmates Merl Lindsey & the Oklahoma Riders. (Lindsey also wrote "Water Baby Blues," an instrumental release for the Maddoxes in 1950.) Fueled by the combination of offbeat songs, gags Fred and Don cooked up (and the many additional ones they stole), and the loose, fun-house atmosphere the group maintained in the studio, the Maddoxes' combination show-and-dance took off.

"The people would come and they'd stand at the stage," Fred explained. "It'd be a big dance hall and they'd stand halfway to the back, sometime all the way back, just standin' and watchin.' We figured we had to do somethin' to entertain 'em. Like Bob Wills. Now he had a dance band, ever'body'd go there to dance, but we wasn't strictly a dance band, and we knew it. We'd just play stuff that'd make you stand and pat your foot.

"And Don said, 'I don't want to just stand here and play the fiddle,' so we decided he'd be the comedian and I'd be the straight man, and what jokes we couldn't write, we'd steal. So we started doin' this stuff and it started workin', and it just worked so good that we kep' it up, a show and dance combined. People who wanted to dance would be back of the crowd that was standin' in front of the bandstand, just a-laughin' and bein' happy. They didn't have to dance because they was bein' entertained."

Just as impressive as the Maddoxes' stage show was the diversity of their repertoire. Onstage, a wild novelty like "Red Silk Stockings and Green Perfume" would often be followed by the rich gospel harmonies of "I'd Rather Have Jesus," and the Maddoxes would do full justice to both numbers. It was this versatility as much as their sight-gags and costumes that made the Maddox Brothers & Rose a hot ticket all across California.

"I saw them twice when I was a kid," said rockabilly bassist Ray Campi. "The Maddox Brothers & Rose were the definitive rockabilly, hillbilly boogie-woogie, western swing, country-gospel band. It was everything you ever heard in your life, growing up in the South. You heard blues, you heard gospel, hillbilly, bluegrass—and they threw it all in there and went one, two, three—KICK! Like a mule kicking, that's it. And they were the most wonderful band I've ever seen. Absolutely amazing. They had so much comedy and showmanship, like a medicine-show kind of vitality."

The Maddoxes approached their music career with a single-minded drive, dedication, and unity that was almost startling, considering the different personalities involved. There was Don, who had no desire to be in the music business at all; Cal, who unfailingly toed the mark and "would tell on you" to Mama; Fred, garrulous huckster; Cliff, headstrong and frustrated; Henry, the youngest and a quiet, introverted soul; and Rose, the jealously guarded star. Rose was a romantic, a frustrated young woman who was forced to develop her own personality in secret, away from the prying eyes of her Mama, her first husband, and her legions of fans. This was no easy task; Lula was ever watchful over her girl. Whenever she found Rose chatting with a boy between sets, Lula would sneak over, take aim, and swat her daughter's backside with a cash-heavy shoulder bag, sending Rose skittering halfway across the dancefloor. Just as in Boaz, Lula made sure her clan stuck to themselves.

"Well, we were strictly business, after we got into it. It was our living and that was it," Fred explained. "A lot of entertainers are just in it for, say, a drink and a woman, and that's all they care about. But we's in it strictly the same as runnin' a store or fillin' station that's a business, and music is a business, too. It's the same difference, only ever'body thinks you're havin' such a great time—well, of course you are, and you're makin' the people have a great time while you're a-doin' it, see?"

Of course, behind the scenes, pushing every step of the way, was Lula. Don Pierce marveled at the inexhaustible drive which she instilled in her children.

"How can you imagine any group of people having the energy that they would have, to do the radio show [at six A.M.], then sleep and then get into the car, and they'd drive all over California!" he said. "I mean it's nothing for them to go to Ventura and back [600 miles], nothing for them to go to Redding and back [480 miles], and get back and hit that radio show again. Drivin' in them cars, and to have that kind of energy . . . and they didn't give a damn whether or not the radio stations paid 'em. They just wanted that air time—because they knew where they were gonna get it [from personal appearances] and they knew where they were going. They just did it."

The Maddoxes' dedication to performing is doubly impressive when one realizes that they were working as hard as possible at two occupations, radio and recording, that paid nothing. Even though they were bringing in upwards of two hundred dollars a night (which would soon grow to three and four hundred, a healthy take in the late forties) there was an incredible naiveté at work—an almost blind dedication to performing and entertaining, and the equally blind faith that there was always "plenty more where that came from."

Fame itself must have assuaged many misgivings. The Maddoxes were by now almost folk heroes in the San Joaquin Valley, an exalted status that was extremely gratifying. Even the Hired Hands found themselves considered celebrities. Jimmy Winkle once attended a Spade Cooley dance and wound up playing it. Recognizing Winkle by his Turk uniform, the bandleader invited Jimmy up to sing a few.

True, the Maddoxes sold their 4 Star 78s at all their performances and earned plenty of cash from them. But it is also likely that they would have kept playing just for the applause. For each of them, the nightly rounds of raging cheers were recompense more satisfying than anything they had received in their lives. For Fred, this was the ultimate payoff on his cotton-field gamble. For Lula, who spent each night offstage clutching her large shoulder bag stuffed with cash, constantly scanning the crowd and counting heads, every successful show was sweet vindication for the move west. And Rose, standing center stage as ever, knew through and through—from the pointed toes of her custom-made boots to the snow-white Stetson tilted back upon her head—that every single audience member had come for one reason: to hear her sing, to watch her keeping time to every song with a kinetic shaking, to marvel at the sheer, natural power with which she filled the entire dance hall.

CHAPTER NINE

As her son began to grow up, Rose watched helplessly from a distance, through less and less frequent meetings. It was an uncomfortable situation. For the most part, Donnie lived in Modesto with his grandfather Charlie, or sometimes with Alta. After Alta's second marriage (to a "nice Mexican man," with whom she bore two children) ended in divorce, Alta was glad to look after her nephew. But shortly after the war ended, Alta took her third and final husband, Charlie Troxel, and moved out into the country.

"We were living out at Oakdale then, on a ranch," Alta said. "I was married to Troxel then and one day Mama, Rose, and little Donnie came by. They was on their way south and they came to visit. Donnie was a little bitty feller. I remember we had an outdoor toilet, because we was a-buildin' the place we was livin' on, and he wanted to go [use the toilet]. So we took him to the outhouse and he looked down into that hole and he says, 'I ain't goin' to get up there!' Rose was gonna go ahead and tell him to do it, but he started to cry, and you never heard such a noise. In that little building, it sounded so loud! He wanted nothing to do with it, and he wouldn't go on the ground, because he'd never did that! I've laughed so many times about that. It was so funny."

To a family of ex–fruit tramps for whom a sturdy outhouse would represent a marvelous creature comfort, such a reaction *would* be hilarious. Donald Douglas Byford Hale, son of the Sweetheart of Hillbilly Swing, was born into a life of quilted playpens, plush toys, and ceramic toilets. He was a stranger to the canvas tents, stagnant water, and the long, cold nights that his mother grew up with.

The family sought to obtain anything and everything modern and convenient. They bought a house on Modesto's Emerald Avenue. More than anything else, the house symbolized all the good fortune that a career in music had brought. Neither Charlie nor Lula had ever owned property, nor scarcely before dreamt of it. For the first time, the family had a real place of their own.

Rose, though, saw her child growing up in many ways a stranger. Even if they were not estranged or unable to communicate, Rose's career nevertheless kept pulling her away from Donnie. Her life was her music, and everything and everyone else came second.

A breath of hope came into Rose's life when Jimmy Winkle, the soft-spoken guitar picker, became romantically involved with her. Surprisingly, Lula saw the affection between the two and said nothing. Lingering guilt at having engineered Rose's failed marriage may have caused her to look the other way.

Rose and Jimmy's relationship was ardent yet completely innocent, in as much as they were constantly together on the road but never alone with one another. "She had an affair with Jimmy Winkle, and they were in love, so to speak," said Don. "She was still married to E. B., and he'd decided to make the army his career and had gone overseas, but they hadn't divorced or anything.

"Rose didn't go out on dates with him or anything like that. When we'd drive to the dance, well, she'd sit in the back seat with him."

The image of Rose and Jimmy as chaste sweethearts offers a strange and touching tableau: the splendor of their Turk uniforms glimmering in the darkness as they rolled up Highway 99, the slight flush of excitement and affection, the low whispers punctuated by the occasional sharp inquiry from Lula, her two-cents' worth being tossed at the lovers regardless of their interest in it. For the moment, Rose was happy.

Jimmy had worked with the Maddoxes for six months before Rose found herself drawn to him. She described it as "a romantic little affair. We went together about a year, and had even planned to get married. Well, we talked about it, put it that way."

For her to consider remarrying, it was certainly more than "a little affair." Practically, she saw a hope to tie her personal life directly into the band's and thereby create a spot for Donnie. For as long as Rose continued as a single girl, her son would remain consigned to the on-again/off-again netherworld Lula reserved for in-laws and relatives.

With Rose and Jimmy closer than ever, the band as a whole was finally becoming an ensemble. The Maddoxes' growing command of their material was clearly evident on "George's Playhouse Boogie," a song they wrote about one of the many roadhouses on Stockton's notorious Waterloo Road.

On their 4 Star recording of the song (released in October 1949), "George's Playhouse Boogie" opens with Winkle's guitar playing a funky, alternating octave pattern that leads into a very hard mandolin solo from Henry. "That's Friendly Henry, the Working Girl's Friend!" Fred bellows on the record, his slap bass keeping steady time, "Le's all go to George's Playhouse, . . ." he adds and Rose sings:

"There's a real hot spot on the Waterloo Road, got a hillbilly band called Maddox & Rose / George's Playhouse so the story goes, where they play a boogie-woogie that'll wiggle your toes / Pull off your shoes and boy what a sight, where they all do the boogie on a Friiiiday night. . . ."

Winkle kicks in with a red-hot vamp typical of their boogies, soloing with a crude call-and-response pattern that builds, with Fred's slapping bass, to create a distinct, seductive, and rocking groove.

As the guitar moves up front, Cal is laughing and Fred yells: "Stop it! I cain't stand it—it's drivin' me sane!" (this was an obvious play on one of his favorite stage gags, "Stop, you're drivin' me crazy!" to Cal's "How can you tell?!") As Don takes his fiddle solo, Fred asks, "Have you ever seen anything like that?"

"No!" Rose answers, and Fred screams, "That's my brother!"

It's an atmosphere of lunacy, specifically tailored for their fans (already familiar enough with his gags that they could appreciate Fred's plea for his insanity), played against a backdrop of some of the hottest music recorded that year, a yoking of overt r&b influence with the Maddoxes' own idiosyncratic drive.

"That's what the public liked," Rose explained. "They felt we were a part of them, because we did what they wanted to hear, and what they asked to hear. With our type of music and the type of show we put on, well, they felt like it related to them, which is the way we figured it was supposed to be."

"George's Playhouse Boogie" was an ideal convergence of their personalities, musical style, and conscious efforts to provide the audience with exactly what they wanted. It was hot, fast, hard roadhouse music that bore little relation to the musical approach of most of their contemporaries, and like many of their 4 Star records it was very close to a rock & roll sound. The fact that Rose also carried her own bass fiddle, for use when Fred took lead vocals, added even more big beat heat to the clattering sound. But, as Fred was fond of saying, the Maddoxes were always "ten years ahead of ourselves" ("Twenty!" Rose invariably snapped in response). Like an advertisement for both band and nightclub, the record carried an incredible live-wire charge; the response when they performed it at George's must have been overwhelming.

"We'd play at George's Playhouse and the House of Blue Lights out on the Waterloo Road," said Jimmy Winkle, "and they got pretty rough sometimes. One time, I don't remember which club it was, we had a stabbing on the floor, right in front of the bandstand."

"It was like a typical West Texas club, just a bar and a dancefloor," recalled booker and personal manager Jack McFadden, who got into the music business at George's Playhouse. "It was what was known as a 'skull orchard.' It wouldn't be on the high end, know what I mean?" He laughs. "You could sure tell the difference between Harrah's Tahoe and George's Playhouse!"

The Maddoxes were well equipped to deal with troublemakers: the entire family had been deputized by the Modesto Police Department around 1947, and they carried the badges to prove it. Though intended mostly as an honorary distinction, the right to wear a deputy's badge also carried with it the tacit understanding that should any real trouble arise, such as a post-dance stickup, the Maddoxes could flash their badges and exercise their "powers of arrest." All the same, the Maddoxes never actually acted in any official law enforcement capacity. Prudently, they hired their own bouncers for dates at the rougher night spots.

"Well, it's better to have somebody to kinda handle people," Fred explained. "For a while we had Jimmy Wakely's brother, John. We had him hired for fifteen or twenty dollars a night, and then we had one big guy from Modesto . . . I can't remember what his name was, I think he was using a fictitious name 'cause he'd been in prison, but he was a good ol' guy. There was nobody got to bother him, because he was so big. I remember one night at Grower's Hall in Stockton, it was upstairs [on the second floor], and he picked up two guys and threw 'em both down [the flight of] stairs!" Fred laughed, and continued: "We didn't take 'em on the road, just to local dates around Modesto. I think we paid 'em fifteen or twenty dollars a night."

On and off the bandstand, Rose and Jimmy, more and more openly, drew closer together. They even recorded the Fred Rose ballad "Blue Eyes Crying in the Rain" with Jimmy singing lead and Rose adding full, melancholy harmony. A soft, sweet record, it is flavored by a sense of the romantic gloom bound to accompany any romance with the daughter of Lula Maddox. "Love is like a dying ember," they sang, "only memories remain." It was as if they anticipated what was to come. Such contentment was far too good to last.

It was not Lula, though, who broke up this romance but a higher authority. "When we got up to where we were workin' seven nights a week, that kinda bothered me." Jimmy said. "Not the work itself, but the workin' on Sundays, because I had never done that and it kinda got my old puritanical upbringing wondering if I wasn't desecrating the Lord's day. And then it got to where it didn't bother me, and then it bothered me because it didn't bother me!"

If there is such a thing as the devil's music, the Maddox Brothers & Rose were playing it, side by side with gospel standards, on the stages of the wickedest dives west of the Mississippi. Winkle's was an age-old struggle, the conflict of secular versus sacred, which has tormented country artists through the years, from Molly O'Day on up to Jerry Lee Lewis. In Winkle's case, a war-time experience helped cast the deciding vote.

"About two weeks before I quit 'em," Jimmy recalled, "I was driving Fred's Chrysler back from Sacramento. It was just me, Fred, and Bud Duncan. They were both asleep. I was drivin' along and the Lord spoke to me, told me to go to Sunday school that day. It's a long story, but when I was overseas I had promised Him that if He got me back safely, I would serve Him. Now it was two and a half years later and I had forgot all about it—but He hadn't! I remember that Saturday night, and the next Saturday night the same thing happened again, and it was just the three of us in the car."

Jimmy felt that commitment gnawing at him and could no longer perform with the Maddoxes in good conscience. That second Sunday, after the Lord had somehow reached him at the wheel of Fred's '48 Chrysler, Jimmy resolved to attend the Riverbank Assembly of God, a Pentecostal church where the most fervent of Holy Rollers gathered to speak in tongues and celebrate their militant faith.

As Jimmy approached the small church that bright, cold morning, he shut from his mind the wild boogie and dazzling glitter, the applause and celebrity. He tried not to think of the Maddox Brothers & Rose, but was unable to shut it from his mind. After all, he had been with them twenty months, playing hundreds of dates and recording dozens of songs with them.

"We drew crowds that were just unbelievable," he said, much as he might have said to himself that morning. "We were playin' at the Rainbow Gardens in Sacramento, a big roller rink there. Spade Cooley was playin' a dance downtown, and Roy Acuff was at another'n downtown. People kept comin' out to tell us that hardly anybody was downtown, and we had that place just jammed . . . they were a live-wire group, never a dull moment. Sometimes we'd have a hundred and fifty, two hundred people just standin' around the stage, watchin' what all we was doin'."

But his mind was made up, and he invited Rose to join him at church for the momentous day. He had not counted, though, on Rose's hopes. She attended that service resolving all the while to keep Jimmy within the family. What a scene: the Assembly of God packed with faithful congregants, all eyes on the Sweetheart of Hillbilly Swing. Rose was never seen at any church, yet she was well known to all. In the close-knit communities of Riverbank and Modesto, there were no secrets, and the appearance of Jimmy and Rose sent a murmur of curiosity through the pews. Rose drew herself inward and took the seat next to Jimmy. Thin, nervous, and devout, he ignored the brethren's whispering.

The service got underway. They sang hymns. While Rose barely mouthed the words, Jimmy attacked the lyrics with fervent passion. Minutes crawled by. When the preacher called for those who wished to be saved to step forward, Jimmy rose eagerly. Rose also stood, reached out, and grasped Jimmy's arm, pulling him back.

At that, the congregation erupted and leapt to its feet, exploding into a righteous roar of disapproval. Rose pleaded with Jimmy to understand, to leave with her. He shook her off. Weeping, she pulled Jimmy to her again, but the devout fell upon the pair and pried them apart. She fought them, struggled and thrashed along the aisle in a bizarre ideological tug of war.

"He went up there and I wouldn't," Rose recalled years later. "Ever'-body in the church knew me, and they literally got me and dragged me out of that pew, up the aisle, all the way up there—and me fightin' 'em the whole way! That's the way the fanatics are, the Holy Rollers. They go at it!

"Well, I figured my soul belonged to God anyway. I didn't have to go do it in public. And I was black and blue from them people. I was in hysterics, but I finally got loose from them that had dragged me up there. I was crying, just trying to get away from them. And there was a friend of mine and Jimmy's there and he said 'Do you want me to take you home, Rose?' I said, 'Please!' So, he took me home, and then Mama took me down to my doctor, who gave me a shot to settle me down.

"I never went with him again, after that," Rose added with finality.

Lula, who had shown admirable restraint throughout the romance with Jimmy, was now disgusted with the whole affair, ashamed at Rose's desperate sorrow, and extremely angry with Jimmy. To Lula, it was a sign. She had given her child free rein and saw that it had been a mistake. Her daughter had been hurt, the band had been hurt, and the entire family had been embarrassed by a scripture-spouting guitar picker. Lula resolved that nothing like this would ever happen to any of them again. She would keep a surer grip and a keener eye on every aspect of the Maddox Brothers & Rose's career and personal lives.

Still, the band needed a lead guitar player. Fred fought to keep Jimmy with them, even after the Riverbank debacle. "I was under contract until September of that year [1948]," said Jimmy, "but they saw that I was really serious and meant business. I told Fred I'd give him thirty days' notice, according to union rules, and Fred said, 'Well, we're gonna take it to the union,' and I said, 'That's all right, you take it to the union and I'll take it to the Lord!'

"So, finally Fred says, 'Well, will you play with us until we can get somebody else?' and I said, 'No, I'll just give you my thirty days' notice,' because I knew they wouldn't even look for anybody else. They'd just go on, hopin' it would wear off of me.

"I stayed with 'em that thirty days, and I just couldn't do anything right after that, in my own mind. I didn't mean to, but I'd forget to 'take-off' [solo] the song or I'd take it off in the wrong key, or I'd forget to take it off the second time around, stuff like that. I guess I made them so miserable, unintentionally of course, that they let me go after two weeks! I left them around the first of February 1948." (The recording of "Blue Eyes Crying in the Rain" with Winkle's lead vocal was never released by 4 Star. Arhoolie Records issued it some thirty years later.)

Meanwhile, the family was also contending with major personal problems. For several years, Charlie and Lula had drifted further and further apart. Lula spent very little time with him and was usually gone nights. Rumor had it that Charlie had been slipping around with other women. After thirty years, the marriage was over. Charlie and Lula sought a divorce, and it was granted in early 1949. Rose accompanied Lula to a Hollywood courthouse for the final dissolution.

The divorce seems to have had surprisingly little impact on Rose and her brothers; the family had been divided into two camps for so long that all were used to seeing Charlie for only brief periods of time, a habit that the Maddoxes would maintain up until his death. For his own part, Charlie was doubtless relieved at being cut loose. Although Lula was responsible for all the good that had befallen the family, marriage to such a domineering woman must have been tiresome at best. Charlie was content to enjoy his children's considerable success and savor a parent's vicarious sense of pride. His children, no doubt, were happy that the old boy had, for once, gotten his way.

CHAPTER TEN

While the years after the war continued to be emotionally turbulent for Rose, they were also the most professionally rewarding of her career. Operating out of their Emerald Avenue home, the Maddoxes promoted their name with greater effect than any other West Coast artists except major-label hit makers like Spade Cooley, Merle Travis, and Jimmy Wakely. The recognition their recordings for 4 Star brought, together with the barrage of personal appearances and radio work, began to pay off (although not in the form of record royalties from the tight-fisted Bill McCall).

The loss of Jimmy Winkle was a blow to the group, but they almost immediately replaced him with another Valley guitarist, Gene LeMasters, a good-looking man who wore his Turk stage costumes with flair. His guitar playing did not quite suit Fred or Lula, however, and he was cut loose after six months. This situation made the brothers realize that they could not rely on outsiders, so they began to concentrate seriously on perfecting their own playing. They got an unexpected crash course when musicians' union boss James Petrillo decided that jukeboxes were bleeding his men dry and called a strike, effective January 1, 1948.

"Petrillo said: 'Look, we are putting ourselves out of business with these records, because we are depriving musicians of a chance to perform live—it is all being replaced by the jukebox,'" recalled Don Pierce. "'Therefore, we are cutting our own throats by letting union members make records, and so the only way we will permit them to make records is if they pay royalties to our trust fund.' So there was a strike for a year over that."

The Maddox Brothers & Rose had never been partial to the union. When word of the impending strike reached them (now reluctant card-carrying union members all) they knew it was time to act.

"The companies all knew they were fixin' to strike, so 4 Star had us to go in and record ever'thing we knew, practically," said Rose. "We went in ever' day for two weeks, so we had records coming out for the entire time the strike was, and the union couldn't do anything, because they'd been recorded before the strike went into effect."

While this was a shrewd move (at Capitol, Cliffie Stone had done the same, recording everything they could: "good, bad or indifferent"), Pierce soon devised an even more effective strategy: "I suggested to them, and it came as the result of the recording ban, that we make some transcriptions. 'Well, what're we gonna do with them?' they asked, and I said, 'I'm personally gonna carry them mothers across the border and see my friend, Polo Juaquez, who is DJ at XERB down there. And if you will give me enough material so that he can do fifteen minutes a night, without repeating all the time, I think we can make a trade: he will play your music every night at prime time, seven o'clock—and he will announce your dates for the whole damn week. You give me the transcriptions."

Pierce, who regularly covered a circuit up and down the West Coast, knew it was wise to cater to the band, the hottest act on 4 Star's roster, in such an unusually accommodating manner. As Rose said, "He did it to keep us happy. They'd promised us publicity and this let everyone know what we were doin'." Pierce also realized that making recordings to acetate discs known as "electrical transcriptions" was the only way to allow the Maddoxes to appear regularly on XERB and maintain their lucrative touring schedule. Recording to magnetic tape was only just then becoming a possibility in the music business in the late 1940s, though not for budget operations like 4 Star.

XERB, a giant border station in Rosarita Beach, Mexico, reached farther than any FCC licensed station and was a force to be reckoned with. Ten years earlier, XERA, its sister station in Del Rio, Texas, had helped establish the Carter Family as one of the nation's leading hillbilly acts. These border stations had huge, loyal audiences rivaling those of leading stations like WSM in Nashville and WLS in Chicago, and these border blasters reached virtually the entire western half of the country and into Canada.

"Well, 4 Star paid for the studio, and we'd all go in and stay up all night long—and they didn't ask for one dime," said Pierce. "They were willing to make the transcriptions, and I'd carry 'em down to Polo every week, with their dates for the week, and he'd play their music and read off their dates—and they cleaned up. It was a hell of a trade.

"And to give it a more big-time air, I had Fred do some kind of ad-lib commercials for Folgers Coffee. Now, Folgers had never even heard of the Maddox Brothers & Rose, but it made them sound so goddamn big, that even Folgers was hiring 'em! Oh, yeah, it worked. And if you suggested anything like that to Fred and them, why, they'd go right along with it. They'd just say, 'What does it take to get ther'?' And they would do it. Which was one of the reasons they didn't care if they got paid or not. They just wanted to have records out there. The Maddoxes were willing to do something out in front, to achieve what they were setting out to do, which was knocking people dead at the box office."

The Folgers spots opened the door for other major brand-name sponsorships; Regal Pale Beer hired them to promote their brew and Fred sounded especially persuasive as he called out, "Remember, folks: winter, spring, summer or fall, it's Regal Pale Beer for y'all."

Those nightly XERB broadcasts were instrumental in breaking the Maddox name outside of California, reaching a far greater audience than the McClatchy network had. Without these fifteen-minute programs, pre-recorded on acetate discs, they might have remained a West Coast act, but the 150,000-watt clear-channel signal that XERB generated, as Rose put it, "flat reached out." Thus, they not only comfortably weathered Petrillo's jukebox strike (most other labels took to recording illegally before it was over) but with Pierce's aid they were actually able to increase their fame.

"You know, it's a peculiar thing, the role of transcriptions," Pierce added. "Transcriptions enabled them to introduce themselves to 4 Star. It was through transcriptions that we had got 'Deck of Cards' from T. Texas Tyler, and it was through transcriptions that they learned 'Philadelphia Lawyer,' which Woody Guthrie had made years before.

"But most important out of this transcription thing is, that was how I was introduced to XERB, which was very important. I was the record salesman, too. I'd sell from Tehachapi to Bakersfield to Visalia, Tulare, Lindsay, up to Red Bluff, Redding . . . and I'm on the road, selling records out of my car, taking records to radio stations, and they would ask me for certain songs. And I'd say, 'There is no such record!' 'Well, we keep gettin' requests for it.' And you would find out, more often than not, that it was one that had been done on an XERB transcription."

The Maddoxes recorded, by Rose's reckoning, several hundred songs on transcription; while approximately 116 remain in private collections today, there are doubtless far more scattered between Rosarita Beach and Shreveport, Louisiana, where they cut dozens of acetates during their later stint at the "Louisiana Hayride." These radio recordings represent a considerable body of work that today lives on only in the hearts of their aging fans and the memories of the Maddoxes themselves.

Meanwhile, the songs they cut for 4 Star Records became increasingly theatrical. "Philadelphia Lawyer" is a case in point. Guthrie's tongue-in-cheek tale of the city slicker who woos a cowboy's girl, only to perish at the rival's hand, was a sure-fire crowd pleaser. The Maddoxes' recording, enhanced by Bud Duncan's marvelously expressive, jokey steel lines, also features the pistol shot which drops the lawyer, a rather startling effect the Maddoxes always used in performance.

One of their 'hired hands' recalled the stage routine: "Henry would come after Don, who wore the lawyer's stovepipe hat, with a water pistol, and Don would jump into Bud Duncan's arms, so the water pistol would 'accidentally' hit Fred, and he'd fall down dead!"

The musician still laughed recalling the routine thirty-seven years later, and the lightning-quick timing necessary to be back at the microphones for harmony on the closing line must have been impressive. They were slick performers, indeed, and "Philadelphia Lawyer" was one of their best sellers. Eventually, "Philadelphia Lawyer" became Rose's signature number and the most requested song at any of her performances.

The Maddoxes had hit their stride, and it was during this period that the Maddoxes recorded the songs for which they are best known. After the success of "Honky Tonkin'," they cut Hank Williams's "Move It on Over," using the same shaking octave pattern and call-and-response guitar lines as on "George's Playhouse," which was their standard arrangement for many of the boogie tunes they played. Rose significantly codified her forthright social stance and onstage persona with two classic 4 Star numbers, "I Wish I Was a Single Girl" and "Pay Me Alimony," both of which came across as eyebrow-raising statements of an almost proto-feminist nature.

From the titles alone, one might assume these were subjects very close to Rose's heart, but she insisted years later that "they were just songs to me." Still, her performances on both these records—rousing, dynamic, full of color and a sense of independence—belied this indifferent attitude. Abetted by her brothers' nonstop braying, bellowing, and wise-cracking, Rose sang at full throttle, and these records faithfully captured the free-wheeling atmosphere that epitomized the Maddox Brothers & Rose's live show.

The Maddoxes were also recording a lot of sacred material at the time, and their harmony singing on such sides was similarly effective. In "I'd Rather Have Jesus," the organic sympathy with which Don highlights Rose's lead is undeniably sophisticated, yet it never departs from the realm of traditional hillbilly. In the late 1950s King Records reissued several of the band's 4 Star gospel numbers on *A Collection of Standard Sacred Songs* (King 669). It was a marvelous showcase for the band's gospel side, offering yet another proof of the family's innate musical talent and a strong suggestion of how dazzling the Maddoxes must have been as a live act in these peak years.

Only a few months after signing to 4 Star, the Maddoxes were so much in demand that Fred, who had handled all their bookings since the beginning, found he needed an assistant and brought on a young Jack McFadden to help. Then a novice booking agent, McFadden was impressed both by the Maddoxes' expanding popularity and by what a ferociously single-minded business woman Lula was. McFadden would learn well from her and go on to represent Buck Owens, Keith Whitley, and Billy Ray Cyrus.

"The first time I seen 'em was at the Uptown Ballroom," McFadden recalled years later. "Heard about it on the radio. Fred would always say, 'We'll be at the Uptown Ballroom in downtown Modesto this Thursday.' Then Cal would do that laugh of his, all that. So I walked in there, I happened to be with Truitt Cunningham [then lead singer in Al Brown & the Alabamans], and I was dazzled—I mean totally dazzled—just awed by all that glitter. So later on I went out to KTRB, met Fred and we really hit it off." McFadden laughed, as anyone who knew Fred will do when reminiscing. "He was an entertainer on and offstage; I think he could've been brushing his teeth and he'd still entertain you!

"My next encounter was with Mrs. Maddox. Now there, I've got to tell you, was the Queen of the Pocketbook! She sat on the mountain, brother, and she ruled it with an iron hand. Mama ruled that bunch, hand and foot. She gave the boys the money they were supposed to have, took the rest of it, and bought equipment."

"But you've got to figure this out: they came from a damned place of starvation. They had to give each other a bite of one item. They had it rough, so I understand what made Mrs. Maddox like that. And I've never seen a family as tight as they were. They might fight amongst themselves, but don't let an outsider step in!

"Here I was, eighteen years old and already decided that I'm going to be the world's greatest agent and manager, so I started talkin' to Mrs. Maddox, sayin', 'You know, Mrs. Maddox, that you and I are gonna do business together.' So she says, 'Waall, we'll see, Jack, we'll see. See, what's a-happenin', my kids is a-gettin' goin' now. We're gonna get a couple more cars, start livin' like white folks.'

"So, I booked 'em into a place called the Red Barn, on the river in Sacramento. We had got three hundred and fifty dollars for the date, against a percentage. This was on some crazy week night. . . . So I go out there, and I tell you, I had to walk half a mile to get to the gig, there was so many cars there already. I get in there and see Mrs. Maddox. She had a purse, a shoulder bag, right? And it was always full of money! She says, 'Hiii, Jack. Things is lookin' pretty good tonight. The kids drew a healthy crowd and I'm a-settin' here lookin' after the money.' So anyway, we settled up, she gave me my forty or fifty bucks, and that's how we got started."

McFadden recalled another occasion several years later when Lula had him booking dates in northern California with orders "not to take less than four hundred dollars," which was not a problem, given the group's ever growing popularity. "So I set one date here, four hundred dollars, another date there, five hundred dollars, and I came across what I thought was a really great deal. There was a drive-in movie in Redding, and the guy said, 'I'll give you three hundred dollars, or a percentage.' And it was a really good, high percentage, 'cause it was his merchants' night or something, and he only needed so much for himself. So I said, 'Well, I think we can work that out,' and I put all the contracts in a big envelope and sent 'em off. I had deposits on all these dates, with the checks all made out to Lula Maddox / Maddox Brothers & Rose.

"Anyhow, I get home. It's about two-thirty in the morning, I'm sound asleep, and the phone rings. It's Lula. She says, 'Jack, I got the contracts on the kids and that Redding date. I ain't a-gonna do it." I said, 'Mrs. Maddox, you could walk out of there with maybe one thousand dollars!' 'I ain't in the promotin' business, I'm in the talent sellin' business,' she says, or something like that about musicians. And I say, 'But I got you three hundred dollars on a Monday night!' and there ain't nobody playin' for that kind of money on a Monday night. 'Well, we ain't a-gonna do it.' So finally I said, 'You just sign the contract, mark it four hundred dollars and I'll give you the extra hundred.' I took the percentages. She says, 'Waall, Jack, that'll be fine.' Went up there, and the Maddox Brothers & Rose made—I'll never forget it—they made eight hundred and sixty-two dollars! She like to come apart! And she just raised hell, but as the old story proves, you're never too old to learn. Mama Maddox was a great lady. I wish I could have worked with her some more. It was a great experience."

Tiny Moore, the late swing mandolin great who worked with Bob Wills after World War II, was booking bands at Wills Point, the resort that Bob and Betty Wills had constructed in the late forties. Tired of the road, Moore gladly accepted the chance to operate out of his home base, Sacramento. Wills Point (destroyed on June 15, 1956, in a blaze attributed to arson) included a ballroom, olympic-size swimming pool, amusement park, and apartment complex. It was home to many of the Texas Playboys, who were also broadcasting over KFBK at the time. Moore recalled employing the Maddox Brothers & Rose every chance he could:

"They always did a good show. Fred would clown around and ride that bass like it was a donkey, but what I remember most was the total dominance of Mama. After the show, when I was paying them, it was always both of 'em, Fred and Mama. They'd usually get four hundred dollars, which was a lot, but they were very popular. Fred would count the money, fill out a receipt—now, Mama would want that money right away. I remember that if Fred didn't hand it right over, why, she would punch him! I have the idea that if anybody tried to pay less, they'd be in serious trouble with Mama. Like I say, it is that total dominance that she had over them that I really remember." Her pummeling physical style had great effect. Fred himself described Lula as having a hand "like hardwood."

Soon Mama's reputation preceded them wherever they were booked, and stories of her controlling behavior spread all over California. Hank Thompson, who worked a few brief West Coast tours with the Maddoxes ("Yeah, Hank was always tryin' to get you onto his bus to show you his wardrobe!" Fred would tease Rose), recalled what Steve Stebbins, a leading West Coast hillbilly promoter, had told him of his experiences on the road with Lula:

"Steve would handle the door, and whenever the dance was over Mama'd go over to the hotel where they were staying, to Steve's room to count the money and settle up on ever'thing. Now, he smoked cigars, see, and she would not let him smoke a cigar when he was working the door, with all the people comin' in and out, because she didn't smoke, see? So after the dance he'd run up to his room, close all the doors and windows, and just smoke up that room, puffin' on a cigar! So that when she got there, she'd always say, 'Steve, it smells like a hog pen in here!' He used to laugh and say, 'It's the only way I can get back at her! By golly, this is my room and she can't tell me not to smoke in it!'" Even a roughneck like Stebbins, who was a former Los Angeles police officer, could not match Lula's bluster. Though Don Pierce accurately described Lula as "crude and unlettered," her demanding style always got results.

By now, the Maddox Brothers & Rose were driving several dark blue Chrysler New Yorkers, with both Fred and Rose's bass fiddles strapped on top. The Maddoxes always strove to make a deliberately grand entrance, cruising the main street of whatever town where they were booked, rolling back and forth in their fleet of cars several times to make sure they were noticed. As they arrived in a cloud of dust and emerged clad in their Turk uniforms, it was inevitably a charged, thrilling moment. Then they would invade a local cafe, decked out in full regalia, for a bite to eat and some promotional gladhanding. They were mobbed wherever they went.

"Oh folks! Were they hot!" said Buck Owens. "And not only were they hot, they were fun. [There was] a little radio station there in Mesa, Arizona. KTYL, they called it. 'The World's First Drive-In Radio Station,' and that's where I first saw the Maddox Brothers & Rose. This radio station had a great big plate-glass window in the studio. They built 'em so they could have live stuff there. This was about 1948. What they did was, people would come and park their cars, just like at a drive-in movie. You'd park, watch 'em perform, and hear it on your car radio.

"They had advertised that the Maddox Brothers & Rose were gonna do a thirty-minute program at drive-in radio station KTYL. That was the first place I seen 'em, and then I went that night to the Civic Auditorium and seen them Chrysler New Yorkers, with the dog-house basses on top.

"Oh, Friendly Henry, and Don Juan and Fred with all that comedy, and Rose playing the bass. . . . They were just a lot of fun!" Although Owens was already broadcasting over KTYL by this time with "a little band called Mike and the Skillet Lickers," he still credits the Maddoxes as being the catalyst that drew him into the music business.

Even though the Maddoxes were able to command higher and higher fees and were working outside the state more and more, they had yet to work up to the level of prestige and national recognition each craved; despite a decade of broadcasting, they had not yet become an established act in Los Angeles. The band's only appearance in the area had been at Hoot Gibson's Painted Post (whose sign read "Where the sidewalk ends and the West begins"), a popular nightclub on the San Fernando Valley's Ventura Boulevard. It was a brief, impromptu guest set which Rose, Fred, and Cal had played after Wesley Tuttle (leading the house band there between his own tours) invited them onstage when they dropped in one night. Finally, the time and energy so long invested began to pay off. As it had so often before, the aid and influence of friendly outsiders eventually enabled the family to get a key booking that had thus far eluded them.

"I remember how hard it was to get them into the Riverside Rancho," said Don Pierce. "We'd talk to Marty Landau and tell him what great business we were doin' up and down the state. I'd get Steve Stebbins to call him and tell him what kind of box office they were doin', but it finally took Cliffie Stone to get 'em in there. Cliffie called Marty—and here's Cliffie, he's A&R man at Capitol, for Christ sakes. He's our competition! And he's a disc jockey, he's playin' their records, but he's not bookin' them, he's not makin' five cents with them, but he just dug 'em, know what I mean? And he says, 'Marty, you put 'em in here and I'll underwrite it. Any losses that you have, I'll pay you for.' They went in on a Tuesday night and they filled the damn joint. I've got to give Cliffie credit, because who's gonna do that? He's with Capitol! Maybe he was tryin' to show them what a mistake they'd made . . . but he was true to his word, and when he had a chance to help 'em, he stepped out and did somethin' for them. I really respect that."

Getting booked into the Riverside Rancho was a major break for the Maddoxes. Opened in the early forties and run by Marty Landau, a former big band promoter bitten by the country bug after attending a Bob Wills dance, the Rancho boasted ten thousand square feet of dancefloor, three bars, and a restaurant. Located at Los Feliz Boulevard and Riverside Drive, it routinely drew hundreds of Hollywood hillbillies, and nearby Griffith Park was filled almost nightly with the overflow fisticuffs, boozing, and necking of Rancho patrons. It was a major showcase for touring country acts and the main gathering spot for the growing community of country artists based on the West Coast. Merle Travis, Tex Ritter, Ferlin Husky (then still known professionally as Terry Preston), Eddie Kirk, Joe and Rose Lee Maphis, Spade Cooley, Tex Williams, Johnny Bond, and Tennessee Ernie Ford all operated out of the Rancho, which soon became the site of several television shows as well as the Squeakin' Deacon radio program. (After the Rancho burned down in the early sixties, Landau busied himself as Marty Robbins's booking agent, a fifteen-year association that continued right up until Landau's death in 1970.)

The acts that frequented the Rancho were then developing a style of hillbilly music that owed little to the more sedate and conservative country music that still held sway in the Southeast. While Red Foley was crooning "Old Shep," the Rancho's regulars were working up a distinctive, groove-oriented West Coast country sound, typified by Merle Travis's "So Round, So Firm, So Fully Packed," Tex Williams's million-seller "Smoke, Smoke, Smoke (That Cigarette)," and Ernie Ford's "Shotgun Boogie." The Maddox Brothers & Rose easily fell in alongside these folks, and they were soon playing not only at the Rancho, but also at Dave Ming's 97th Street Corral, a now-forgotten L.A. dance hall located at 97th street and South Main. The Corral featured big-name talent and was the site of regular live remote radio broadcasts; Fred described it as "the 'Grand Ole Opry' of the West Coast, kinda."

Around this time, the Maddoxes started selling eight-by-ten glossies of the band after their performances, which was standard procedure among hillbilly acts. The Maddoxes went one step further, though, having a wallet-size photo and key fob manufactured, which they also sold together for a dollar. The wallet photo was emblazoned with their title "The Most Colorful Hillbilly Band in America." The key fob offered a picture of Rose on one side, the boys on the other. Along with the 4 Star 78s the Maddoxes also sold at shows, these items provided a lucrative sideline. How lucrative? Rose has a photo of the band taken after a "Town Hall Party" radio show in Compton, California. All the brothers' fists clutch bundles of cash; prominent among Henry's fistful are several C notes.

Having set Hollywood on its ear, the Maddoxes turned their attentions to the South, and again it was an outside supporter who made it possible, Harold W. "Pappy" Daily. Since the mid-1930s, Daily had built a considerable business network, virtually controlling jukeboxes, wholesale and retail record distribution, and song publishing through much of the Southwest. Of course, as a 4 Star distributor, he had a professional stake in the Maddoxes' success. Don Pierce explained Daily's role in the Maddox Brothers & Rose's career:

"Daily, because he was a distributor in Texas and he liked their music and was having some success with it, he thought that if they came down there, it would open up Texas, for records. Now, we couldn't get anybody to book 'em. So Pappy put his own money on the line, and he booked about eight dates for 'em in Texas. I believe he lost some money, but he felt it was worth it to establish the act. And he knew that even if he did lose the first time around, after the word-of-mouth, he would clean up on the second time. And he did."

Soon the Maddoxes were embarking on regular, lengthy tours of the Southwest that spread their name. At the same time, 4 Star Records developed a new method for encouraging airplay of the label's latest releases.

"The major companies, at that time, did service the radio stations with promotional 78s, but they had to charge 'em a subscription," Don Pierce said. "Well, there was no way that we could charge 'em, and there was no way that we could afford to send Tyler and Maddox 78s to five hundred radio stations, in a carton with enough padding and postage to get it through in one piece. We just didn't have that kind of money.

"The radio stations could play 33⅓, though, and we found that we could make a break-resistant, flexible record and put three or four songs by different artists on each side, and mail out five or six hundred of those. Like, when we had 'Philadelphia Lawyer,' we made that the outside track, along with songs by three other artists. It was a ten-inch disc in semivinylite, and those we could afford to send out."

4 Star was one of the first outfits in the business to press anything on semivinylite, rather than the brittle shellac still being used by most labels. Thus, even though 4 Star might have been a exploitive operation, run by a man who unfailingly took advantage of anyone he possibly could (and whose eye was more and more focused on building up a lucrative publishing catalog of song titles), 4 Star helped make history. The new ten-inch, flexible 33⅓–rpm discs' significance was not lost on the industry, and this was a vital step towards developing the long-playing albums that dominated the industry for four decades.

Between the promo records ("4 Star Electrical Transcriptions") and Pappy Daily's distribution, the Maddox Brothers & Rose became known throughout the country. The stage was set for their records to hit on a national basis. One release finally did. It was a back-to-back sacred offering that showcased the family's emotion-packed camp-meeting harmonies: "Gathering Flowers for the Master's Bouquet" and "Tramp on the Street." Written by Marvin E. Baumgardner and originally published in a 1940 Stamps-Baxter shape-note hymnal, "Gathering Flowers" was a gospel tune with a hint of Tin Pan Alley whose mordant lyrics perfectly suited the Maddoxes' singing style. The flip side, "Tramp on the Street" (adapted ten years earlier by Hazel and Grady Cole from an 1877 sacred song) had recently been a hit for Molly O'Day and was fast becoming a country standard. Whatever it is that makes a hit record, "Gathering Flowers" had it. Released in July 1948, the disc started selling faster than any other the Maddoxes had done.

"That was the biggest record we had on them, nationally," confirmed Don Pierce. "That's what established them in the South and got them east of the Mississippi. We had a distributor in Charlotte, North Carolina, who said: 'Send me five hundred of them suckers every day until I tell you to stop!' That's what established them beyond Texas was the sacred stuff."

Apart from his record-selling jaunts on the coast, Pierce often went to Nashville, scouting songs for 4 Star artists to record. His recollections offer an interesting perspective at how the fledgling Music City publishers operated:

"I would always go see the Acuff-Rose and 'Opry' people. They were always nice, but they knew that 4 Star didn't amount to a hell of a lot. One thing, Fred Rose [the Nashville based songwriter-publisher who handled Hank Williams], he knew that T. Texas Tyler was an important artist. So whenever he had a good song, he'd send us a dub of it and say: 'You can give this to Tyler, but do not put it out before our release date.' Like 'Chattanoogie Shoeshine Boy' [a huge hit for Red Foley]. We got that thing three or four weeks before Foley hit with it.

"Fred Rose was a publisher, and a publisher is a whore for his music. Who cares about Decca and Foley? Rose knew that we weren't a threat to them, and he knew that we'd do a few extra copies, twenty or thirty thousand, on the West Coast. But we dare not interfere with that release date, see?"

Pierce was on just such a trip to Nashville in early 1949, talking up his hit group, scrounging material, and generally hobnobbing: "I went to see Fred Rose, and I tell him, 'Rose Maddox wants to know if we can find any more of these Molly O'Day type of songs, like "Matthew Twenty-Four" or "Thirty Pieces of Silver," that kind of stuff.' And he says, 'Hell, Don, I don't even know about her [Molly's] songs till she's cut 'em and she sends 'em down to me and I send her a contract . . . I can't do nothin'.' And then in comes Hank Williams. We get to talkin', go across the street for some beer and some barbecue.

"And Hank says, 'Don, I don't think that Tex Tyler is all so damn great, but I'll tell you the act that you've got who is really something—it's that Rose Maddox. Now, that is something. I've got a song for that broad.'

"We went from there out to Fred Rose's house, and he puts a little old mike down there. He's always tryin' to get Hank to sing whatever songs he can, because he knows he'll be publishing 'em. So anytime Hank wants to sing, well, brother, Fred is ready! So, ol' Hank takes his damn boots off, gets in his stocking feet, gets on there and sings that 'How Can You Refuse Him Now?'

"And he says, 'I wrote this with Rose in mind. I'll tell you why: when she sings those sacred songs like "Tramp on the Street" and "Gathering Flowers," she sounds just like an angel that's as pure as the drifted snow. Then she'll turn around and do that song of mine, 'Honky Tonkin',' and she'll sound like a gal that's straight out of a cat house!' And he says, 'What's she like? What is she like anyway?' I says, 'Well, straight out of a boxcar, you know.' 'My kind of gal! Right out of Alabam', where I'm from!' You know, that's the way ol' Hank would talk. And I took that damn acetate out there and Rose made it, and Hank was delighted."

Hank was quite an admirer of the Maddox Brothers & Rose. It is likely that appreciation for the group's colorful costumes prompted him to purchase his first Nudie suits in late 1949. Meanwhile, he was including the Maddox theme song "I Want to Live and Love" in his stage show as well. He and the Maddoxes often played the same towns within a day or two of each other, but they had yet to actually meet.

Shortly after Pierce brought Hank's song to the Maddoxes, Williams was booked at the Riverside Rancho in Los Angeles and asked Marty Landau to call Rose and arrange a meeting between them.

"Marty Landau called me up and said, 'There's someone here wants to meet you,'" Rose recalled. "I said, 'Who is it?' and he said, 'Hank Williams—he is one of your biggest fans and really wants to talk to you.'" A meeting between the Hillbilly Shakespeare and the Sweetheart of Hillbilly Swing, this was an artistic summit between the West Coast and the Southeast.

"So Mama and Cal and I went down there. One of the highest compliments I have ever been paid came from Hank Williams that night. Marty introduced me to him and he said, 'I never thought I'd get to meet you.'

He said, 'To me, you are what Roy Acuff was ten years ago.' That was a big compliment. There wasn't a dance that night, so we just sat back in the office and talked for three or four hours, and then went our separate ways."

The meeting with Hank Williams coincided with a propitious new development. "Gathering Flowers for the Master's Bouquet" had boosted the Maddoxes' career in a big way and had established them among the top hillbilly acts in the land. It also won them an invitation to appear on WSM's "Grand Ole Opry."

CHAPTER ELEVEN

The **"Grand Ole Opry"** of February 1949 was ill prepared for the Maddox Brothers & Rose. WSM still actively promoted the throwback stringband music of cast members like Grandpappy Wilkerson & his Fruit Jar Drinkers, along with a variety of Gully Jumpers and Possum Hunters. Roy Acuff and Uncle Dave Macon were the stars, Red Foley the smooth master of ceremonies for the Prince Albert segment of the program, broadcast nationally over the NBC radio network. Along with the old-time stringbands and the antics of comics Rod Brasfield and Minnie Pearl, "Opry" listeners cheered the most notable recent addition to the cast, Little Jimmy Dickens, the West Virginian dynamo who blended novelty corn with tough hillbilly boogie (Roy Acuff, in a moment of rare prescience, personally welcomed him aboard in late 1948.)

At the time, only two "Opry" artists had significantly expanded the artistic parameters of hillbilly music: Ernest Tubb and Bill Monroe. Hank Williams's fabled showstoppping "Opry" debut with "Lovesick Blues" would not occur for another four months, and the "Opry" for the most part ignored the radical shifts and expanded vision that country music developed after the war.

Once WSM and "Opry" officials came face to face with honky-tonk men like Hank Williams and Webb Pierce, conflict was inevitable, sooner or later. Both Williams and Pierce were fired from the "Opry" at the height of their popularity, Williams in 1952 and Pierce in 1956. After Pierce's manager convinced WSM that "Webb'd be a good boy if they'd take him back," he was rehired. On his first night back, Pierce strolled up to the microphone and announced his resignation, effective immediately, over the air. When Bob Wills was grudgingly allowed on back in 1944, his appearance was almost canceled because his band used drums, heresy to the self-appointed arbiters of hillbilly music at the "Opry." Nonetheless, the "Opry" unfailingly acknowledged commercial success; during this period it was primarily West Coast artists who provided fresh sounds to their stage. Capitol's Jimmy Wakely and pop thrush Margaret Whiting, for example, brought their first "crossover" hit to WSM in 1949, after an unlikely duet on Floyd Tillman's "Slipping Around," featuring a wheezing organ, sold a million copies.

When in Nashville, Don Pierce regularly pitched the Maddoxes to "Opry" boss Jack Stapp, and his tireless lobbying finally paid off. "Gathering Flowers" was perfectly suited to "Opry" standards. After the record hit during Christmas 1948, WSM was almost obliged to invite them for a guest appearance. The date that was announced, February 26, 1949, coincided with a planned tour of Texas and Oklahoma, kicking off on February 17. KTRB, which usually did not carry the national Prince Albert segment of the "Opry," made special arrangements with WSM to broadcast it that evening and record it onto acetate for the Maddoxes' collection. 4 Star took out a half-page advertisement in *Billboard*'s February 12 issue:

"They've Done It Again!! The Most Colorful Hillbilly Band In America. Newest Release . . . 'Philadelphia Lawyer'" read the headlines. Beneath that a "Flash Announcement!! Maddox Bros and Rose will appear on the 'Grand Ole Opry' February 26th."

The accompanying photo showed the Maddoxes in dazzling white uniforms embellished with elaborate cacti and desert scenes. Both Cliff and Bud Duncan are shown, as Cliff had occasionally been playing guitar with them between Winkle's departure and LeMasters's hiring. By that

February, LeMasters was out. Bud Duncan was the only hired hand who traveled to Nashville, and Henry's mandolin took the lead. While Cliff's increasingly poor health probably prevented him from accompanying them, Lula's disfavor was doubtless another factor.

Rose, only twenty-three years old, was beside herself with excitement. Fred was at his most prideful, swaggering into Nashville in his hand-made cowboy boots. "I had just got my first Cadillac," he recalled, pleased to be on one of his favorite topics. "It was a '49 Fleetwood, two-tone gray. Cal had him a maroon one. They're about half a mile long, you know, and we pulled up back of the Ryman Auditorium, and Roy Acuff, who I had already met in Hollywood, was out there, and we got to talkin'. Now, all the musicians, ever'body back there was a-drivin' Chryslers—I'd been drivin' a Chrysler myself, till I found out there was such a thing as a Cadillac! But, Acuff, finally he says, 'Fred, I have got to have me one of them.' And the very next week, he had one, just the same two-tone gray."

If the Cadillacs impressed Acuff, the Turk uniforms probably startled him. At that time, "Opry" artists favored either plain dress suits or the corny bib overalls and checked shirts of the stage hayseed. Bill Monroe usually worked in a business suit, but would occasionally go so far as to appear in riding gear. Only Tubb and Cowboy Copas affected western wear, though their conservatively tailored suits were nothing like the Maddoxes' flamboyant attire.

The family's reputation preceded them in Nashville. Little Jimmy Dickens had followed them through Texas the year before, on a tour which brought him into the same dance halls the Maddoxes worked, a scant two or three days after their appearances. "The worst time I ever had in my life," he later told California club owner Jim Brogdon, "was when A. V. Bamford was bookin' me, and he run me through Texas at the same time as Maddox Brothers & Rose. I had never met 'em, but after three days I hated those people! Ever'where I'd go, people would say, 'Yeah, you're all right—but you should see those Maddox Brothers & Rose!' Ten days of that and I was ready to quit. I got so sick of hearin' about them hillbillies!"

On arriving at the "Opry," the Maddoxes, inevitably, cooked up a conflict of their own. When program director Jack Stapp said he wanted Rose to do all the talking onstage with Foley, Fred, understandably, got angry. "I was always the announcer," he maintained, "but they said, 'We'll have Rose do the announcin'.' I said, 'I'm the announcer!' But Jack Stapp said, 'You do things our way around here.' And that kinda threw me. So I told Mama, I said, 'Let's just get out of here.' But we got to talkin': 'Well, we come all this way. Let's just go ahead and do it.'"

Fred's hard-headed reaction typified the growing country music rivalry between California and Tennessee. The West Coast posse circa 1949 vied with Nashville in popularity, record sales, and influence. Gene Autry, Tex Ritter, Spade Cooley, Merle Travis, and Tex Williams were as big, nationally, as Roy Acuff, Ernest Tubb, and Red Foley. After June 11, however, when Hank Williams tumultuously debuted on the "Opry," the commercial and spiritual focus of hillbilly music began to shift to Nashville, though neither side has ever really given up the feud. (Fred stayed mad about not being that night's announcer for the rest of his life.)

The Maddoxes were somewhat disappointed to find the backstage facilities at the Ryman uncomfortably cramped and also by the chilly reception they got from other "Opry" performers. "Basically, most of the musicians were snobbish towards us," said Rose. "Bill Monroe wasn't and Ernest Tubb wasn't. He was great to us and had us on his 'Midnight Jamboree' after the 'Opry.' But we were based on the West Coast, and most of 'em thought the West Coast could not be connected to the 'Opry.' They just didn't like it. Even though we're from Alabama, they just figured that . . . well, they were 'cordial' to us, let's put it that way. So we just went in and did our show.

"All they had backstage for rehearsal and dressing rooms was three or four little stalls, and we had left our instruments in there. When we came back later, there was Bill Monroe & the Bluegrass Boys, they had all our instruments out, playin' 'em!"

"That was a long time ago," recalled Bill Monroe. "I can't remember that, and I always played my own mandolin. I was just taking care of our friendship, getting acquainted. That's all that interested me that night, was gettin' to see her and to get acquainted. I had heard their records quite a bit and was really glad to meet 'em when they got to Nashville. She had a beautiful voice and was a beautiful lady."

Darkness fell over the Ryman, and the 7:30 Prince Albert portion of the "Opry" was going out over the NBC radio network. Red Foley, looking the distinguished businessman in his blue suit, stood before the microphone: "Well, we're always kinda on our best behavior whenever we have folks comin' to visit with us for the first time here on the Prince Albert "Grand Ole Opry," and tonight each and ever' one of us is in our best bib and tucker, because we've got us some wonderful entertainers all the way from Modesto, California. That's way out in the West there."

A murmur rippled through the crowd as the Maddoxes elbowed their way past the "Opry" cast.

"And they think so much of 'em out there in California," Foley continued as the audience, amazed by the Turk uniforms, broke into whistles and cheers, forcing Foley to raise his voice, "that the local radio station is carryin' our radio program tonight. Folks, let's give a great big Prince Albert hello to one of the most popular recording and radio groups in the country, the Maddox Brothers & Rose!"

The crowd was still cheering as Rose stepped up to Foley (with Fred lurking a surly distance behind). "Well, Rose, you're the prettiest one in the bunch," Foley said. "So you tell us what you and the boys have cooked up for your first 'P. A.' appearance."

"Well, we're a-gonna do one that ever'body's been askin' for," she said, "'Flowers for the Master's Bouquet.'"

When the Maddoxes finished and drifted toward the wings, comic Rod Brasfield joined Foley at the mike: "Well, sir, Mr. Foley, they shore do sing pretty, don't they?"

"Yes, they sure do, Rod," came Foley's well-modulated response.

"And ain't they dressed-upinnest buncha folks you ever saw?" Brasfield sputtered. "Lookit them grapes on them britches!"

"Boy, you ain't kiddin'," said Foley. "They got grapes and vines and flowers all over 'em."

The Maddoxes performed another song, ("I Couldn't Believe It Was

True," written by the "Opry"'s own Wally Fowler) and spent the rest of the evening swapping tales with Ernest Tubb until it was time to appear on Tubb's "Midnight Jamboree" radio show, held a couple of blocks away at the Ernest Tubb Record Shop. And that, it seems, was that. If the "Opry"'s management realized that the Maddox Brothers & Rose represented the future of country music, they gave no such indication. They did not extend any invitation to the Maddoxes to become full-time "Opry" cast members. For their part, the Maddox gang by and large had no interest in competing in Nashville. It was enough for them that they had been baptized at country's Mother Church, a major step in their twelve-year quest for national stardom.

Following the remaining southwestern tour dates, the Maddoxes returned to Modesto and Fred began searching for a new hired hand. It would be sixteen-year-old Roy Nichols, whom Fred had heard playing on Fresno DJ Barney Lee's Saturday morning show.

"Somebody introduced me to Fred," Nichols recalled, "and he took me out to the parking lot, told me all the rules, and I was hired."

In order to secure his services, Fred had to go the local school administration and take elaborate steps to become not only Roy's legal guardian, but also a sanctioned tutor, as the band's schedule often took them out of state for weeks at a stretch. Though Fred was named guardian, it was actually Henry who tutored Roy. Like Duncan before him, Roy often had to sneak into nightclubs to play with the Maddoxes.

"The best part," Nichols said, "was that I already liked them so much. I'd been goin' to the dances for a year before they hired me. I was really sold on 'em, they were really great. They played hillbilly music, but it sounded real hot."

This was ideal for Nichols, who had already developed his tricky, string-bending guitar style. The Maddoxes gave him his first professional road job. From there, he went on to work with several of the greatest artists in country music: Lefty Frizzell, Wynn Stewart, and Merle Haggard, all of whom knew that (as Haggard pointed out in his autobiography) "the Maddox Brothers & Rose wouldn't have nobody playin' for them who wasn't first-rate." Despite his tender age, Nichols brought to the band a sense of musical sophistication that Winkle could never have managed. Nichols contributed swinging, savagely eloquent solos on the Maddoxes' instrumental record "Water Baby Blues" as well as amazing breaks on their recording of jazz man Bennie Moten's "South," on which the entire family, in deference to the teen's potency, shouted out: "Roy Nichols, play that thang!" "Water Baby Blues" became a hit on jukeboxes across the nation.

"Let's see, I went with them in early '49, and stayed on till early '50, just a year or so." said Nichols. "They paid me well—ninety dollars a week—and that was when I was sixteen!

"I think that Mama was the most interestin' one, to me. She sat right over at the sidelines. Whatever we was doin', she was right there, and if anything went wrong, she'd get off that chair, come right over to you and tell you off, then go sit down again."

This was not mere dominant whim; Lula was an accomplished mandolinist, had sung harmony with the kids on at least one record ("I'm Sending Daffydills"), and even dabbled in songwriting. She knew exactly what she wanted to hear. One of Nichols's trademark guitar gimmicks, the rushed, descending note used to punctuate his solos was a favorite. "Roy, play that thing that sounds like a horsey fartin'," she would command.

"She did this to me," Nichols recalled with a laugh. "I had just learned a little blues thing that I really liked, so I tried it in a song one night, and she walks right up to me and says, 'If you take another break like that one, I'll fire you!' She would always listen to the music. She was the one who suggested the real flashy clothes. She was the backbone of the whole thing.

"The way she run them kids was fascinatin'. One time, me and Henry went to the drugstore to pick somethin' up for Mama. We were late comin' back. You know, we were young and caught up with somethin' in town. Anyway, when we finally get back, Mama was waitin' in front of the motel, and she just grabbed Henry and started spankin' him, right there in front of me!" (Henry was probably twenty-one years old at the time.)

"We weren't allowed to sit in with any other band or anything. One time, me and Fred and Don Juan went to a union party and got to drinkin'. Don, he usually toed the mark, but that night he was drinkin', had about three beers, and just wasn't thinkin' about what Mama might think—and she really thought! And we all got up, sat in with the band. Well, when she found out about that—golly! You can't believe what she said! We were out of favor for about a month. First, she gave you a lecture and from then on you'd get the silent treatment. All the other kids got good treatment, but not you."

Fred, ever the slick operator, got away with more extra-curricular high jinks than the rest of the kids combined. He had in fact been the first of the band (apart from Cliff) to marry and the only one to do so and maintain favor with Mama. On leave from the army in 1943, Fred wed his Modesto sweetheart Clotha Reynolds, affectionately known as Kitty, and managed to avoid Lula's condemnation. No doubt Kitty's quiet charm—and her ability to adapt to the bizarre situations and standards the Maddoxes lived with—helped her fit in. She traveled with the band extensively. Fred recalled numerous visits to roadside cafes where, by the time the family had bolted their orders, Kitty would have enjoyed only two or three bites of her meal when Lula would rush them out of the cafe. "Poor Kitty, she never got to finish her food before Mama'd say, 'Let's blow this joint,'" he recalled.

While Fred's marriage was a rock-solid union that lasted some fifty years, at the time Fred was living up, more and more, to his "Meanest Man in Town" stage persona. Leering and slapping his bass, he'd stare down into thousands of rapt eyes and growl: "Let me tell you 'bout a man named Fred / He never goes home and goes to bed / He's got a big fat wife that's a-doggin' him down / That's why he's called the meanest man in town." The song is a wild tale of back-alley trysts and "drinkin' red-hot gin," and Fred delivered it with delightful, oozing bawdiness. The Meanest Man in Town spoke from experience.

"Fred and I would slip out almost every night," recalled Roy Nichols. "See, during intermission, I'd roam around the dance hall and explain to girls what the situation was [with Mama lurking to squelch any hanky-panky], and they didn't seem to mind! So, anyway, one night we had a couple of girls, and Fred took one into our motel room, and I took the other one into his Cadillac.

"I oughtn't to tell this story, but I'm gonna anyway," he said with a laugh. "We're messin' around in the front seat, and I don't know how it happened, but my elbow kept slippin' and honkin' the horn of that Cadillac! And I did that five or six times. How come she never heard that and came out to investigate, I'll never know!

"Don was on our side. He'd say, 'I know what you guys are doin'!' Calvin was straitlaced, though. He'd tell on you. It was Cal who found out about that union party we sat in on, and he'd told Mama. But Fred always told me that she was the boss, and if I messed up, she'd fire me."

Jimmy Winkle recalled Bud Duncan's frequent protest-in-vain: "Fred hired me—he's the boss."

"Oh no, he's not!" Lula always shot back, "You do what I tell you to do!"

Following Gene LeMasters's departure, Henry was encouraged to play more and more leads. By the time Roy Nichols was added, Henry's idiosyncratic mandolin had established itself as an important part of the sound. Nichols recalls that not only did the Maddoxes play their music "hot," but they also played it at a higher volume than most other bands of the day.

"The mandolin was a lot of that hot feeling," said Nichols. "Plus they got two basses behind it. He played real loud. Nobody else turned it up as loud as they did, and Henry would really crank it up, and it sounded good. I'll say this: it was all right for them to play that loud, whereas it wouldn't have been all right for somebody else to."

Had Lula encouraged them to do so? "I'm sure she did," he replied. "If she hadn't've liked it, she sure would've stopped them. The guitars stayed loud, but I remember the mandolin standin' out more than the rest of 'em. She had a lot of influence, and for that group, she had great judgment."

Though Lula was the group's inspiration and boss, the real spirit came from the kids alone. The combination show-and-dance had developed into a full-blown stage act; Don now carried a large trunk stuffed with various props, masks, and magic-store joke items. According to Cliffie Stone, by this time the band's stage props even included an old toilet seat and an outhouse! The band's radio announcements began to emphasize, more and more, both the costumes and comedy used at dances.

"Howdy all you folks out ther' in radio land," Rose would begin, sounding both brash and bashful, then proudly boasting, "Our uniforms are the best in the business, but you got to see 'em to appreciate 'em! And even if you don't dance, all our songs are stage show numbers, so come on out. We want to meet the whole family!"

Don Maddox recalled how their show-and-dance numbers were created: "It was more or less spontaneous. Most everything we did was spontaneous. On actin' out the songs, mostly, I would usually take a nap in the afternoon. They'd accuse me of goofin' off, but actually, I was thinkin' these songs through, thinkin' what I could do to make 'em funnier. So I would visualize all that in my mind, put it together in my mind, while I was lyin' there supposedly takin' a nap. And the next time we'd go onstage, why, I do whatever I'd thought up.

"I remember one routine on New Year's Eve 1950. I dressed up as old Father Time goin' out, and we had Roy get into a diaper (he didn't want to do it). I carried him out onstage, as the New Year was comin' in!

"Another gag, I wore a mask, and then after the song, I'd go up to Fred, pull the mask off and he'd say, "Is that your face?" and I'd say, "Well, it's nobody else's butt!" Such low comedy, which reads as less than amusing, was transformed in performance by the Maddoxes' keen timing.

"And I was doin' magic tricks. I'd break an egg in Fred's hat and pull a dressed chicken out of it, and then we'd sing, 'Patty Cake Patty Cake,' and I'd bake a cake onstage in a magic pan, stuff like that.

"When Rose sang 'Whoa, Sailor,' I'd put on my sailor cap. And I had some of these trick binoculars; when I was the sailor lookin' at the girl, why, the lenses, the 'eyes' would bulge right out when I was lookin' at her. And at the end of the song, when the sailor 'breaks out six months pay,' I'd take out my wallet, show it to her, and she'd go, 'Ooooh! Sailor, I think you've won my heart .'"

Don, who happily retired from the music business in the late 1950s, lights up when discussing his stage antics. The sight of the brothers, clad in purple satin, cutting up on the bandstand, with Rose moving around like wildfire, must have been an unforgettable one.

"Let's see . . . I didn't have too many props, but when we'd do 'Cherokee Maiden,' then I'd put on my Indian feathers, and Fred would be down beatin' on his bass like it was a tom-tom, all stooped over. So I'd take my fiddle and bow, use it like a bow and arrow, and shoot him in the rear! When they sang 'Send Me the Pillow You Dream On,' I'd get my pillow out, that I'd dream on, and I'd open it up, and it would be a bunch of women's breasts—that's the pillow I dream on!"

While the Maddox Brothers & Rose did indeed "want to meet the whole family" at their dances, such risqué gags became a large part of the show. Another favorite trick of Don's, recalled by Roy Nichols, was to have two handkerchiefs knotted together and—with some deft sleight-of-hand—make it appear that it was Rose's bra, whisked off from beneath her blouse.

Gene Albright (who led a western swing band in Sacramento) recalls seeing the Maddoxes at Wills Point in the early fifties. Jammed up against the bandstand by a capacity crowd, he found himself directly in front of Rose, who was tearing up a typically hot boogie song.

"She was just kickin' and kickin' her leg up in the air, kickin' durin' the whole song, really goin', and after it was over, she looked down at me and said right into the microphone, 'YOU are lookin' up my SKIRT!' Now, you couldn't have seen nothin' anyway, but ever'body in the place was laughin' at me, and I like to've died!"

Even as the band's fame and popularity grew, they were not without setbacks. In the midst of a 1950 Texas tour, Bud Duncan was abruptly fired by Lula. He had recently married, always an unwelcome condition in Mama's eyes, and when she discovered Rose and Duncan sharing a quiet moment outside their motel rooms late one night, it was reason enough to let him go.

They hadn't been caught in flagrante delicto by any means, and Rose says, "Him and Mama had always gotten along fine, as far as I could tell. A while after Bud got married, she decided she didn't want him in the band no more."

Years later, she discussed the matter with the delicate, tentative air of a schoolgirl: "Now, I was never interested in Bud until after he got married. Ain't that terrible, though?" She laughed, then continued: "And I didn't think he was, until he came to me, after he had got this girl pregnant and didn't want to marry her, so he asked if I would marry him. I told him no, and he went ahead and married the other girl. I'd never been with Bud, except for workin', but one thing led to another, and . . ."

It ultimately led Lula to dismiss him, probably due to equal parts fear of scandal (especially since the Riverbank scene with Jimmy Winkle became a notorious piece of Valley gossip) and her own ingrained distaste for dealing with married musicians.

Roy Nichols says that Duncan's firing left a very real void in their sound, even cutting their draw in certain areas. For the past four years, Duncan's steel guitar had been an important part of their music, live and on record. To compensate, they relied heavily on Nichols's guitar and put Henry's raging mandolin right in front. The Maddox Brothers & Rose would never again use a steel guitar onstage, and this led their music ever closer to hillbilly boogie and rockabilly.

Their recording of "Step It Up and Go" (a song learned from bluesman Blind Boy Fuller's disk) with Fred's slap bass and Roy's playful, fiery guitar runs, is a prime example of their leaner, foward-looking sound. It's only one step away from being standard rockabilly; without Don Juan's fiddle, it would be a quintessential example. Conversely, their version of Merle Travis's mournful "Dark As a Dungeon" would have been mightily enhanced by Duncan's steel. Still, their fine harmony singing makes this a memorable, lovely record.

Nichols must be given a great deal of credit. Without him at this point the brothers would have been sorely pressed to maintain a credible sense of musical ability on the bandstand. Between commercial 4 Star releases and radio show transcriptions, routinely cut in marathon between-tour sessions, Nichols recorded over one hundred songs with the Maddox Brothers & Rose in the year he was with them, and any selection he appears on stands out dramatically from those featuring Winkle or LeMasters. Many artists cite him as the best player the Maddoxes ever employed.

He got plenty of practice, too, as the band continued to work seven nights almost every week. There were no more worries about having to sneak him into clubs like George's Playhouse; the majority of their appearances were at large dance halls and auditoriums open to all ages, usually with a bar or beer garden fenced off at one end of the room. By 1949, the Maddox Brothers & Rose were far too big to play any of the smaller clubs or beer joints. They were pulling down a minimum of two thousand dollars a week, and more often than not two thousand five hundred—with souvenir and record sales being pure gravy above that figure.

In 1949 Maddox Bros. & Rose became, as Fred proudly recalled, "The first hillbilly band to play on the Strip in Las Vegas—not the first hillbilly band to play Vegas, but the first one on the Strip!" They debuted at the Last Frontier, headlining a bill that included the comic Professor Backwards and the casino's resident pianist, Liberace. On opening night, though, as Don Juan faced the crowded showroom—a sea of linen-draped tables behind which floated a blur of white shirt fronts, fur stoles, strands of pearls, cocktails, and cigarettes—he completely froze. The bout of stage fright had consequences for the whole band: the next night found Liberace headlining and the Maddoxes opening.

While Don suffered the dreaded "treatment" from Mama, there was a matter of greater worry for the family: Cliff's rapidly worsening health. Always frail, he nonetheless worked incessantly. After the war, he played with Al Brown's Alabamans, then formed his own group, the Rhythm Ramblers, with Gordie on vocals. Even broadcasting over KTRB, it was difficult for him to establish his own identity and following, as the Maddox name was inevitably linked to the family band. Cliff and Gordie maintained a migratory lifestyle, following crops as well as musical bookings. The couple had two sons, Tom and Benny, and the family's needs often pushed Cliff's weak condition to its limits.

Jack McFadden recalled Cliff calling on him in 1948. "He was the outcast there, but he was a real good musician. In fact, he was the only musician in the bunch, and a lot of people said that he could outpick anybody in the family, which was why he wasn't included. I asked Fred about it one time and he said, 'I don't want to talk of it.'"

When Cliff arrived at McFadden's Modesto office, the agent was already booking the Maddox Brothers & Rose. "He didn't have any money and he wanted me to represent him," McFadden recalled. "I said, 'Why can't you be named Cliff Smith? Because every time they mention your name, they'll think of the Maddox Brothers & Rose, and that'll be hard to sell, you know?' He had a hard time dealing with that."

Although Cliff still played occasional shows with the Maddox Brothers & Rose and was featured on some of their 4 Star recordings, he would never again fit in as he had before the war.

"We had switched our style after the boys came back from the service," Rose explained, "and Cliff wanted to stick with the old blues and country stuff, Jimmie Rodgers and all such as this. You have to progress with the times. Whether you still do the old stuff or not, you have to progress, or you're out of a job. There was no real sore spot about it, that I know anything about. It was more a natural kind of break.

"Cliff wanted Gordie to sing, and Mama didn't go for that, and Gordie did a lot of talkin' to get Cliff to start his own group, rather than stay with the boys. Cliff didn't like to be dominated by Mama after he was married, and anybody in our band had to go along with what Mama said. But he was with us, off and on, and then he got his own group and started playin', but he wasn't well."

"Cliff and his Mama got along real good." Gordie maintained. "He just wouldn't do ever'thing she told him to. She was very demanding. And if anybody ever asked him why he wasn't with them full time, he'd say, 'I've got a family.' So they got along but he'd disagree with her, and he knew that she had to have her way. So he just didn't say much! Just like Charlie, he lived in Modesto for years and years and just stayed in the background. A lot of people thought he was dead!"

Gordie recalled that Cliff performed with seven other musicians in the

Rhythm Ramblers and that she broadcast with them over KTRB until the group disbanded, when she and Cliff went down to El Centro (in the Imperial Valley), where they had their own radio show, even as Cliff continued to work in the fields. Having suffered from rheumatic fever twice, Cliff was in increasingly frail health. McFadden recalled that he looked very emaciated when they met in Modesto. "His appearance wasn't that bad," Rose claimed, though she tellingly added, "the fever had left him apparently, but it had done its damage."

Now thirty-seven, with two sons and a lifelong ambition to be a success in the music business still burning within, Cliff had to work whatever day jobs he could. "He got a loggin' job up in Susanville," Rose said. "Him and Gordie and Tom and Benny moved up there. They had been there awhile and there was somethin' wrong with Cliff. He went to a doctor to get checked out and the doctor told him, 'If you want to see your kids grown, get out of here,' 'cause his blood pressure was sky high, with the altitude. And the doctor could get him into that big hospital at UC-Berkeley, so they all moved back down to Modesto and Cliff went into the hospital." Her voice trailed off. "And they said that his insides was just ate away."

Even after leaving the band, Jimmy Winkle maintained a friendship with Henry, and he had also known Cliff. When Jimmy heard the bad news, he went to visit Cliff in the hospital. "I didn't know him too well, but he seemed like a good, level-headed person," Winkle said. "I never worked a job with him, because they claimed that he wasn't good enough to play with 'em. I went to visit him and told him how I had quit. 'Your family's not too happy with me,' I said. 'Well, Jimmy,' he said, 'a guy's got to look out for his own soul, and I think you did the right thing.' Just before he died, he told me that."

The ravages of rheumatic fever, coupled with years of poverty and malnutrition, ultimately took their toll. "He was just a young guy when he first had it, and the third time he got it his kidneys just closed on him, for eleven days," said Fred of his brother's rheumatic fever. "He just got in such a mess. The old story is, if you had it a third time, you might as well forget it. That's all she wrote."

Cliff continued playing almost right up to his death. In its March 19, 1949, issue *Billboard* magazine mentions that a "Danny Dedmon, formerly with Bill Nettles and Jerry Elliot and his Singing Cowboys, is working with Cliff Maddox and the Dixieland Playboys on KTRB."

Shortly after that, his kidneys failed and he died, still just thirty-seven years old. Deeply shaken, the family had him interred at Modesto's Masonic Cemetery, paying for all outstanding hospital bills and the funeral. They felt a keen sense of loss, and even regret. Cliff had taught them well. Even though he wasn't able to realize his full potential, either on his own or with the band, Cliff's legacy to the family—the marriage of traditional hillbilly, low-down blues and uptown jazz, learned at his uncle Foncy's side—was doubtless the basis of their music, the catalyst that gave them the vision to develop, even further, what Cliff had begun back in Alabama.

Gordie took the boys and moved to Anaheim, then just a small rural town full of orange groves and ranches. She, Tom, and Benny made their home there, stayed in close contact with Rose and Fred, and maintained the memory of Cliff Maddox and his sadly unsung contributions to the course of country music. The rest of the family was stunned at the loss and decided to pull up stakes, leave Modesto, and make their home in Hollywood.

Hollywood. You couldn't get farther from a sharecropper's shack. The Maddoxes worked harder at their manifest destiny than any other of the modern pioneers of country music. They had come so far from their desperate, squalid background that this move was symbolic, pure vindication. If only ol' Uncle Roscoe could see them now!

Yet it was a logical choice. They were spending a great deal of time in the Los Angeles area, at the 4 Star offices, and at various Hollywood recording studios. Cliffie Stone was airing "Hometown Jamboree" five times a week on radio and every Saturday on television (live on KTLA channel five), and was as eager to use them on the show as they were to appear. They arranged to continue providing KTRB with enough transcribed material to satisfy their Valley fans and prepared to leave Modesto.

The move to Hollywood, where they rented a lavish home perched on a hillside at 1905 North Curson Place, was another major psychological shift for the family, particularly Rose. The rent in Hollywood was three hundred dollars a month. Most of their friends in the Valley were paying fifteen or twenty dollars a month for their homes, yet the Maddoxes could make more than their rent in one night's work.

Rose became more conscious of her image, the type of songs she performed, and the effect she had on an audience. Shortly after moving to Tinsel Town, she enrolled in a modeling school's self-improvement course; one of the instructors there was Dorothy Ritter, Tex's wife. Rose joined at the tail end of the course and resented the fact that having missed the start, she was nonetheless expected to keep up. "So I left that one," she said, "and of course they sued me for breach of contract, but I went to a lawyer and got out of it."

She was already dealing in matters completely foreign to her, and on a very personal basis. Obviously, this woman had a clear idea of what she intended to make of herself, and it did not include remaining a mere hillbilly singer.

"So I went to another school and learned to model, and self-improvement of all types. I figured that in the modeling, you learned how to walk, how to stand. I took all that and switched it around, used it to my advantage. I went to a diction teacher, also, because I used to talk real flat, more so than I do now, but I never tried to lose my Southern accent, and she didn't try to make me. She was an excellent teacher. I was going for pronunciation, and how to control my voice when talking, and it helped me in my singing at the same time.

"She didn't try to teach me anything about singing, just the control of the voice and the diction. I learned it, ever' bit and I did what I wanted to do with it—just like I always do! That helped me a great deal and gave me a great advantage over a lot of the females in the country business."

At the time, girl singers were still fairly scarce in the field. Molly O'Day was soon recording nothing but sacred material, and Patsy Montana and Lulu Belle's influence had dimmed, as the WLS "National Barn Dance" had been greatly eclipsed by the "Opry." Kitty Wells was still vainly trying to make a name for herself: she had recorded "Gathering

Flowers for the Master's Bouquet" shortly after the Maddoxes' version had hit. (*Billboard* shows the Wells version was released March 19, 1949, barely a month after the Maddoxes' "Opry" appearance.) Other girl singers like Laura Lee Owens, Carolina Cotton, and Rosalie Allen operated almost exclusively as featured vocalists in other men's bands, onstage for only a brief portion of the show. Rose Maddox was the only true national female country music star in the years 1949 to 1951.

She knew it, too. Cruising Hollywood Boulevard in her Cadillac, popping into Musso & Frank's for a Caesar salad, looking more like Ida Lupino than Daisy Mae from Dogpatch, Rose was a television star, box-office dynamite, and a famous celebrity. Her appearances as a guest on "Hometown Jamboree" were a vital step forward, exposing Rose and her brothers to an entirely new urban audience. It allowed them to work alongside innovative artists like Joe and Rose Lee Maphis, Tennessee Ernie Ford, and Merle Travis.

"The Maddox Brothers & Rose came down from Modesto and hit this part of the country by storm," said Cliffie Stone. "They came up with stuff nobody had ever heard. The boys were wild. They weren't great musicians, but it doesn't make any difference how good a musician somebody is. If the public likes 'em, who the hell cares? I can go and hire a great guitar player for scale and nobody'll come to see 'em, or I can hire Fred Maddox of the Maddox Brothers & Rose and we'll draw twenty-five hundred people.

"They were the hottest thing around at that time. They billed themselves as 'The Most Colorful Hillbilly Band in America,' and they certainly were that. When they hit the stage, it was exciting, and of course it was all built around Rose. She'd start stompin' her foot, sing for an hour, and wipe these people out. I figure with Rose, you could have played a suitcase behind her and had her sing! And of course Mama Maddox herded 'em around. She ran a tight ship. She was something of a problem on the television show, but I had an aunt just like her, so I knew where she was comin' from. They were itinerant workers. They'd been scroungin' and starvin' to death, and she raised these kids and put 'em together and kept 'em together. I don't think without her that it would've ever happened."

The Maddox Brothers & Rose worked on several local television shows in Southern California: Bill Wagnon's "Town Hall Party" (a long-running Saturday night broadcast out of Compton, emceed by Tex Ritter, and the leading competitor of "Hometown Jamboree"), "Western Varieties," and later, "Cal's Corral," a live three-hour Sunday afternoon show (sponsored by the king of the used car dealers, Cal Worthington). Roy Nichols recalled that every time they appeared on "Hometown Jamboree" "there were people hangin' off the rafters."

The 4 Star releases were doing very well, too. After the substantial sales of "Philadelphia Lawyer" (which could not have been hurt by Woody Guthrie singing the band's praises in the all-purpose promotional letter reprinted as the foreword to this book), the January 1950 release of "Sally Let Your Bangs Hang Down" brought the Maddoxes redoubled attention. The record did very well considering, or perhaps because of, its suggestive lyrics. It couldn't be played on radio; one Bakersfield DJ was fired for playing it on the air. Though the line "I saw Sally changin' clothes, she was in a perfect pose" seems tame today, for its time Fred's low-down delivery was nothing short of inflammatory.

"In about 1949, I rode with a friend back to a little mountain hollow village in Virginia," recalled longtime Maddox fan Paul Groah. "He told me before we got there that the one store in town, a combination post office/general store/cafe, had a jukebox and that there was a 'real dirty record' on it that he wanted me to hear. When we opened the door of the place that 'dirty' record was playin': 'Sally Let Your Bangs Hang Down' by the Maddox Brothers & Rose on 4 Star Records. You could play a record for a nickel then, and we must have heard it at least a dozen times that wintry afternoon."

Of course, the Maddoxes did not introduce lascivious lyrics to hillbilly music, but their kaleidoscopic juxtaposition of song styles, however, was something new and different. They tackled everything and made it their own: from the leering "Sally Let Your Bangs Hang Down" to the traditional gospel sounds of "Tramp on the Street" and "Gathering Flowers for the Master's Bouquet," from distinctive covers of recent hits like "Honky Tonkin'" and "Whoa, Sailor" to wild rearrangements of older classics like "Mule Skinner Blues" and "Milk Cow Blues," and on up to the wise-guy retooling of Woody Guthrie's "Philadelphia Lawyer." From such wildly diverse songs the Maddoxes compiled a catalogue that many other performers would never dream of integrating into a cohesive set. They were consciously and consistently appealing to as many different types of fans as was humanly possible. In the process, they were making a discernible impact on the growing country music business.

FAMILY ROAMS U.S. FOR WORK

A hitch-hiking family of seven found shelter at Oakland's "Pipe City" after a cross-country trip from Alabama seeking work. The family comprises (left to right): **Calvin Maddux,** his father, **Charles; Rose, Fred** (standing), **Mrs. Lulu Maddux, Henry** and **Kenneth**. They have "ridden the rails" in their westward trek, and hope to make their home in California—*Tribune Photo.*

(reprinted from the Oakland Tribune, April 11, 1933)

1. Hungry eyes: the family at Pipe City shortly after arriving in California.

2. Lula Maddox at Land's End, San Francisco, California, mid-1930s.

3. Lula, Charlie, and Rose in Modesto, ca. 1938.

4. Rose, the yodeling cowgirl, posing with Cal's guitar in the foothills of the Sierra Nevada, late 1930s.

5. Rose shows off her bass-playing form in the Arizona desert, late 1930s.

6. Fred, Rose, Cliff, and Don, ready to hog-tie their destiny, late 1930s.

7. Cal, Cliff, Fred, and Rose take in the sights of downtown Modesto, late 1930s.

8. Rose and Mama relishing their prewar happiness.

9. Modesto bandleader Uncle Si (left) with Cal, Rose, Cliff, and Fred, 1938.

10. Ready for the big time: Fred, Rose, Cliff, and Cal pose for an early publicity shot, Sacramento, Ca.

11. Rose jives, along with Fred and Cal, for a KGDM publicity photographer, Stockton, California, 1938.

12. The Maddoxes in a 1939 photo taken at the California Centennial State Fair's Livestock Pavilion, in Sacramento, California, shortly after they were named best hillbilly band in a state-wide talent contest. Note Don's (a.k.a. Ken) fiddle case with NBC lettering.

13. Cal, Rose, Don, and Fred, ready to broadcast over the McClatchy Network at Sacramento's KFBK, ca. 1940.

14. Fred, serving in the Pacific Theater, poses with one of his fellow "Khaki Mountaineers," ca. 1943.

15

15–21. The Most Colorful Hillbilly Band in America, showing off their custom-tailored Nathan Turk finery, 1946–1953. Shot #16 shows Fred's "battle star bass," emblazoned with stars and battle sites from his army stint; note the curtain rod used to support the neck after a jeep ran over the instrument. Fred played the bass for years. It's now displayed in a Modesto church.

16

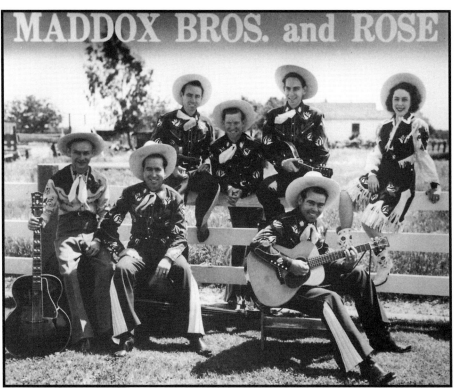

MADDOX BROS. and ROSE

17

18

19

20

21

22. Rose, the star-spangled single girl, raising blood pressure at Pappy Daily's Houston, Texas, record shop, ca. 1947.

23. From left: Fred ("your announcer"), "Friendly" Henry, "Honky Tonkin'" Duncan, an unidentified cowpoke, sister Rose, Don Juan, "Hired Hand" Gene LeMasters, and Cal "the laughing cowboy," at Visalia, California's KKIN, ca. 1949.

24. Fred, Don, Henry, Rose, Bud Duncan, Cal, and Gene LeMasters at Dinuba, California's KRDU; kneeling front and center is radio preacher John Banks.

25. Wowing 'em in San Diego, ca. 1948, with Bud Duncan, far left, and Gene LeMasters, far right.

26. Note program times on this page from a KTRB schedule. The Maddoxes would likely be doing that 6:35 A.M. show after driving several hundred miles back to Modesto following a late-night dance job.

27. Rose, with E. B. Hale on their wedding day, hopes for the best.

28. Enoch Byford Hale
and his teenage bride,
1943.

29. Rose and Bob Wills
reminisce about the
time she threatened to
"put him out of busi-
ness," mid-1950s *(photo
courtesy of Johnny Bond)*.

31. Rose and seven-year-old Donnie, on furlough from the Black Fox Military Institute.

30. Rose and Donnie, ca. 1947.

32. A big time in Porterville, California, ca. 1954.

33. The Sweetheart of Hillbilly Swing in a publicity shot from the Music Corporation of America, the same agency that booked Frank Sinatra.

34. Rose and Fred, road weary but ever ready, early 1950s.

35. Cal, in a particularly wild Turk suit, with formal Rose and "Grand Ole Opry" star Hawkshaw Hawkins, back stage at Nashville's Ryman Auditorium, 1956.

Made at The
Grand Ole Opry
1/21/'56

36. Rose aims for the "Opry," with an assist from stage manager Vito Pellettieri, eight months before her "Tall Men" appearance.

37. Rose entertains visitors at the "Grand Ole Opry"—Fred, Henry, Don, Cal, and Columbia A&R head Mitch Miller.

38. Rose, Cal, and Jim Reeves onstage at the "Opry," late 1956.

39. Rose comes into her own at Capitol, late 1959.

40. A Columbia promo shot, mid-1950s.

41. A Columbia promo shot, mid-1950s.

42. Rosie and Retta offer some flamenco thrills, ca. 1954.

43. Rose and Retta shake up the fans, mid-1950s.

44. Columbia promo shot for the duet act, 1953.

45. Fred, Don, and Henry, braced for Rose's departure, ca. 1957.

46. The show-and-dance in action. Fred: "Is that your face?" Don: "It's nobody else's but!"

47. Rose, in mod mini-dress, meets the 1970s head-on at an appearance in Columbia, California.

48. The cover of Rose's 1967 Starday album.

49. Rose in action, ca. 1986, Santa Maria, California.

50. Rose, "the walking miracle," back in action nine months after her three-month coma, San Bernardino, California, 1990. *(Photo: Ken McKnight)*

CHAPTER TWELVE

Mama's boys, Lula discovered, were growing up. Although Lula had been unable to stop Fred from marrying because of wartime uncertainties over the band's future, she still did her best to keep the others single. Jimmy Winkle recalled Cal's attempt to wed: "He was sweet on a little gal, just about seventeen years old, and he was gonna get married, but Mama said: 'No, you're not goin' to marry her!' And he didn't." Cal remained a bachelor for life.

Don and Henry both bucked Lula's authority and married in 1949. "I remember when the two of 'em married," said Roy Nichols. "Friendly Henry, he did it without askin' and was out of favor for a while, and then Don Juan slipped off and did it. He was in the doghouse for a long time, but they both got back in favor." Henry wed high school sweetheart Loretta Graham, who, like Kitty, traveled with the band. Nila Bussey, Don's chosen, stayed prudently in the background.

The spiritual core of Lula's realm—her favorites, Cal and Rose—remained intact. With Cliff's death heavy on her mind and the loss of her other sons to wedlock, Lula's grip on Rose tightened. These three took up residence on North Curson Place; Fred and Kitty leased a home in Beverly Hills; and Don, Nila, Henry, and Loretta (nicknamed Retta) resided at different Hollywood addresses. In the wake of Charlie and Lula's divorce, Cliff's death and the boys' marriages, the old family bonds were sorely taxed. Each member of the tribe began to view his or her role in the music business differently, even if they remained as dedicated as ever.

In both the mother's and the daughter's case, change was obvious. Rose had grown into a sophisticated woman, with charm school and elocution classes under her belt. Lula, still crude, unlettered, and ambitious, exerted an even greater degree of control over Rose, drawing pleasure and satisfaction from her daughter's onstage exploits. Rose sensed this hunger growing stronger within Lula after moving to Hollywood, but she had another concern: her son Donnie, now seven years old. Rose was unable to care for him, because of her hectic schedule. She would have been happy to bring him along, but neither the back seat of a Cadillac nor a dance hall dressing room was an appropriate place for an impressionable youngster to spend his nights.

It was a frustrating situation, as Rose readily admitted. "Well, there was really nothing to enjoy about it, because I was out on the road all the time. When I was around Donnie, I enjoyed it, but . . . My mother, who was very dominant and in control of everything, she never actually let me be a mother, in the true sense of the word . . . because . . . well, it's hard to explain, but it was like I was her daughter and that was it. Period. Even though Donnie lived with us, and she was partial to him . . ." Rose trailed off here, unable even today to rationalize the bizarre circumstances of a personal life entirely determined by the demands of another.

"As far as my being a mother to him. . . . Well, I had him educated, the best education I could get. I knew he'd need it, because times were changing. I was on the road all the time, and he couldn't get to school without me, and I couldn't find reliable babysitters to do all this stuff, so I enrolled him in a military school, when he was in first grade. I'd checked out military schools all over the country, and one of the best ones was the Black Fox Military Institute, right here in Hollywood. This was another reason we had moved down here, so I could be near to his school during the holidays."

Rose felt terrific shame and doubt even before the decision was made; the reality was even worse. "I think that just about tore me up, when I left that little thing standin' there cryin' in that little uniform," she said. "I told him: 'It's the only way I got of makin' a livin', and I've got to be gone to do it.' And he understood—not that he approved of it. He stayed there year round, and summertime he went to a camp out of Flagstaff, Arizona."

That was how their relationship stood for the next ten years. Naturally, Donnie's side of the matter was an entirely different story. Lula had no time for anyone other than her own kids and tried to keep Rose's mind on anything but Donnie.

There was plenty to deal with. Following their move to Hollywood the Maddoxes signed with the Music Corporation of America (MCA), then the largest booking agency on the West Coast. Surprisingly, it appears that MCA was unable to match Fred's abilities as a booker for the band. Though the company's agents were able to arrange shows at established venues like the Riverside Rancho, they failed to connect with the barns and dance halls out in the hills, the obscure, far-flung rural settings that were the bread and butter of the hillbilly artists. As it turned out, the various small-time promoters much preferred dealing personally and directly with Fred himself.

The Maddoxes were appearing all over the country now, working longer and longer stretches every time out. Each of their four Cadillacs averaged one hundred thousand miles a year. "After 1950, I'd have two Cadillacs each year," Fred recalled. "I'd put so many miles on it, then get another one and give the first one to my wife. Then I'd drive the new one for six months, give her that one, and get a new one for the road, because it'd be nearly wore out. I was gettin' two a year till '58."

He paused, seeming to recall the feel of the road, the easy ride of those majestic Fleetwoods and De Villes. "Sometimes we'd have five on the road at one time." Gene Albright recalls his own band's stretch roadster eating the Maddoxes' dust as their fleet of Caddies whipped past. Fans were often pelted with gravel as they roared off after finishing a dance or radio show.

Unfortunately, they were doing these national tours without Roy Nichols. Though he had enjoyed his year with them, the intense, rigid discipline that Lula insisted on became impossible to accept. "The rules were so strict," he said. "It was a hard routine to go by. It really set them apart from any artists I've met, then or now. I enjoyed playing with them, but I just didn't want to do it anymore. Like when we played Las Vegas, Mama told me to go to my room after the job, not to go out and play the slots or anything. Of course, I did it anyway, and she caught me and gave me a big lecture!"

Nichols laughed. The sight of an irate Lula chewing out the tiny hired hand amidst Vegas's glitter must have been an amusing one. "So the next night I turned around and done it again. She fired me, and that was it." Nichols landed on his feet. He already had another job waiting back in the Valley, and within two years he would be playing lead guitar for Lefty Frizzell.

The loss of another hired hand, which had brought panic to the band two years earlier, was now only a minor annoyance. Since Bud Duncan's departure, Henry consistently played lead on the mandolin—the only one of the rhythm-strumming brothers to do so—and with five years' full-time experience under his belt, he could now quite ably do the job. This brought about even further development of his unique style; as the need for experienced sidemen diminished, the band's own originality flourished.

On the other hand, Since Nichols's flawless technique and distinctive contributions had become so popular with the fans, there was a sense that he needed to be replaced by an equally impressive guitar man, lest the crowd feel cheated. Understanding this, and to make clear there was no animosity over his firing, Roy recommended another local picker to fill the bill: Gene Breeden, at the time only fifteen years old.

"I idolized Roy Nichols," said Breeden, who now runs a Nashville recording studio, "and had met him while he was still playin' with the Maddoxes, but was lookin' to get off the road and settle near his parents. I don't know if Roy had even heard me play guitar when he recommended they audition me, along with some other people. When my father told me that Fred had called and asked me to audition, boy, I beat a trail there, I want to tell you!"

Like Nichols, Gene had attended several of the Maddoxes' combination show-and-dances around the area, and they were one of his favorite groups. He had been playing guitar since the age of ten. Originally from Arkansas, Breeden was himself the son of fruit tramps; he knew the only way out of life as a fieldhand was in the music business, and what better opportunity than playing with the Most Colorful Hillbilly Band in America?

As it had been with Nichols, getting permission from the local high school was an important step. But being only fifteen, Breeden found it a much more complicated proposition. Breeden eventually worked out an agreement where his teachers provided him with schoolwork to do while out on tour, as long as he faithfully mailed the lessons back at the close of each week. Rose was named his legal guardian, and Breeden officially became a member of the band.

"We traveled every single day, averaged three hundred miles a day, I think," said Breeden. "We were on the road at eight in the morning and went to bed as soon as we could get through. It was a very clean, tight, straight organization.

"No drinkin', no smokin', no cussin'. No nothin'!" He laughingly emphasized. "And it was all work. We'd travel till three or four in the afternoon, and then get a chance to lay down for an hour or two before the dance. Well, while everybody rested, I had to do my school work! They just about wore me out, man, but I wouldn't trade it for anything."

Lula was doubly pleased, figuring that Breeden, at age fifteen, would be even easier to handle than the seventeen-year-old Nichols or twenty-year-old Duncan, and that there was no chance of involvement with Rose.

"They pushed me around a little, but they'd never had anybody my age workin' for 'em. With this kind of thing, though, Mama didn't care if you were fifty years old! I love 'em, still do to this day, but they had some really weird ideas.

"One time, when I was first with 'em, we were in Baker, Oregon. We had finished the show and there was a little display window, and the box-office guy just whipped down the pictures of Rose and the band, and I said, 'If you're gonna throw those away, can I have 'em?' Because the corners were all tore off and ever'thing. He said, 'Sure.' Rose and them was standin' there, and I asked if they wouldn't mind signin' the pictures for me, so I could take 'em home. They all said yeah, made some joke about it. And then Mama said to Rose, 'Rose, remember to be *careful* of what you write on there.' She was really nasty like that."

Lula ruled every aspect of life on the road. Breeden soon found that her control over the music was as complete as her dominance of the children. "When we worked the 'Town Hall Party,' I still hadn't been with them very long," Breeden recalled. "Billy Strange was there. He was the big guitar player at the time, and here we are in Hollywood, right? Well, I had just heard Tennessee Ernie's 'Shotgun Boogie,' with Jimmy Bryant playing on it, and I thought, Whoa, boy, wham! What a great solo! And I played it there, just exactly like on the record. When I got through, she told me that if I ever played anything like that again, I'd be fired.

"And then, one mornin' we had just checked out of our hotel and we were sittin' in the bottom there, grabbing a bite to eat at the counter, and they had these little jukebox things on it, so I put in my dime and played Les Paul & Mary Ford, I was a big fan of theirs. It started playin' and we're all lined up there at the counter and now the old lady sticks her head around there and says, 'Who played that mess a shit?'

"'I did,' I answered.

"'Well, if you ever play anything like that again, you're fired! If you're a-gonna play the jukebox, you play the Maddox Brothers & Rose or don't play it.'"

Even today, Breeden seems appalled by memories of Lula, still trying to comprehend these scenes of brutal admonishment. "When she'd pull somethin' like that on me, Cal would just shake his head. He knew it was out of line. Maybe that was one of the reasons I liked him so well, because he'd go, 'Mama, that ain't gonna hurt anything.' He stuck up for me a lot, because I was just a kid and when they started browbeatin' me, it really had an effect."

Gene established friendships with both Cal and Fred, making such pressures easier to take, and, after all, he was playing in one of the nation's top hillbilly acts. Even with the additional workload from his school lessons, such minor discomforts were tolerable. Like Roy Nichols, he never tired of watching the Maddoxes perform. "They did that ol' 'Step It Up and Go' thing, my God, I must've played it a thousand times, and I laughed ever' time I played it."

Don took the lead vocal on "Step It Up and Go" and several other uptempo numbers, usually more in the rock & roll vein. His careless, jokey style suited these tunes but he specialized, more and more, in elaborate stage trickery. "Don got most of his stuff from when they'd go to Las Vegas," said Breeden. "He'd sit and watch 'em and write things down. Stole all his material! And he was slick with them props, too. That's the funniest cat that ever walked, to me. They'd use the same humor that 'Hee Haw' is based on, and they are the only group I ever saw who did that real slapstick, cornball humor.

"He'd bake a cake in Fred's hat, pour lighter fluid in there, and slap a lid down on it, because there'd be flames up to here, and then he'd have a nice, beautiful cake. Or he'd be wipin' his face with a handkerchief and then he'd throw it and it'd become a cane. He didn't do anything super-complicated, but they were cute and quick, real quick, because everything he performed was while there was a song being played, so it was a two-, two-and-a-half-minute affair, see?" If it seems like Don spent more time cutting up and rummaging through his prop trunk, Breeden explained, "Oh, yeah, he did, because he was a bad fiddle player!"

Contradictory elements seemed to drive the band: a fiddler who had no desire to improve his skill, indeed no desire at all to be playing fiddle in the first place; a bassist who could barely tell one key from another and who never even bothered to learn any chords; an unorthodox electric rhythm guitarist, who threw down ringing, open chords at high volume; a mandolinist who played even louder and walked all over the dance hall with crude boogie riffs and a razor sharp, metallic tone. And yet for all their clumsy, amateur bluster, they had an unequaled fire and skill in performance, standing as strong competition to the best bands in the country.

"A lot of the other artists thought we weren't musicians," Rose said. "They viewed us as amateurs, as far as music was concerned, and I guess maybe we were. None of us read music; we were not accomplished musicians. We didn't do music this way, that way, or any other way. We just did what we felt and what came natural."

"The Maddox Brothers & Rose had a strange mixture of ignorance and supreme intelligence," explained Tommy Collins, the Oklahoma born singer-songwriter who got his start on Capitol Records while sharing an apartment with Ferlin Husky in Bakersfield. "They had confidence, an almost unwarranted confidence. I think that Mama had a lot to do with it. They had a sense of self-importance, or self-esteem that they never got away from, and I really appreciated their audacious presentation. I personally don't care if Fred can't hit a note on that bass, and it's the same with Don Juan. I liked 'em, because they were exciting and sort of brazen."

Collins, who first saw the Maddoxes at Bakersfield's Rainbow Gardens, recalled Lula stalking out to the microphone, glaring at the horde of people crushed against the stage and snarling, "I paid five thousand dollars for my kids' clothes and y'all are gonna have ta move back so's other folks can see 'em!"

Gene Breeden joined at the most critical period in the band's career, after the hired hands had established an accomplished, original sound, and just as the brothers themselves were coming into their own as players, yet still relying on the anchor of Breeden's lead guitar. "I thought the energy and everything else was what sold the group," he said. "But, really, they had their own personal style of music and there was no other group in the world like them.

"I don't think they took it from anybody. They just did the best they could with each other, learning. Like how Don and Henry, for example, were forced to learn to play. And now that I have progressed in music, I remember, or now know, how they played—or didn't play. Let's say both. I believe they shaped their playing to each other, and I believe they complemented each other in their playing."

"They were very limited, such as we couldn't do songs in B-flat, because Fred couldn't play in B-flat on the bass, and Fred didn't play in any particular key on the bass anyway. But as a unit they were good. And they had a harmony between them, I don't care who was singin'. It could be Henry, Fred, and Rose, or Don and Cal, whatever, the blend was excellent. I remember to this day, and I haven't worked with them since I was eighteen. It was really a pure harmony. And you have to remember, too, that we didn't have any guidelines. We were pioneers in what was going to happen, in what the music scene would become."

There were night after night of these dances, an endless stream of towns, stages, motels, and radio studios. "Sometimes we'd go out for four or five days," Breeden recalled. "In a lot of cases, it was four or five weeks. Sometimes it was four months. We went out for sixteen weeks, and that meant we worked ever' day for sixteen weeks, seven nights a week, and I don't remember workin' any one place for two nights in a row." For the Maddox Brothers and Rose, time flew by as swiftly as the landmarks and cities their cars passed.

In Pasadena, Bill McCall was ecstatic. Signing the Maddoxes had been the best move of his career thus far. They worked harder than any artists he had ever seen, and they never complained. Though their contract with 4 Star would not lapse for another year and a half, both McCall and Don Pierce were eagerly pressing the Maddoxes to renew with them, hoping to obligate the group for as long as possible.

Lula wanted to remain with 4 Star, because she knew McCall and felt she could control him, but the kids were by now sick and tired of being handed paychecks after every recording session and then giving them straight back to McCall. By 1951, after five years of handing their pay to the boss, they saw this arrangement for the travesty it was and acted accordingly.

The Maddoxes, after all, were not the only artists who accepted this treatment from McCall. Webb Pierce, a man renowned for his business acumen, had worked under the same terms, and he was also the first to call Bill McCall on it.

"It was a terrible thing!" Pierce declared years later. "He felt it was a sin to pay anybody, see? I didn't get any money. I just got loose from him, and when I met the Maddoxes, Rose says, 'You are the only one ever been able to get loose from him—how'd you do it?' I said, 'I used my head, just got a lawyer and threatened to sue him.' Took it to the union, and the union called on him for all the back money. McCall says, 'I ain't payin' this!' I says, 'Well, write me a letter of release, then.' So he did." (The shrewd Pierce later bought all his record masters from McCall to ensure 4 Star would no longer profit from them.)

After hearing Pierce's story, the kids ignored Lula's advice and went to the musicians union themselves. At last, the union dues they had grudgingly paid out seemed justified. McCall had gotten so much from them. They recorded stacks of records for 4 Star since 1946, many of which were dubbed onto the 33⅓ r.p.m. promo discs, as well as countless others on acetate for XERB and KTRB, and they had done all of this for free.

According to Don Pierce, none of the Maddox releases ever sold as much as one hundred thousand copies, but "Gathering Flowers" must have sold at least tens of thousands. Otherwise, why would the "Opry" have asked them to appear? In any event, McCall's one-sided way of doing business had soured the Maddox Brothers & Rose on continuing the relationship.

After the Maddoxes approached the union and explained the situation, word of their impending release reached the ears of "Uncle" Art Satherley, the legendary British-born A&R man for Columbia Records. Satherley and his protégé, Don Law, another Briton, had put together some of the greatest recording sessions in history. Uncle Art organized early sessions for Bob Wills and Gene Autry, and Law had recorded Delta blues legend Robert Johnson. Satherley wasted no time in signing the Maddoxes, regardless of whatever claim 4 Star had on them, knowing that any paper McCall held was essentially worthless.

"The Maddoxes were on 4 Star until 1951, when they signed with Columbia," Don Pierce said. "I remember I went up and saw Uncle Art at the Knickerbocker Hotel in Hollywood, and I said, 'Art, I know you signed the Maddox Brothers & Rose, but we've spent a lot of money of them, and they are still under contract to us.' And he says, 'Yeah? We've got it pretty well documented that the sessions weren't paid at union scale, so they feel they can go to Petrillo and get the whole thing canceled." Pierce knew 4 Star did not have a leg to stand on, and it was a gloomy time for the label. "Oh hell, we were hurtin' then," Pierce said.

McCall and Pierce eventually lost this battle, but 4 Star was able to come out ahead, in one respect, because of the Maddoxes. This is an ideal illustration of how McCall operated, and it all started in Cliffie Stone's office at Capitol. Stone was by then personal manager to Tennessee Ernie Ford. Looking for material to record one day, he played Ford the Maddoxes' "Philadelphia Lawyer."

"He flipped when he heard that pistol," Stone recalled, "and said, 'I have got to record this!'" The decision led to a complex situation. 4 Star owned the publishing rights to "Philadelphia Lawyer," which Cliffie was sure would be "an important record" for Tennessee Ernie. T. Texas Tyler had previously recorded Jack Guthrie's beautiful "Oklahoma Hills" as the flipside to "Remember Me," which had been one of 4 Star's biggest sellers. But Capitol Songs owned the rights to "Oklahoma Hills" and 4 Star, naturally, never paid Capitol a cent for its use. Don Pierce explained how the deal went down:

"We tried to pay as few people as we could, and Capitol had never received anything for our use of 'Oklahoma Hills.' So when they came around and wanted to get the copyright on 'Philadelphia Lawyer,' we said, 'We'll sign it over to you, if you will forgive all royalties owed on 'Oklahoma Hills,' and they did. So, in that respect, the Maddoxes helped us quite a bit."

This seat-of-the-pants scam was typical of 4 Star, but the label could not operate on such a basis forever. Shortly after losing Maddox Brothers & Rose, at the time 4 Star's most prestigious act, McCall turned his attention towards building a song publishing empire, 4 Star Music. Apart from saddling Patsy Cline with a restrictive recording contract and mediocre songs from 1955 to 1960, McCall more or less scrapped the 4 Star label and eventually disappeared from the music business, though not before selling off his catalog. It, too, is now fragmented and scattered among dozens of other publishing firms.

It would seem that the Maddox Brothers & Rose had made the ideal career move. Columbia had been home to many top-selling hillbilly artists during the 1940s, and Satherley was instrumental in signing the label's "Big Three": Bob Wills, Roy Acuff, and Gene Autry. By 1950, however, all of the "Big Three" had experienced a sharp decline in popularity and record sales. Unhappy Columbia executives in the label's New York headquarters felt that the sixty-one-year-old Satherley was resting on his laurels and considered shutting down the entire country division. Deciding it wiser to turn the reins over to a younger man, they replaced Satherley with Don Law, only months after Satherley signed the Maddox Brothers & Rose. With Satherley's sympathetic ear gone shortly after their first Columbia session, the Maddoxes soon found themselves lost in a corporate shuffle and came up against forces even Lula could not contend with.

Even before Satherley's ouster, however, there were problems. Owing to continuing legal tangles with the Maddoxes' 4 Star contract, months passed before any recording sessions were scheduled for the Maddoxes. When the date finally arrived for their first session, at Columbia's Hollywood studio on January 29, 1952, the Maddoxes were hampered by misjudgments from Satherley as well as their own artistic growing pains. In an effort to shape them into a more commercially viable unit, Satherley suggested they record with Joe Maphis on guitar and Wesley Tuttle on bass. Furthermore, he would not allow either Henry Maddox or Gene Breeden to play their instruments, only Cal contributing emasculated rhythm and singing harmony with Fred and Don, neither of whom played a lick on the session either. Though both Maphis and Tuttle were first-rate talents and friends of the family (from numerous dates on "Hometown Jamboree" and "Town Hall Party"), the arrangement was, as Fred says, "a disaster." Though the Maddoxes' primitive Okie style made perfect sense to them and their fans, the studio pickers were baffled by it. So Columbia's A&R men naturally assumed that this bizarre music, coming from such "amateurs," could be more easily popularized if made to sound like the predominant country music styles of the day.

"With us," Fred said, "it was so hard for anybody who wasn't in the band to do our stuff, because we did it so different from anybody else, that they just couldn't get it. The style we did was so simple that it was hard for them to play it."

That first session was also marred by poor judgment on the part of the family itself, who were left to their own devices in choosing material. The songs and performances reflected a distinct change in approach. "I'm Coquita of Laredo," a south-of-the-border-style pop record, found Rose in fine voice but hampered by a gratingly cute chorus ("chickalittle, chickalittle, chickalittle Coquita"). The brothers' lackluster contributions—except for Fred's leering interjection, during the bridge: "Chili beans an' Pepsi Cola"—created an altogether forgettable record. Another side, "I'll Make Sweet Love to You," was a honky-tonk number similar to the 4 Star efforts. A fine, jokey duet between Rose and Cal, it was all about implicit fornication and Cadillacs, though it was a mere ghost of the full-bore attack that 4 Star had captured so well. To add insult to injury, the Maddoxes' first Columbia single, "I'll Make Sweet Love to You" / "Wedding Blues," was not even released until June 13, 1952, nearly six full months after their session because of continuing legal snags with 4 Star. The week it was released, *Billboard* announced that Art Satherley "has resigned his post as h.b. [hillbilly] and Western cutting chief for Columbia, with Don Law, long his aide-de-camp, taking over."

Unfortunately, Don Law seems to have understood the Maddox Brothers & Rose even less than Satherley. Law viewed the brothers more as a back-up band for solo vocalist Rose. This was a disastrous misunderstanding of the band, but Law nonetheless went ahead with the notion that here was a fine singing star saddled with a rough-hewn and inappropriate group. Meanwhile, Don Law had his hands full out at Jim Beck's Dallas studio where in the early 1950s he was regularly recording Lefty Frizzell, Ray Price, and Carl Smith. The level of activity at Beck's was so intense that Columbia was at one point considering moving its country division to Dallas. (When Beck died in May 1956 that plan was shelved forever.) The type of music Law was working with in Dallas, classic honky-tonk, was a formula soon to become standard after being transplanted to Nashville. But it was meticulously conceived and arranged music, nothing like the frantic West Coast honky-tonk that the Maddox Brothers & Rose played.

As Rose pointed out, "We were a live group, even on records—singin', hollerin', cuttin' up, and the people would just go wild over it. We had become one of the biggest things in hillbilly music and figured we could do even better if we were on a bigger label." But they had not counted on the refinement that Don Law insisted on in the studio.

"Columbia didn't want us like we was," Fred explained. "We had to use the staff band they had. They didn't use us at all, and I didn't like that, did not go for that. Don Law was okay, but he just didn't understand us . . . and when they take away from you what you got, you just don't want to do nothin'. They wanted it a certain way, but 4 Star wanted it like we had it. Still, they had the contract. There was nothin' we could do about it.

"See, 4 Star understood us," said Fred. "Hank Williams had told me to stick with what I had, because they was a-pushin' us. Columbia already had the acts they was gonna push, but they didn't push our records." He paused. "I kinda hated that."

Rose knew change was inevitable. She began to wonder whether Don Law was not, after all, correct in his assessment of the band. She said nothing to Fred or Mama but was prepared for it. In fact, she welcomed a change.

CHAPTER THIRTEEN

If the Maddoxes' first Columbia recordings were under par, it made little difference in their career momentum. Throughout 1952, their radio work remained just as prolific as ever, and 4 Star also continued releasing back-logged Maddox records. Their fans remained loyal, knowing that the band was capable of so many different sounds and styles that the Columbia misfires were easily forgiven. The Columbia material was, at least, well-recorded. In contrast, most of the 4 Star releases had been murky slabs of chaotic din, with shouts and vocal peaks often crashing into the realm of over-modulated distortion.

In a way, it was almost as if Don Law's lack of faith in the Maddoxes as an integral unit only spurred them on to play even harder and more cohesively. Radio transcriptions from the early 1950s demonstrate that they were more than able to operate as a hot country band. A live recording of a 1951 dance at Compton's McDonald Ballroom is almost overwhelming in its raw idiosyncrasy, particularly in the intensity, volume, and drive of Henry's mandolin.

Their tours now took them as far east as Washington, D.C., where they played numerous shows for promoter Connie B. Gay, often on a steamboat churning along the Potomac River. Now nationally recognized, the Maddox Brothers & Rose attracted the attention of one of country music's best-known promoters, the Cuban-born talent broker A. V. Bamford. A ruthless, colorful figure with an eye for the ladies, Bamford was best known for the grueling cross-country package tours he assembled, and, later, for booking Hank Williams's 1953 New Year's Day show in Canton, Ohio. After the "Opry"'s Jim Denny, Bamford was probably country music's top booker of the day, in terms of artists represented and fees commanded.

"He was a real small, skinny little guy," said Rose, "I don't remember where he was from. He wasn't our nationality. He was one of these that I call 'an outlandish person.' He had already booked us, from here in Hollywood. He'd 'buy' us for a certain price for so many dates and then he'd 'sell' us for more, so he got his money above ours, see? That's how it was done. And one day he called me and said that he could get us on the 'Louisiana Hayride,' which was more or less like the 'Grand Ole Opry.'"

Established in 1948 in Shreveport, just across the Texas state line, the KWKH "Louisiana Hayride" was the "Opry"'s most important rival for national prominence. Chicago's WLS "National Barn Dance" had lost Patsy Montana to the "Hayride" almost as soon as the Shreveport show started broadcasting and had added only two stars of any significance since the war (Bob Atcher and singing cowboy Rex Allen, who soon fled to Hollywood). Although WLS stalwarts Lulu Belle & Scotty remained popular, they were no competition for the more contemporary artists that both the "Opry" and the "Hayride" featured.

It was on the "Hayride" that both Hank Williams and Elvis Presley enjoyed their earliest successes of consequence; other names to come out of the show were Jim Reeves (initially an announcer on the program), Webb Pierce, Faron Young, Red Sovine, and Johnny Horton, although almost all of these men abandoned the "Hayride" for the "Opry" as soon they were able. Known as "the Cradle of the Stars," the "Hayride" was certainly an estimable gig.

"Bamford said he could get us on the 'Hayride,'" said Rose, "but that I would have to come back there to Louisiana, where he was at the time, to talk it over. So me and Mama went—I didn't go anywhere without

Mama. She saw to that." This was a fact of life Rose was beginning to resent, but in this case, Rose was fortunate Lula accompanied her. They arrived in Shreveport in late 1951.

"Bamford got us on the 'Hayride' as regulars," Rose continued, "and he also told me why he had got us back there. He and his wife had split, they were in the process of divorce, she was back in Hollywood—and he wanted me to live with him! He decided he had to have a woman, and he picked me. Well, I told Mama and she flat blew her stack! We had already made the deal with the 'Hayride,' so I just told Bamford no, and that was it. He went to Nashville and got himself another woman." After a failed attempt to turn Audrey Williams into a country music star, Bamford quit promoting by the late 1950s and bought a radio station in San Antonio, Texas, which he operated up until the mid-1980s.

Being part of the "Hayride" cast brought the Maddox Brothers & Rose further in the Southern country music establishment than ever before. It also compounded an already demanding schedule of travel, radio, recording, and personal appearance obligations. "We'd go back to Shreveport and stay there for four months," Rose recalled. "On Saturday nights we'd do the 'Hayride' broadcast over KWKH. On Sundays, we'd tape all day long for the early morning radio programs. Those were sponsored by a company that sold mail-order baby chicks out of Chicago. We also had a fifteen-minute program that aired at midnight, which reached all over the South and Midwest. During the week we'd work every night, travel around that part of the country, but we were always back in Shreveport for the Saturday night broadcast."

They debuted on the "Hayride" in January 1952. Gene Breeden recalled the first night: "I never wore one of them Turk uniforms except for once in my life and that was on our first night on the 'Louisiana Hayride.' They usually didn't want the hired hands dressed exactly like them, but that night we all had white outfits, totally white, silk lined, with rhinestones all over 'em. They'd cost four hundred dollars apiece and the designs were taken from stained glass church windows. Roy Nichols had recorded 'Water Baby Blues' with them and it had been a big thing. The first time on the 'Hayride,' Roy hadn't been with 'em for over a year, but we did 'Water Baby Blues' and got a standing ovation for it."

Their easy conquest of KWKH was gratifying and, from Fred's point of view, called for celebration. Just as he had with Roy Nichols, Fred now roomed and roamed with Gene Breeden. "When we checked into the motel," Breeden said, "the kid who worked there was settin' our luggage down. Fred calls him over and says, 'Listen, we're gonna go out, do the show, and be back around eleven o'clock. Here's five dollars. I want you to go get a six-pack of beer and some ice, put it in the bathroom sink and make sure'—I remember distinctly that he said this—'make sure and close the bathroom door in case Mama follows me in. I don't want her to see it.' So the kid says okay and does just that. Well, we come back in and Fred's waitin' for everybody to settle and go to sleep. He has a couple of beers while he's waitin, and he's peekin' out the window. Finally, he says 'Okay, we'll go!'

"Now, he won't start his car because he knows Mama will hear it. He'd always park it at an angle where we could push it out of the driveway and then start it. So we get out there, gee whiz, pushin' that brand new Fleetwood Cadillac, the biggest one they made, across them motel parkin' lots. If anybody could've seen us, we must've looked really stupid. And once in awhile he would climb out the bathroom window, just raise that window and crawl out, then wake me up comin' back in at one or two in the mornin'. Of course, he didn't need a fifteen-, sixteen-year-old kid taggin' along anyway. I didn't run around as much as Roy, so Fred finally just put me with Cal, because he stayed straight and did what Mama told him."

Getting around Lula was no easy feat, but the attempts Fred made became a favorite subject among country performers. "I had already met them when I was in California at the Riverside Rancho," Webb Pierce recalled. "They all came out to see me, but Mama wasn't there that night. I met her in Texas, at a fair we were all working, and she was just a domineering old woman, one that told them boys and girls what to do—and them, thirty-five years old! One of them boys would get up and slip out at night, and she'd get on his butt about it when she found out. I told him, 'Tell her to go to hell!'"

Pierce laughed and mimicked Fred's response: "'An' git fired?' he said. 'She owns this band!' I said, 'Well, I don't know, you'll have to work it out yourself.' And he says, 'That's what I'm a-doin.'"

Fred recalled there was many a morning when it was hard work indeed "not to look tired" after a round of late-night escapades. Rose has maintained that she and Fred were the black sheep of the family, but with Mama's attentions focused so intently on Rose, it was Fred who had a better chance for slipping around.

"Mama has drug me out of bed in the middle of the night more than one time, huntin' Fred," Rose recalled. "Oh, yes. Mama didn't drive, so I had to go with her—and she always found him, too. Said, 'Come on, Fred!' and he went. There were no ifs, ands, or buts. He went. She knew the things he did and she could just home right in on him. He and Roy would slip out at night and she always knew, but unless she got worried and decided to go after him, why, she'd usually let it slide by."

This cat-and-mouse routine went on almost nightly. Late one evening, after the Maddoxes had finished a gig, Lula was hungry, so she and Rose strolled over to a nearby coffee shop when who should turn the corner but Fred, holding a six-pack of beer. "Mama got so mad she was like to kill him," Rose said. Although they were at the tail end of a Texas tour, Mama resolved to fix his wagon. She took Rose first for a bite to eat and then directly to their Sedan de Ville, driving straight through to California. Before leaving, Mama rounded up Loretta as well; she had accompanied Henry on the tour and, being a fair singer herself, she might otherwise have been drafted to fill in for Rose. The brothers sheepishly played the remaining dates, announcing that Rose was ill.

While Lula's punishment may have taught Fred a lesson—to be more sneaky in the future—the disappointment of several thousand Texas fans was surely more damaging to the band then any clandestine late-night beer guzzling. Such flare-ups of rash judgment, of course, had characterized Lula's approach to family business from the very beginning. Despite all her driving ambitions for her brood, Lula often seemed to show a complete and paradoxical disregard for the band's welfare.

Rose recalled another episode of Lula's capricious attitude. "We were working every night and I was doing the majority of the singing," she said. "I had this horrible cold and I was still singing. My ears plugged up and it got to the point where I couldn't hear anything on stage. My doctor said, 'There's nothing I can do. Go to Arizona and get in that dry heat. Your ears will open up.' Well, Mama and I drove over to Yuma, was there one day and she decided that she didn't like it. So we went to Phoenix and she didn't like it there, either."

There they were, on doctor's orders to stay in Arizona until Rose recovered, but Lula was dissatisfied and would not stay, regardless of her daughter's condition. "When we were driving over, we heard on the radio that T. Texas Tyler was appearing in San Diego, and after Mama heard that she said, 'Let's go see Tex Tyler.' So we started back over the mountains when my ears opened up—I had got enough of that dry heat to do it. So we went and seen T. Texas Tyler, then turned around and went home."

Thus it was only by sheer chance that Rose was exposed to enough dry heat to help her condition. Or so it seemed. Rose often referred to Lula's presentiment (which seemed particularly strong where she was concerned) as an inescapable phenomena. "Mama knew what I was thinkin' most all the time," Rose explained, "and would say it before I did." This ability was a key aspect of the dominance and control that mother increasingly exercised over daughter.

Another source of frustration for Rose was that she was never allowed to enjoy the company of any man, save for her brothers. Not that there hadn't been suitors. ("Oh, man, she had a body that would break you up," said Jack McFadden.) At the "Hayride," Johnny Horton proposed to her. "One night he came up to me," said Rose. "He'd decided it was time to take a wife, and out of the blue he says to me, 'Rose, will you go out with me?' and I said, 'No, I won't.'

"And then he says, 'Rose, will you marry me?'

"'Johnny, I think the world of you, but I don't want to marry you.' He was in the mood, says, 'Well, it is time to get married.'"

She recalls that two weeks later Billie Jean Eshliman Williams (Hank's second wife) was backstage at the "Hayride." "And she says, 'I predict the next big star will be Johnny Horton!' And shortly after that, they were married, and sure enough, he was the star!" (Horton did indeed go on to major stardom with his million-selling "Battle of New Orleans"; unfortunately, Billie Jean was widowed again when Horton was killed in a car wreck in Texas, so badly disfigured that his toupee and jewelry were the only means of identification at the site.)

Forced to content herself with the fulfillment her music and her audiences brought, Rose persuaded herself that all was well. She was justifiably proud of her reputation as one of the best female singers in country music. In the back of her mind, though, she began to wonder if perhaps the antics of her brothers detracted from her performance, if in fact Don Law might be right. As she grew more conscious of her image, Rose noticed that she was being mimicked at the "Hayride."

"When we was on the 'Hayride,' for instance, all the girls on there—and there was several—started tryin' to copy what I was wearin'," she said, adding that they were "just local girls who haven't been in the business for years.

"I thought, Well, I'll get me a nice evenin' dress. So I had several of 'em made up, formal stage dresses, instead of the western stuff. I showed up one Saturday night wearin' one of 'em, and the very next weekend every girl on the 'Hayride' was wearin' that type of dress!"

She laughed, recalling her day as a trendsetter. "Oh, it made me mad! So I went back to the other type of clothes, even though that was why I'd switched in the first place, because so many others wore 'em. They thought I was a leader in the stuff, which actually, after I thought about it, I guess I was! Because there wasn't a lot of female singers in the business back then."

Rose had to work even harder to stay on top after the spring of 1952, when Kitty Wells scored a #1 smash with "It Wasn't God Who Made Honky Tonk Angels." With that record Wells became the first female solo singer in history to top the *Billboard* country charts, which was an indication of how few female artists there were in country music and how poorly accepted they were. Before long, Wells assumed the unofficial title "Queen of Country Music," an honor that up until then Rose Maddox had claimed. But Rose did not resent the success of Kitty Wells at all. In fact, she was a big fan of Wells's record and must have instinctively realized that there was a world of difference between Kitty's staid, tradition-bound presentation and Rose's high-powered, increasingly elegant whirl-wind.

Meanwhile, it was time for another Maddox Brothers & Rose record-ing date with Columbia. For their second recording session, Don Law let the group handle the music on their own, without any additional session players. Held on October 26, 1952, in Hollywood, the session yielded some decent material: "Green Grow the Lilacs," a sentimental nine-teenth-century chestnut with fine harmony singing; "The Hiccough Song," a novelty much more in step with the crazed spontaneity they were known for; and yet another foray into country-pop, "Little Willie Waltz."

Law arranged their next session in Dallas on December 13. Jim Beck's studio was booked solid, so they recorded in, as Fred remembered, "a big barn type of thing. Well, it was a warehouse, really." Although admon-ished by Law to "tone down the hollering," they were back to recording much as they had with 4 Star.

Law insisted the Maddoxes cut the Carlisles' "No Help Wanted," which would hit the charts the following January before inspiring a hit cover by Hank Thompson and a hit duet reworking ("No Help Wanted No. 2") by Red Foley and Ernest Tubb. The Maddoxes made an amazing record, better than anything else they had yet done for Columbia. Henry's mandolin took the lead (Gene Breeden never played on any com-mercial releases), and he played imaginative, jazzy solos, as sophisticated as they were rude and driving. Fred's vocal was superlative, though years later he still scoffed at Law's choice of material. The song was ideally suited to the Maddoxes, but the other stars' versions blacked theirs out, and it foundered at the retail counters. And yet this Dallas session, where Fred was given a lead vocal, was a breakthrough. The Maddoxes' first eighteen months on Columbia had been artistically disastrous, but now Law finally understood what the group was all about.

Despite a year and a half of inferior record releases, the Maddox Brothers & Rose became more and more popular. What with appear-ances on the "Hayride," "Hometown Jamboree," and "Town Hall Party," as well as transcribed broadcasts from KTRB, live from the Riverside Rancho and Ming's 97th Street Corral, and daily programs on KWKH, their name and music were getting big play.

In a way, perhaps, this abundance of exposure contributed to the poor sales Columbia had with them, since the Maddoxes were there every time anyone turned on the radio or television, or heard a jukebox play. Columbia's virtually nonexistent promotion for the band certainly didn't help matters. Without any professional management or big-picture business acumen, the Maddox Brothers & Rose just about out-promoted themselves. They were still giving it away, routinely recording far more material on acetate for radio broadcasts than for commercial releases, content to get the majority of their income from gate receipts.

For all their successes, and there were many, the Maddoxes' career was also marked by a number of factors that held them back. All these were caused primarily by Lula's domineering style. Although she inspired fierce loyalty and had sound, steady judgment for the most part, her inflexible attitude just could not carry the group into the upper strata of country music's firmament.

Lula knew it, too. She had wanted to stay with 4 Star, even though she knew her children were being swindled, because she thought it was a company she could, as Fred and Rose both said, "boss around." To her mind the Maddoxes' road show sales of photos, key fobs, and records evened up the injustice of all those unpaid recording sessions. Besides, she still had thousands of dollars from sales of these socked away in a Hollywood safety deposit box.

She conducted business as if she were still leading her children through perilous badlands, relying on simple survival techniques. She had the basic drive of the frontiersman, not the shrewd strategies of music business professionals. Though her primitive methods kept the all-important family pride intact, they afforded the band only a minimum of professional progress. The Maddoxes ignored increasingly important aspects of the business, such as publicity and song publishing, which were fast becoming fundamental to success in the business of country music.

Back at the "Hayride," the Maddoxes continued wowing all comers. Hank Williams had returned to the show in September 1952, fallen like

Lucifer from the paradise of WSM back into the Cradle of the Stars. The Maddoxes worked alongside him and the Carlisles (from whom they also picked up "Too Old to Cut the Mustard," one of their best transcription recordings from this period), but Mama's "stick to yourself" dictates held true. Gene Breeden had to sneak into the "Hayride" basement to swap licks with Johnny Horton's guitar player; Don Maddox recalled working numerous shows there with Hank Williams but never actually watched him perform. (This may speak more of Don's own lack of interest in music than any family policy; Rose and Fred were always right at the sidelines.)

If spontaneity was the rule on the bandstand, after the show it was all strictly business, and the organization cut no slack for any of them. For teenaged Breeden the stifling restrictions all came to a head one night in Oklahoma City.

"We'd been on the road for about eight or nine weeks, and we were booked in at Hank Thompson's place," Breeden recalled. "I'd played the program a thousand times, but I would get so lost, man, because they'd do somethin' a little bit different or funnier, every time. Say I'd be really into watchin' Don, and Fred would catch me and he'd get right behind me and slap me—real hard—right in the middle of the back. I mean, he'd knock you to your knees almost! And this in Oklahoma City. The stage was as high as your shoulders, with a little ol' thing like a picket fence right in front.

"I was standin' there, lookin' off, and there was hundreds on the dance floor, Mama's over on the bench, and I'm daydreamin'. Fred come up and slapped me so hard that I went right straight over the front. That's the hardest he ever hit me. He really laid it on—BANG! And up off that bench comes Mama, yellin', 'I told you not to hit that kid!' And the both of 'em, Fred and Mama, just barely managed to catch me in time, and right in the middle of a tune."

The shaken sixteen-year-old struggled through the rest of the show, having barely missed being impaled, or trampled. He glanced down into the crowd and saw his next-door neighbor from Visalia, with her teenage daughter, a girl from Gene's own class in high school.

"I hadn't seen anybody from home in nine weeks," he said. "They were out visiting relatives in Oklahoma and came up while we were playing, said hi. Man, was I surprised to see 'em. We took a break right after that, and I got down and walked to the bar with 'em. The mother bought me and her daughter a Coke."

Unbeknownst to Gene, Cal stood on the bandstand alongside Lula, pointed out the three to her with a sly grin and chuckled: "You better watch your little boy; there's a girl after him!" As Lula wedged her bulk and money bag through the crowd, Cal let out his cackle and sat back to watch the fireworks. He often dispatched her on such needless missions simply to get a laugh from observing the effect she had on innocent bystanders.

"So Lula walks right up to us," Breeden continued, "butts in between and says, 'You're breakin' one of our laws, ain't you?'

"'What law's that?'

"'You can't be associatin' with people like this.'

"'No, these are my neighbors. I go to school with this girl. They're out here visitin' relatives.'"

Lula threw out her chest and gave Breeden her hardest tone:

"'You let them buy you that coke, didn't you?'

"'Yes, I did.'

"'Well, you know that nobody can buy you a drink, or anything!'

"And the lady says, 'Hey, wait a minute, this boy lives next door to us. . . .'

"And Lula turns to her and says, 'You ought to be ashamed, lettin' your daughter hustle musicians like this.'

"And the lady says, 'That's all you need to say to me.'

"And Lula whips out a badge, because they were all deputies and she says, 'If you say one more word to me, I'll arrest you.' And it embarrassed me so badly."

Breeden shook his head at the memory. "Right then, Cal came runnin' up and tried to call his mother off, but it had gotten totally out of hand, right in front of everybody. 'Gene, I'm sorry,' Cal says. 'I was teasin' Mama. I didn't know she was gonna do this. . . .' And I loved Cal, man. He was the one I rode with most of the time.

"So that night, I told 'em, 'Look, I've never caused you any trouble,

I've done everything your way, but this time you are wrong and I'm through.' And they all said, 'No! You can't just leave.' And I said, 'I am. First thing in the mornin'.' And the mother was one of these: 'Go ahead—you'll be sorry! You'll never work for us again.' But I got on a bus the next day and went back to California."

So they lost Gene Breeden, who would prove to be their final hired hand. Despite the circumstances under which he left the band, Breeden stayed in close contact with the family and did return on several occasions to fill in on brief tours when health problems arose, such as when Henry was hospitalized for removal of a spinal cyst. (Rose underwent similar surgery in the mid-1940s, only a minor case in comparison to Henry's.)

Between a permanent ban on hired hands—Lula would tolerate no more meddling outsiders, and the brothers were eager to play—and Columbia's "half-sweet, half-acid" (as Fred liked to say) treatment of the band, Cal and Henry came into their own on records, both trading off leads that became more economical and evocative. The band was definitely tightening up. Even so, 1953 was a lean year for Maddox Brothers & Rose releases, limited to several sessions that produced mostly remakes of previously recorded stage and radio show favorites.

It was during this period that Fred cut one of his greatest vehicles, "Kiss Me Quick and Go," a sly, licentious tale of front-porch wooing cut short by an enraged dad who turns loose his dog on the unlucky suitor. Fred was in top form with his wry, drawling delivery on the record, offering lines like: "Through the window I had business, 'round the corner I went whizzin', with that big white English bulldog on my trail." The Maddoxes had previously recorded the song as a transcription for KTRB, with Cal singing harmony, but the commercial release, as a duet with Rose, was (for once) far superior. The band also recorded "Baby, You Should Live So Long" (which they had previously recorded for 4 Star) and "Just A-Walkin' in My Sleep," another jump folk-growler from Fred, one of his most popular songs, which had been cut as an acetate for KTRB.

But 1953 was also the year that Columbia offered Rose a contract as a solo artist, allowing her to explore different types of songs and moods while still maintaining her identity as leader of the family band. It was an opportunity she relished. While the brothers were cutting remakes of familiar favorites, her song choices reflected the shift she had made with her image at the "Hayride." Rose knew that variety had been a crucial part of the Maddoxes' success and that it was time to move on. They had been singing stone-country oldies like "Sally Let Your Bangs Hang Down" for nearly fifteen years. She began picking songs with an increasingly mainstream pop slant. In retrospect, it was not a very surprising turn at all. Tony Bennett and Joni James may have had best-selling records with their pop covers of Hank Williams's songs, but hillbilly music was still a subject ripe for derision in the major cities of America. Corny antics may have been all well and good for the Maddox Brothers, but Rose, gussied up in fur-stole-topped formal gowns, wanted to bring some glamour and sophistication to both her image and her act.

Her first session as a single was on May 19, 1953, during which she waxed the mournful lover's plea "I'd Rather Die Young," and a sprightly "The Nightingale Song." The next recording date was September 1, just weeks after her twenty-eighth birthday. She took a fine lead on "I'm a Little Red Caboose," a mix of uptown sass and down-home metaphor that, while far from a hit, demonstrated Rose's artistic instincts were far from those of a back-hills country gal. As showcases for her expanded interests, most of these songs were less than ideal, but they made it clear that, years before Marty Robbins and Johnny Horton began dabbling in the field, Rose had taken some of the earliest steps towards a country-pop blend.

The Maddoxes were booked so heavily that Rose rarely saw Donnie and was never able to visit the Arizona camp where he spent each summer. Still attending military school, Donnie turned ten years old in December 1953.

"Of course I felt bad about it, but what could I do?" Rose asked years later, sounding as if she was still questioning herself about the situation. "He resented the fact that he was never home like the other kids for holiday vacations. He had to stay there in school, and usually there was one or two other boys whose parents weren't home at the time.

"But we were very close," she insisted. "As far as he and I were concerned, it was just me and him and that's all there was."

But it was a relationship built on phone calls, postcards, letters, and brief visits, too few and far between to suit anyone but Lula. Rose's life was dance halls, Cadillacs, highways; the only constants were songs, cash, and the quiet activity of the odometer. The pain of separation from her son gnawed at Rose. She was in a tough spot, both personally and professionally. She desperately wanted to be a mother to Donnie, have him beside her and yet still maintain her career—but how could she do both?

Rose began to see that her life was marked by divisions between her and her son, and between the family band and her potential as a solo act. Most difficult of all to accept was the gulf that Lula kept between Rose and her hopes of romance. At the age of twenty-eight, she was a nationally famous entertainer under two contracts to one of the biggest record companies in America. But her personal life was dictated by Mama and circumstance. It had been wrested completely away from her.

CHAPTER FOURTEEN

Surprisingly, given how many miles the Maddoxes covered year in and year out, not one of the Maddoxes' Cadillacs was ever involved in a serious accident. The road was second nature to the family. Even though they always drove as fast as they could safely get away with, each brother handled his car with meticulous care. The collisions they avoided on the highway, it seemed, occurred instead on the bandstand.

"I've heard Don say, 'Me and Fred used to fight so much,'" when they was a-workin'," Alta recalled, "and he says, 'We'd fight right on stage and ever'body thought we were puttin' on a show, but we weren't!'" The majority of these incidents amounted to standard sibling rivalry, but twenty years on the road produced plenty of strains. This cranky dissatisfaction was not limited to the boys. The chance to record on her own also affected Rose, both in how the public perceived her and in the way she saw herself.

"Rose always felt that she was a better singer than they were performers," observed Gene Breeden, who last worked with the Maddoxes in 1954, when Henry was temporarily hospitalized. "After we did the 'Hayride' and really got accepted on there, she didn't feel the musicianship of her brothers was good enough to support where she could go. Now, it was a confidential situation, but they fought a lot in front of me. I guess they thought, with my age at the time, they didn't think it made much difference to me."

When the bickering was over, though, music and career superseded all else. Rose's separate recording contract as a solo act ultimately benefited the Maddoxes tremendously. With Rose able to choose the songs and go her own artistic way on her records, Columbia was content to let the Maddoxes have free rein in the studio. As a result, when they recorded together, Rose and her brothers concentrated on recording material that was solidly representative of the band's singular brand of honky-tonk thrills. In short, they became more focused.

One of their best Columbia sides, 1955's "I've Got Four Big Brothers (To Look After Me)" was an ideal example. Rose was in top form on the recording, playing the coquettish mountain gal. For their part, the brothers contributed a spirited accompaniment. It became one of their most popular records and their best seller since the release of "Sally, Let Your Bangs Hang Down."

That February 7, 1955 session was one of the Maddoxes' finest. In addition to "Four Big Brothers," they cut "No More Time," a clattering answer to Webb Pierce's "There Stands the Glass," and "Rusty Old Halo," still a Rose Maddox standard today. The playfully sexy "I Gotta Go Get My Baby" (a Top Ten hit for Justin Tubb that year) with Rose's lingering, "feathered" drawl on the title line was another unforgettable performance. Throughout the session, the brothers made several tempo changes to great effect, much as they had previously in their arrangements of "Milk Cow Blues" and "New Mule Skinner Blues." Their next session, on October 1, continued to produce high quality records. On "I'll Find Her," the brothers' own harmony and lead vocals sounded better than ever, and Rose's lead on "Let This Be the Last Time" was a model of world-weary, blue romanticism.

On her solo records, Rose continued to experiment with smooth love songs cast in the country-pop mold (such as the wistful, moody plea of "When the Sun Goes Down"), but she never went so far as to shed her image as a high-powered honky-tonk angel. At the suggestion of Cliffie

Stone (who, still at Capitol, never let competition get in the way of advising a friend), Rose recorded a steamy, supercharged version of r&b belter Ruth Brown's "Wild, Wild Young Men," one of the flat-out raving-est performances of her career. Released in May 1955, still a year before Elvis Presley's national breakout, it was as definitive a piece of proto-rockabilly as there was in pre-Elvis country music.

During this period, Rose also made a startling addition to their stage show: flamenco dancing. "I had seen flamenco dancers on Olvera Street [in Los Angeles] and had gone to Vegas to see José Greco, and I thought it was just great," she said, enthusiastically recalling the days when she pushed the accepted boundaries of the "girl singer" in country music far beyond what any of her rivals ever attempted. "Then Mama, Cal, Henry, Loretta, and me took a week's vacation, and flew down to Mexico City, where we saw all of these Spanish and flamenco dancers, and also Aztec Indians dancing there, and I decided it was just something I wanted to do.

"So when we got home, Loretta and I went down to Hollywood, where there was a teacher who taught flamenco. We both learned it and had costumes made up for it. That's when Loretta joined the group, because her and I were dancing together. We were doing lots of auditorium dates, and it was good variety. Of course, your country people weren't educated to that type of dancing." She paused to laugh, still amused to recall the fans' bewildered reaction.

"We had the costumes for it, and I had just fallen in love with the dancing. It fit in very well, just because it was so different. We'd do our regular show and then Loretta and I would come out. We'd just do a couple of songs, singin' and dancin'. It was interesting, it really was. We did that for about a year."

Rose had found something that she could throw herself into, without seeking Mama's approval—though she had that—and relished being able to do something simply because she wanted to. And not only did the dancing rivet the audience's attention to her (and away from the brothers), it also drew Loretta into the act. Loretta became probably one of the first real girlfriends Rose was allowed to have, apart from Alta and Gordie, whom Rose now rarely saw.

That Lula allowed Loretta to continue traveling with the family suggests she realized the band had reached a new plateau and that she could no longer exercise the same degree of control over her brood. Fred still booked the band and Lula definitely ruled them, but more on a personal basis, rather than controlling all business. The brothers, after all, were grown men with wives and children, each of whom, according to Rose, addressed Lula as "Mrs. Maddox," never "Grandma." All except Donnie. Anything having to do with Rose was viewed differently by Lula, who now came to focus her attentions, demands, and needs almost exclusively on Rose alone.

Encouraged by the creativity of the flamenco portion of the Maddoxes' stage show, Columbia signed Rose and Loretta as a vocal duo, billing them as Rosie & Retta. By 1955, Rose was under three separate, concurrent contracts to the label, a claim no other female singer in country music—or pop music, for that matter—could make. Unfortunately, the duets did not do well. "That was a one-year contract," Rose said. "We put out four sides during that year, two or three singles, I think, but they didn't sell, so Columbia dropped the contract."

But Rose's solo sides were making more and more noise in the marketplace. On December 21, 1955, Rose recorded "Tall Men" (an adaptation of the old "Get Along Home, Cindy" folk song) which, after its release the following month, slowly but steadily became a popular regional jukebox hit. With Merle Travis's agile guitar and Rose's aroused vocal, it was one of her best records as a solo act, and it remains one of her personal favorites. At the same session, she cut "Burrito Joe," another south-of-the-border pop foray and "Hey Little Dreamboat," a bubblegum-flavored rocker. Rose was trying everything she could, hoping that one of these songs would finally win her recognition as an individual.

Meanwhile, rock & roll had caused total panic within the country music field. Artists like Elvis Presley, Bill Haley, and Carl Perkins were blurring the distinctions between country, pop, and r&b fields and charts. A commercially disorienting phenomenon that caught country off guard, rock & roll was all the more difficult for the country music establishment to accept due to its emphatic reliance on unwelcome Negro influences and unbridled sexuality. Rock & roll was a hard slap in the face for Nashville, where this kind of "crossover" was far too radical to understand. Record companies and artists alike were desperately scrambling to keep pace, often with embarrassing results, or were simply burying their heads in the sand.

By 1956, the Maddox Brothers & Rose had been serving up music that blended country and r&b for a full ten years, yet they always managed to keep their music within the hillbilly framework. They certainly were not unaware of what was going on; indeed, they were at the heart of it. "We knew we were ahead of ourselves," said Fred, discussing the rise of rock & roll. "We was a-doin' it ourself with the hillbilly thing. We was always about ten or twelve years ahead of ourselves, but it was just a-happenin', so we just let it happen. I don't know if we started it, or who started it. It just fell in, just came into the world."

For years prior to this, many of rock & roll's progenitors had watched Fred growl and slap the bass, had admired Cal's hard, screeching rhythm guitar and Henry's wickedly terse, blues-tinged breaks. Some of these fans did more than just watch. They wanted to get in on the action.

"We were playin' the Cotton Club in Lubbock, Texas," Fred said, "and the radio station guy who promoted the deals said, 'We got a band we're tryin' to get started, can you help 'em out?' So they come out to the club, and we let 'em on. It was Buddy Holly and the gang. So they got started kinda, doin' two or three shows with us, and later a lot more, on up to Nashville. I'm kinda proud, we helped out a lot then. Buddy wasn't even twenty when we met him in Lubbock."

By 1954, the Maddoxes had, of course, seen the avatar of the revolution in the flesh. "Elvis was on the 'Hayride' with us, and we worked with him a lot." said Fred. "See, we'd use a package deal out of the 'Hayride,' to work auditoriums. We were all workin' in Beaumont, Texas, and it was real hot down there. We had our pink uniforms on, because it was April, so we had pink for Easter. I had taken my jacket off, 'course the pink shirt's underneath, you could wear the jacket, or not."

The occasion was a two-day stand to benefit the Beaumont Police Department, with Marty Robbins, Elvis, the Maddox Brothers & Rose,

Sonny James, and the Belew Twins. "Elvis was back in our dressin' room, kiddin' around, and he put on my pink jacket," Fred continued. "Boy, he really liked that! Then my mother comes in there and said, 'Fred! Tell him to take off that jacket!' I said, 'Mama, he wants to try it on, I'm not gonna do it.' And she said, 'Well, I will,' and takes my jacket offa Elvis. And all he said was, 'One of these days, I'm gonna have me a pink jacket.'"

To the Maddoxes, who had jumped the boogie since before the war and who worked alongside Elvis and Buddy Holly before anyone outside of the South ever heard of them, rock & roll was, as Fred put it, "Real neat, to us. When Bill Haley came out, we started doin' more of that, 'cause it just fit us, we already knew that."

The Maddoxes had continually moved forward, exploring both the latest hits and any number of older songs and diverse influences ignored by other country artists, as exemplified by Rose's interest in flamenco. Along the way, dozens of other performers would note how a specific element was employed by the Maddoxes, then translate that into their own method, expanding on what the Maddoxes began.

A fascinating example of this impact was chronicled by Hank Williams biographer Roger M. Williams in an interview with guitarist Zeke Turner, who played on all but one of Hank's sessions. Turner described how he developed the rhythm technique known as "dead string," in which muffled, amplified guitar strings produced a sound akin to drums. It was an important rhythm technique because at the time drums were frowned upon in Music City, and for years it was standard procedure in Nashville studios.

"Freddie [Rose] liked what I did," Turner said. "I played a good, heavy rhythm behind Hank on the electric guitar, when I wasn't playing lead. See, you can't play rhythm on an electric guitar and let it ring. I heard this group, the Maddox Brothers and Rose, and this guy played rhythm on an electric. To me, it sounded like hell, but I thought, 'That would be a good deal if it just didn't ring like that,' so I'd whop it on the back of my hand, sort the back palm, or ball of my hand."

Turner was discussing Hank's November 6, 1947, remake of "Honky

Tonkin'" for the MGM label; at that point, the Maddox Brothers & Rose had been releasing records for just over a year, and the boys in Nashville clearly were already paying close attention.

Friendly Henry, in turn, took dead-string one step further—by muffling all the strings on his mandolin. But instead of "whopping," he fingered them. This produced a very distinctive, staccato effect, similar to the dry percussive rattle (almost like the minstrel's "bones") that Fred's bass produced. On record, the two instruments lent an unmistakable Maddox feel, a playful syncopation that Cal's rhythm guitar also played off of, with distinctive rhythmic results.

Even though rock & roll's dominance of the market in 1956 and 1957 had country music scrambling in profound confusion, the Maddox Brothers & Rose were ready for anything. Characteristically, they made a point to keep their sense of humor on display with one of their most notorious records, "The Death of Rock and Roll." By no means an attack on the form, it is instead a manic send up, and the "death" referred to is how they murder "I Got a Woman," the Ray Charles tune they often heard Elvis perform on the "Hayride."

"We didn't really change anything; all the times were changin'," said Don, who sang lead on the record. "When Elvis first started, we just started doin' more rock & roll 'cause that's what the people wanted, but we just more or less kept the same style that we'd always had. 'The Death of Rock and Roll,' well, that was when Elvis was gettin' real hot, and I was just doin' a take off on him, just foolin' around and doin' it for laughs. I started doin' it onstage and it went over real big in person, so we decided to record it."

Undoubtedly one of the goofiest songs they ever waxed, it resembles nothing so much as the early sixties garage records done by groups like the Fendermen and Trashmen. It is all twisted vocals above a driving guitar and string-bass rhythm, with little rhyme or reason in either, save for sheer lunacy. Though "The Death of Rock and Roll" did not start any fires on the charts, it remains a testament to the brothers' endless capacity to act as wise guys. But it really was not, as they soon discovered, a laughing matter.

By 1956, country music's dance hall era was dead. Eclipsed by rock & roll, drive-in movies, and television, even Bob Wills could no longer pull in the thousands that were once routine for him. Beyond whatever internecine dissatisfactions the Maddox Brothers & Rose might have been troubled by, it was clear that their show-and-dance format couldn't survive the drift in public tastes.

After the spectacular successes of first Roy Acuff and Eddy Arnold, then Hank, Lefty, and Elvis, the solo vocalist became the performer of choice in country music. As dance halls closed down, nightclub operators began insisting that headline artists perform with the house band. It became necessary for the Maddoxes to forego their hard earned title as "Kings of the Roadshow."

Many country artists survived by assembling package shows, revues with several guest artists backed up by the headliner's band. Before long, a "single" was able to command the same pay that an entire band previously got, and touring bands were more and more often refused. At least, this is how the Maddox Brothers & Rose perceived the situation.

For them, the signs were clear. "Tall Men" was a modest hit, while "The Death of Rock and Roll" only gathered dust. The band maintained a healthy following and certainly could have continued operating, playing at rural halls and rodeos. But they had become accustomed to the bright lights, brisk ticket sales, and prestige accorded Columbia recording artists. They considered themselves top of the line, just like their Cadillacs and clothing.

Yet the Maddoxes saw the handwriting on the wall and agreed to end the family act. As disturbing as the breakup must have been, the accrued weight of petty sibling squabbles, the constant accountability to Mama, the round-the-clock exhaustion brought on by the travel between one-night stands, not to mention the draining effect of the shows themselves, made the end of the family act easier to accept. The brothers, still under contract to Columbia, hoped for the best and even posed for publicity shots without Rose, but Fred was unable to convince the label to retain them as a band. Cal was already committed to traveling with Rose as her accompanist; Henry, never one to speak his mind, was content to stick close to his brothers and play out their career, whichever direction it took. Don, who had never wanted to be a musician in the first place, was actually relieved by the turn of events. Under these circumstances, Lula was more than content to split up the group: she would go with Rose and Cal, and earn the same money with far lower expenses. Too, it was the perfect chance to end all unnecessary contact with in-laws. Finally, she would be traveling with her two favorite kids, now even more accessible to her demands and whims.

Despite great mutual sadness that, typically, went unspoken, there was little animosity among the family, with one big exception. Fred saw blood when the reality of the situation hit home. "Fred got all upset," said Rose, "because I was quitting, and I had gotten all these offers as a single. And I think the wives wanted the husbands to get out of the music business, because they was gone all the time. So they were pullin' in one direction, and the times were changin', I could see that. A group couldn't go in as a guest. That's the way it was. It had to be a single, and I could get as much money by myself as the whole group was getting.

"Fred resented the fact that I pulled out and Cal stayed with me, because neither of us was married, and that left them without Cal and it left them without me. They had to hire some others and try to stay together. Fred resented it; I'm not sure whether the others did or not. Don wanted to get out of it anyway, but he and Henry stayed on for awhile. Loretta took my place, but that didn't go over with the public."

It was a messy situation; toward the end, Fred took to announcing the group on the air as "the Maddox Brothers & Her," due equally to his pique and the knowledge that the public needed to become accustomed to a band without Rose. He found himself in the same disadvantageous position that dogged Cliff: competing against his own name.

The Maddox Brothers & Rose had created a distinct, lively sound and a totally unique stage show, the likes of which would never be seen again. The artists influenced by the family were amazingly numerous and varied, and the Maddox impact was so strong that it continued to echo through country music for decades after the break up. Their unparalleled catalog of never-before-attempted gimmicks, like "Philadelphia Lawyer"'s pistol shot, Don Juan's theatrical fiddle (which simulated screeching brakes, a braying mule, and various other sound effects), and their own nonstop hollering, barnyard sounds, hound dog howls and noisy chatter, the Maddoxes were in many ways forerunners of the numerous studio antics that Nashville later embraced. By comparison, Floyd Cramer hammering a mike boom on "Big Bad John," or Owen Bradley's frequent choice to beat on a suitcase or percussion player's thigh instead of a drum, seems altogether tame.

Cliffie Stone used the Maddoxes' records to introduce specific songs to artists, as with Ernie Ford and "Philadelphia Lawyer" and later (to little avail) Polly Bergen and "Honky Tonkin'." Fred's style became deeply ingrained in several West Coast artists, notably Ferlin Husky (whose "I Feel Better All Over," oozes Fred's playful style and features a cloned slap bass sound), Tommy Collins (whose late fifties hits "You Better Not Do That" and "Whatcha Gonna Do Now?" are certainly more than a little reminiscent of Fred's cheery, leering style), and, to a lesser degree, Buck Owens and Merle Haggard. As Jimmy Winkle has suggested, the Maddoxes' brand of corn is certainly a partial basis for the development of Owens's "Hee-Haw" television series, which first aired in 1969 (when Rose was a member of Buck's road show).

Rose, naturally, had the greatest effect on country music. Kitty Wells was acutely aware of Rose's contributions (as her 1949 cover of "Gathering Flowers" proves); Jean Shepard, who came out of the San Joaquin and into national prominence with 1951's "Dear John," started with a vocal style so close to Rose's that it was nearly impossible to tell one from the other; Barbara Mandrell, who worked as a steel guitar child prodigy on "Town Hall Party" in the 1950s, names Rose as a major influence; Wanda Jackson idolized Rose; Dolly Parton has often cited Rose and regularly sang "Tall Men" and "I Gotta Go Get My Baby" during her early career; even Janis Joplin used to follow Rose along the south Texas club circuit.

Just as Buddy Holly had, guest singers ranging from George Jones to Tommy Sands to a teenage Wayne Newton used to ask the Maddoxes if they could "sing one," and the family always let them join in. Later,

Merle Haggard would tell Fred that the Maddoxes' fruit tramp background indirectly inspired him to write "Daddy Frank (The Guitar Man)." Haggard's 1974 hit "Old Man from the Mountain" is nothing short of a tribute to Fred, complete with a bass fiddle track that replicates his slap sound and also mentions "Friendly Henry."

Fred, still steaming-mad at Rose, had little inclination to review their previous successes, but, on the other hand, he realized that this left him and the brothers free to do whatever they pleased. So they took their Okie boogie as far beyond what they had already done as was humanly possible, as "Ugly & Slouchy" (recorded at the same session that produced "The Death of Rock and Roll") ably proved. This was Fred Maddox at his lecherous best: "Ugly and slouchy, that's the way I like 'em. I'll never have no fear of her lovin' someone else. . . ." He got the song from "Black Jack" Wayne, a country performer and promoter who, as Fred put it, "ran the scene up in Oakland."

"'Ugly & Slouchy,'" Fred recalled with enthusiasm, "Man, that was somethin' else! It's us a-playin' on it, and the way we did it, we had Henry—he'd take it on guitar, he'd be doin' lead, rhythm, and singin' harmony—it's almost confusin'!" He laughed at the memory.

"Ugly & Slouchy," the ultimate in white-trash anthems, perfectly captured the Maddoxes' driving, rocked-up brand of honky-tonk. There is no other band, country or rock & roll, who ever came close to capturing down-home lechery as exquisitely as the Maddox Brothers did on this record. Eight months later, in March of 1957, the brothers cut two more songs, "A Short Life and Its Troubles" and "Dig a Hole," with Fred singing lead, and Rose, back in town between bookings as a single, singing harmony.

The brothers never ceased to modify and expand their work, and the arrangements of these two old-time, traditional hillbilly songs were amazingly progressive. A studio drummer (whose name no one remembers) supplied a furious tempo on "A Short Life," throwing in some norteño style snare rolls. The drumming on "Dig a Hole" was equally idiosyncratic and even funkier (although credited to Rose in Columbia's session details, she has no recollection of playing drums), and Henry took a keening, hypnotic solo that sounds more like Lightnin' Hopkins than Joe Maphis. On both cuts, Fred sang like a man with the proverbial hell hound on his trail, yet one who clearly just did not give a damn. If these thrilling, unique, and completely unorthodox sides were an indication of what the brothers were doing without Rose, it is a crying shame that Columbia did not extensively record them. The record company, however, was not ready for a rhythm-drunk hillbilly garage band in 1957, and neither of these were issued until the 1980s.

So Fred, Don, and Henry worked shows up and down the coast, with Loretta singing, now billed as the Maddox Brothers & Retta. Tommy Collins played with the brothers extensively in 1957. After Collins's Capitol sides started hitting, Fred replaced him with a young country singer named Glen Trout, a cousin of Porter Wagoner, whom the family had first met at El Monte Legion Stadium when they appeared on "Hometown Jamboree."

After Fred introduced Trout to Elvis during Presley's 1956 show at Los Angeles' Pan Pacific Auditorium, the twenty-one-year-old Trout went rockabilly crazy. Later known professionally as Glen Glenn, he is best remembered for the outstandingly frosty "Everybody's Movin'." From his days as a Maddox employee, a few memories seemed to stand out, such as the way Fred always announced him as "Glenn Trout, the Stinkin' Fisherman," a play on Johnny Horton's "Singing Fisherman" handle; that the Maddox Brothers & Retta played a lot of rockabilly music and also that Bill Black, Elvis's bass man, often mentioned that he had long idolized Fred's slap-bass flair; and finally that Fred, typically, always tried to beat Glenn out of any extra pay. (Unfortunately for Glenn, several years later, just before his "Laurie Ann" started to hit, he was drafted. Stationed in Hawaii, he was forced to turn down Dick Clark's invitation to appear on "American Bandstand.")

Fred, of course, was still more than able to work a crowd up to the frenzy point, but after Rose's departure, the momentum that had carried the family band so far would never be regained. Nevertheless, they kept a high profile on the West Coast. "Maddox Bros. Open Newest Coast Show," read a headline in the March 16, 1957 issue of *Country Music*

Reporter's "News from Hollywood" section. "San Bernadino, Calif. The Maddox Brothers and Retta, with Glen Trout, have begun a new Friday night show and dance at the Sierra Park Ballroom here under a long-term lease. . . . Fred is also kicking off deejay shows on three Southern California radio stations: KCSB, San Bernadino; KBUC, Corona; and KOCS, Ontario."

The article also mentioned that Fred planned to start Thursday night and Sunday afternoon dances at Sierra Park. A month earlier, the February 16 issue's "Cracker Barrel" column had reported that "the Maddox Brothers and Retta have opened a Saturday morning live television show in Los Angeles." (The three-hour show was known as "Cal's Corral.")

One aspect of their career that Mama's departure had not changed was the staggeringly heavy schedule, something that every brother kept up as long as he was active in the music business. For the next two years, Maddox Brothers & Retta worked dances and TV shows all over the West Coast.

Rose, meanwhile, had other fish to fry—at the "Grand Ole Opry."

CHAPTER FIFTEEN

"Tall Men" was "riding high on the juke boxes around the country," according to *Country Music Reporter,* and as a result the "Opry" invited Rose and Cal back to appear as guests on September 29, 1956. Rose knew this was an ideal chance to establish herself as a single act. The timing seemed perfect, and she lost no time in preparing for what turned out to be one of the most memorable nights in "Opry" history.

"I went to the 'Grand Ole Opry' as a guest, because 'I Love a Tall Man' was a smash hit at the time," said Rose (referring to "Tall Men" by its chorus). "And I had a costume made for it: a short, blue satin skirt with silver fringe, a bare midriff and the top, with long sleeves and the silver fringe hangin' down like that, with my boots, neckerchief, and a cowboy hat. So, at the 'Opry,' I did my first song, and I went back into the rest room and changed into that blue satin."

At the "Opry," each guest performed two songs, separately, within one segment of the show. Rose waited in the makeshift dressing room until the announcer called her name and then she raced out to center stage.

"I came back out to sing 'Tall Men,'" she said with a broad grin. "And I thought that 'Opry' would come apart, right there! Nothing like that had ever happened, and of course the 'Opry' bosses like to come unglued. I just went out there and did my song, and the audience ate it up!"

One can just imagine the impact she made. Rose was just past her thirty-first birthday, with shapely legs arching up from the low-cut boots, the skin of her bare midriff accentuated by the long blue sleeves of her blouse, silver fringe brushing flesh as she vibrated and sang: "I wish I was a kiss tree, a-growin' in the ground/And ev'ry time my sweetie passed by, I'd throw some kisses down . . ." She must have looked like a cowgirl version of the classic forties pinups.

"Whenever I saw Minnie Pearl after that," Rose recalled, "she would say, about that night, 'Ever' one of them ["Opry" bosses] jumped on me, sayin', "Why did you let her do that?" and I said, "I didn't have nothin' to do with that; and if I had known she was gonna do that, I wouldn't have stopped her!"'"

"The crowd went wild, and the officials' mouths was a-hangin' open. They didn't know what to say or do! And Rod Brasfield, he came out, man, he took that up and just carried it to the limit. It was great, all the stuff he said."

That night was one the "Opry" would probably just as soon forget, but it stands as one of the most memorable appearances ever made at Ryman Auditorium. Even more remarkable, considering the tumult, is that the "Opry" did not censure or blacklist Rose. On the contrary, they actually welcomed Rose with open arms.

In its October 6 issue, the *Country Music Reporter* featured a brief item headlined "Rose Maddox Joins Opry As Regular." It read, "Los Angeles—Rose Maddox, Columbia recording artist who has been working the West Coast in what has often been described as 'the most colorful band in show business,' has joined the Grand Ole Opry as a regular performer, it has just been announced by Jack Stapp, WSM program manager. Her first broadcast was on Sept. 29."

Rose joined the "Opry" when its cast boasted many of the greatest names in country music history: Roy Acuff, Chet Atkins, Johnny Cash, Jimmy Dickens, Ferlin Husky and Jean Shepard (both old friends from the San Joaquin Valley), the Louvin Brothers, Moon Mullican, Bill Monroe, Ray Price, Jim Reeves (with whom Rose had occasionally sung duets on the "Louisiana Hayride"), Marty Robbins, Hank Snow, Ernest Tubb, and Kitty Wells. Unfortunately, she also joined during the height of one of the "Opry"'s most bitter internecine feuds.

The dispute centered on the September 24, 1956, firing of Jim Denny, head of the WSM Artist Service Bureau. Since 1946, he had booked every road date for the "Opry" cast, having risen from the lowly position of concessions manager. Instigated in part by Roy Acuff, who charged artist favoritism and misappropriation of funds, and administered by WSM president Jack DeWitt, Denny's departure immediately created a battle of loyalties among "Opry" members.

The issue was whether or not "Opry" artists should continue to rely on the WSM Artist Service Bureau (now headed by W. D. Kilpatrick) for their bookings, or simply continue using Denny as agent. He had immediately opened his own Cedarwood Agency and Publishing Company, just a block away from the "Opry." The vast majority of "Opry" artists signed with Cedarwood, infuriating several WSM stalwarts, notably Acuff, Snow, and Tubb. Jack DeWitt told Denny biographer Albert Cunniff: "What did he do? He corralled a lot of our top stars and tried to take them away from WSM, for booking. And he didn't even want them to appear on the 'Grand Ole Opry.'"

Rose knew there had been some trouble at the "Opry" but was pleased to be there nonetheless. In October of 1956, Rose, Mama, and Cal moved to Nashville, rented a house, and counted their blessings. Apprehension over the band's breakup was eased and Rose's stature as a single seemed assured. Or so it seemed that winter.

"It was a good opportunity to be booked throughout the country, by the biggest bookers there was," she recalled, somewhat sourly. "But it didn't happen that way, for some reason." Over the next six months, Rose sang at the Ryman every weekend, and kept waiting for Kilpatrick to book some dates for her.

"I think they got me three, maybe four dates, that entire time. They either couldn't book me, or they wasn't tryin'. I don't know which. So to compensate for that, they started puttin' me on both Friday and Saturday shows at the 'Opry' and had me doin' all the local television shows."

The *Country Music Reporter*'s "Cracker Barrel" column for December 22, 1956, reported that "Friends of Rose Maddox (Columbia) are expecting big things from her new record set for distribution around Jan. 1. It's entitled 'Your Sweet Mean Heart' backed with 'Looky There Over There.' Rose, together with her brother, Cal Maddox, and their mother, Mrs. Lula Maddox, are in Hollywood for the holidays. They plan to lease their home in Hollywood and return to Nashville Jan. 10. Cal says they drive the distance in three days each way." (That was two thousand and eleven miles, or six hundred and seventy miles a day. What's more, they were making these trips in the days before the interstate highway system had been developed. Behind the wheel, Cal was a demon.)

Even though Donnie, now thirteen, had to stay at his Arizona boarding school, they stopped to see him on the drive back to California, en route to Hollywood. It was a fine Christmas for Rose, except for the separation from Donnie (deemed necessary by Lula). Rose could never get used to that.

In Nashville, the tour bookings still were not coming. Instead, Kilpatrick continued booking Rose for television appearances on the "Opry"'s own short-lived one-hour regional taped broadcast, Red Foley's "Ozark Jubilee," and numerous other local shows. This kept up for six months. In March 1957, things came to a head amongst the close-knit "Opry" clan.

"The other acts that were out working on the road," Rose recalled, "they'd come in for the Saturday night show, and they found out I had been doing all the local television shows. Well, that didn't set very well with 'em. It hadn't set good with 'em when I went back there in the first place, because they had brought a new West Coast artist in. So they all got together, apparently—I don't know if they really did or not—but Jack Stapp called me, says, 'I've got to see you.' So I went down there and he says, 'I hate to tell you this, Rose, but I'm goin' to have to take you off the TV shows.'

"'Why?'

"'Well, the acts who're out on the road are all complainin' about you being on TV so regularly.'

"'Well, they aren't here, they're out on the road—and you're supposed to have me out there, workin' all week long.'

"'I know I'm supposed to, but it hasn't worked out, and due to the number of complaints, I'm goin' to have to take you off the TV shows.'

"'Who is complainin'?'"

Stapp's answer caught Rose completely off guard: "'Roy Acuff is the main one.'

"'You're kidding me!'

"'No. Acuff told me: Either you take her off the TV shows, or I'll leave.'

"And Jack started to apologize to me, so I just said, 'That's all right, the grass is greener out west. I'm goin.'"

She went home, told Mama and Cal what happened, called Sears Roebuck to come and take all the furniture back, then "packed up and headed west." They were cast out of Dixie Land once again, but as before, it was a matter of their own personal pride and choice. Rose knew there was no point in asking Stapp to get the King of Country Music to reconsider his position. The situation that forced Rose off the "Opry" was equally due to the politically charged limbo that the Artist Service Bureau found itself in and Acuff's displeasure over the abundance of TV exposure Rose had enjoyed. Always jealously mindful of the "Opry" performers' welfare and morale (and still rankled over Denny's thriving Cedarwood Agency), Acuff had left neither Jack Stapp nor Rose any real choice in the matter.

Such insider politics were never Rose's style. Although she was "mad about the whole situation," it must have been a relief to get back to Hollywood, where folks knew and understood her. On her return, though, Rose discovered that being a solo act was not the easy path she dreamt of.

"I couldn't get a job anywhere. It was just like when the boys went into the army. Even though Cal had stayed with me, everybody said, 'She can't do a thing without her brothers.' Well, nobody even gave me a chance to see whether I could or couldn't."

Several factors contributed to this fallow period: the "Opry" debacle, Lula's reputation as a behind-the-scenes troublemaker, booking competition from the brothers, and, finally, the inconsistent records she was releasing. "Looky There Over There," for instance, was syrupy pop, a well-intentioned but clumsy stab at crossover success, while other songs, like "1, 2, 3, 4, Anyplace Road," were sheer schmaltz. To this day, however, Rose is proud of these experiments, and with reason. Though they fell short of the mark artistically and commercially, they were nevertheless some of the most ambitious crossover records attempted by a country singer in the 1950s.

"I was doing a lot of things on Columbia. I was one of the first to ever use strings on my records, using these violas, with a bow and all that. And I started doin' more rockabilly singles, although I had been doin' them prior to the band's break-up."

While the pop records were often contrived, her rockabilly sides were some of the most earthy and incandescent in that style. Cliffie Stone still kept Rose informed about the latest r&b and rock & roll releases, often suggesting a particular tune he felt would be good for her. While her brothers were supercharging traditional hillbilly music, Rose was injecting atomic power into contemporary rhythm & blues. But alternating pop with big beat only served to confuse the public and programmers alike; Stone had a better grasp on what would work for her, but Rose, headstrong as any Maddox, would have her own way or nothing.

Speaking of her solo recordings, Rose emphasized that "the label had nothing to do with my songs. Like I said before, you either progress with the times, or you're dead. Things like 'Wild, Wild Young Men' were going good, so I started to do a lot of 'em. The company never told me what to do. They never presented me with songs. I would go into the studio with my songs picked out before, and I could get whatever musicians I wanted to back me." This bunch always included Cal, often Merle Travis and Joe Maphis, even Chet Atkins (on "I'd Rather Die Young").

These sophisticated pickers made a fine counterpoint to Cal's heavy rhythm and Rose's fiery, testifying vocals.

Confused and somewhat disheartened by her lack of commercial success on Columbia, Rose tried her hand at everything she could. When Columbia okayed the release of a Rose Maddox LP, she opted for a gospel album, a style at which she excelled. The *Precious Memories* LP came out in 1958 and captured all the power of Rose in her most traditional revival-meeting voice, albeit with a heavy complement of background singers and a wheezing Hammond organ vying with Joe Maphis's flat picking for instrumental supremacy.

This was the only full-length Rose Maddox album that Columbia released while she was under contract to the company. Ironically, more than half a dozen Maddox Brothers & Rose long players were available at the time on the Decca, King, and Wrangler labels, which were leasing the old 4 Star material. Suffice it to say, Bill McCall was the only one making any money from these. Rose's career plodded on through this rather muddy period, until an old friend once again came to the rescue.

"Then Cliffie Stone hired me to be on 'Hometown Jamboree' every Saturday night, and from the exposure of that I started getting jobs. After we finished the TV show, for as long as we were on it, we was usually booked somewhere else. We'd have to drive from 150 to 200 miles, after the show, to get there in time to make our first club show."

With her career now back in the groove, Rose was able to catch her breath, look around, and assess the state of her personal life. What she saw did not please her. It was the start of what became a fierce struggle between her loyalty to Mama and her conscience as a woman.

Donnie was the catalyst. Now a teenager, he was sick of being ignored and shunted from boarding school to summer camp. Rose was considering relocating to Arizona, where Donnie stayed year round. Having tired of military school, he was enrolled in a "ranch school," a sort of agricultural college for young westerners. At age fifteen, he found it impossible to hold himself in line any longer.

"He'd been in those schools since he was seven and wanted to come home, so he started runnin' away." Rose laughed, recalling her rebel son. "And every time, they always found him, usually downtown in Scottsdale. Finally they called me. I happened to be at home in Hollywood, and they said they were sending him back to me."

She had mixed feelings regarding this development. Rose wanted to give Donnie what had so long been denied him—a home and family life—yet her career was at a critical stage. Knowing it was necessary to bring the boy home and enroll him in a public school, Rose found the dilemma of motherhood versus career more painful than ever. She looked to the family for help.

Rose knew placing Donnie in Hollywood High would be a mistake, and she formulated a plan, more of a hope, that he and Lula could live near wherever Don and Nila were ranching (at the time, Don was enrolled in agricultural college, planning to quit the music business and raise livestock). This would allow her and Cal to go out on the road alone. For the first time in her life, she was trying to separate herself from Mama.

At age thirty-three, the break was long overdue. What began as a mother's concern and devotion had evolved into bondage. Without the boys around to divide her attentions, Lula clamped down tough on Rose. Cal, now over forty, had toed the mark so long and so faithfully that Lula had no suspicions about his behavior. Total obedience was all she required, and Cal never withheld it.

At that time, Don was purchasing a ranch outside of Ashland, Oregon, a small town seventeen miles over the California state line. Rose and Cal bought several acres adjacent to Don's property and built a home, and they all moved up to Oregon. While Don stocked his land with sheep and cattle, Rose, Cal, Donnie, and Lula shared the newly constructed house. Donnie began high school in Ashland, and Rose silently hoped that Lula would agree to stay with the boy when she and Cal went out to work. It would have been an ideal situation. Instead, it became a nightmare.

"Donnie liked Oregon and his school fine, and it was the first public school he'd ever been in. But I was still out on the road, working with

Cal, and Mama always went with us. She wouldn't stay home to look after Donnie. It didn't matter if that was all right with me or not, because she was the boss. You were just supposed to do what she said and never even think of doing anything differently." A pause. "She was a very tough person."

Rose spoke of the conflict with a quiet, mournful tone. "She had become so involved in my life that it was to the point where I had no privacy. I could only talk to people she said I could, only see people she said I could. I never went on a date. Never. I was up in my early thirties, but I was still 'her little girl.' I loved Mama dearly, but it was to the point where anything I did, or wanted to do, she had to approve it or I didn't do it. She was living her life through me. That's what was always in her mind: I was doing exactly what she had wanted to do but couldn't because of the backwoodsy way she was brought up. She was living her dream through me.

"She just became more and more possessive and possessive. I was never out of her sight, anywhere. She went wherever I went. After we moved up to Oregon, I wasn't allowed to open my own mail, I wasn't allowed to answer telephone calls. It became the type of relationship where she thought I was going to try and do something or other, I couldn't tell what exactly."

Well aware of the uncomfortable position she had Rose in, Lula seemed to be waiting for Rose to break and was unwilling to relinquish her grip. She craved that vicarious thrill her daughter provided. Her boys were all married and leading their own careers, Charlie was long gone. Rose was all she had left. Lula had to have that intoxicating perfume of success, fame, and glamour that came so easily to her daughter but was impossible for her to obtain herself.

Rose did not even have anyone to talk to. "Me and the brothers never discussed things like that. We weren't raised to do that. It wouldn't have done any good. I never even considered talking to Mama about it. She was the boss and that was it. I wasn't allowed to have any close friends. I did have two girl friends in Southern California that I confided a lot in, but I had to sneak around to do it.

"I was becoming very resentful of the dominant portion of her. It put so much pressure on me. I felt like I was just completely dominated. I did what she said, or I did nothin'. I was just lookin' for a way to get out from under it."

And so she went from nightclub to nightclub, more and more often a sullen cloud of frustration and dissatisfaction hanging over her. By late 1958, this succession of thwarted friendships, combined with Mama's relentless demands and her total subjugation of Rose's personal life, now turned in on itself and left Rose an angry, numb, and bitter woman.

All Rose had were her songs, and the pleasures that performing brought. She sang her heart out night after night. While the songs did immeasurable good, after the show it was back to reality: Mama standing offstage, shoulder bag full of cash, watching Cal load his guitar and amp into the Cadillac. Driving home, almost always in silence, all Rose thought of was "lookin' for a way to get out from under it."

Certainly, Lula never meant to hurt her daughter, never even admitted to herself that there was any possibility of that. She was devoted, desperately attached to Rose—as Rose was to her, even at the lowest points their relationship sank to. But Lula was doing her wrong, and every day that passed only did more damage.

Picture Rose as she was in 1958: skin, milky pale from twenty years of nightclub work, clad in satin and silk, her body fine and slim, dark hair worn in a short bob. She looked for all the world a star, with a quietly regal air. Yet she was a woman at the height of emotional need, one who had done without the affection and attention of a lover for years. Rose had resolved to make the break, the hardest decision of her life. Not yet, she repeated. But soon.

One afternoon, with work on the *Precious Memories* LP complete, she, Cal, and Mama were burning down the highway, en route to a date in San Diego. Passing by Oceanside, California, a small Marine Corps town strung along the beach, Rose remembered hearing about a country joint, the Wheel Club, and figured they ought to stop in and see if there was any work to be had.

"I'd heard that this club was usin' a lot of guest artists," said Rose, "and I told Mama, 'Let's stop and see if we can get a bookin'.' So, we stopped in and Jimmy Brogdon, the owner, was there. I took one look at him and thought, 'Wow! That's what I want!'"

CHAPTER SIXTEEN

As she stood inside the dark and beery Wheel Club that fair afternoon, looking upon the face and body of Jimmy Brogdon, an inevitable, long overdue journey began. Rose felt in her heart, instantly, that before her stood the one chance to escape from Lula's shackles.

As she introduced herself, Cal, and Mama to Jim Brogdon, chatting casually over business ("Of course you can get a booking here"), Rose felt the duties and commitment that she had so long unquestioningly given Lula pass over and away from her, like a dark cloud. And as it drifted away, she stood gazing at Brogdon's warm eyes, wondering what love really was, and if this was how it felt.

The Wheel Club was quite a joint, with a built-in audience from the area's numerous servicemen, and Brogdon had established excellent connections in the short time he had operated it, employing every up-and-coming country performer on the coast, and many of the biggest names out of the South. Rose and Cal were more than welcome. Brogdon arranged to have them appear the very next weekend. He was no stranger to their music.

"I'd seen them many times, years ago," Brogdon later recalled. "The first time was at the 97th Street Corral in the late forties. 'The

Most Colorful Hillbilly Band in America!' They were good, and they certainly lived up to their reputation. But I thought Rose was the whole show. Of course, the boys wouldn't agree with that, but you can put any group of good musicians around her, and that is the show. So I booked 'em in for Friday and Saturday nights, and we had people lining down the street to get in, night after night."

Brisk business pleased Lula. A good, regular local job to hit after "Hometown Jamboree" was just what they were looking for. "Lula treated me kinda like she treated everybody else," recalled Brogdon, "just kept her distance. You kinda had to get to know Mama. She was going to keep that family as close together as she could. That was her nature, whatever her reasons were. I looked at it as a kind of quirk, like an ol' mother hen that just will not give up." (Brogdon paints a surprisingly sympathetic portrait of Lula; most folks who did business with her recall her as a terror.)

The Wheel Club bookings, to Rose's delight, came steadily. Weeks gave way to months, Rose and Cal's Cadillacs running a constant loop from Los Angeles to Ashland, often into Reno and Las Vegas. One musician recalled playing alongside Rose often during this period, "in Jackpot, Nevada. It was a godforsaken place, five thousand feet elevation and nothing but nightclubs. Every night was like New Year's Eve in Jackpot, and Rose and Cal used to work there all the time." Even without the brothers, with all the changes in the music industry over the last five years, the images remain the same: Cadillacs racing to far-flung pleasure domes, where the citizenry of several distant towns gather for a night of unrepentant and unbridled high living.

Columbia released Rose when her recording contract expired in 1958, resolving a situation that had become unsatisfactory for both parties. Being without a record deal for the first time in twelve years was not a pleasant sensation for Rose. So, shortly afterward, she cut several sides for Black Jack Wayne's label and another session for Uni Records which Cliffie Stone supervised, recording "(Don't the World Look Better through) The Bottom of a Glass" backed with "Step Right In," which have since become two of her rarest recordings.

Hard-to-find, independent releases were not what she wanted, though, and Cliffie Stone knew Rose was more than capable and deserving of national attention. After six years of being fleeced at 4 Star, seven years of mild success at Columbia, Rose was a free agent, and Stone, in concert with A&R man Ken Nelson, finally brought her to Capitol Records—fourteen years after Stone had first wanted to. In January 1959, she and Capitol inked a pact, a five-year contract with a two-year option.

After being welcomed back on "Hometown Jamboree" and signing with Capitol, any lack of exposure Rose might have suffered as a single was alleviated. To fans, Rose was always the leader of the Maddox Brothers & Rose. Besides, she still had the backbone of their sound: Cal, who supplied the throbbing rhythm guitar, harmony vocals, and trademark cackle. He played on all her live appearances, and she used both Cal and Henry on many of her later recordings.

By 1959, with Don preoccupied with building his ranch, Retta frustrated over trying to replace Rose, and Glen Trout whisked into the army, the brothers were forced to abandon performing together. Henry continued to work what club dates he could, and Fred plunged into life as a disc jockey, nightclub owner, and record company boss. He bought the Flat Git It label from Black Jack Wayne, relocated to Norwalk, California, and operated the company primarily as a vanity label that recorded only Cal, Henry, and himself. Fred began a whole new career on the periphery of the music business but never stopped performing. At this point, the Maddox Brothers Band, stymied by circumstance, had run its course. Now it was all up to sister Rose to carry on the dream.

Things were looking up for Rose. She had met an interesting man, her brothers were no longer in competition with her on the club circuit, and she had a new record contract even as her *Precious Memories* LP was still available in record bins nationwide. Seemingly disconnected, all of these converging events worked to Rose's advantage. Major commercial success and true love, the two things Rose always worked for but had so far been denied, seemed just within her reach; only one obstacle stood in the way: Lula. Making the break with Lula was almost impossible for Rose to contemplate, or so she had always told herself. But after so many years of manipulation and subjugation, Rose found herself longing for it.

Jimmy Brogdon, a man she barely knew, was becoming the first and foremost desire of her life. She desperately hoped to win him, yet she was actually unsure of how she felt. Strange as it seems, Rose was unable to tell herself that she loved him, but acted as if she did nonetheless, as if her heart were breaking every moment they were apart. She was inexperienced, certainly, but sick and tired of being that way. Too long had she been kept from the embrace of a man, too long had she been pushed and prodded like an adolescent. She had to command her own life.

"That was my means of getting out, and I was determined to do it," Rose said, "whether I loved him or not. And I thought an awful lot of him. I guess you could call it love, in one sense of the word. I know that I later grew to respect him very much, and to love him, too. At the time, I just guessed I was in love with him, and I told him I was . . . I was looking for a way to get away from Mama. . . . It had gotten worse and worse and worse.

"I had sent him a note through the mail, and all it said on it was, 'I Love You,' and signed it, 'Rose.'" She paused, then, eyes flashing, said, "Well, that was when I started hittin' that mail box early, before Mama could get it!"

Rose's first Capitol recording session was scheduled for February 25, 1959. Supervising the session would be Ken Nelson, then head of Capitol's country division. Nelson had an unlikely background for the country music field. His early music business experience came in Chicago, where he worked as an organist in movie houses, sang in pop dance bands, and announced concerts by the Chicago Symphony Orchestra on WJJD, where he also served as music director. Nelson moved to Hollywood in the late forties, when Capitol chose him to head their transcription library. Four years later, in 1952, he was named head of Capitol's country division. Working closely with Stone, Nelson brought to Capitol artists like Jean Shepard, Ferlin Husky, Faron Young, Tommy Collins, the Louvin Brothers, Wanda Jackson, Buck Owens, Wynn Stewart, Jerry Reed, and Merle Haggard. Capitol's country releases from the mid-1950s through the mid-1960s stand among the best in the music's history and were some of the biggest selling, most influential hillbilly discs ever.

Nelson was also one of the very few industry figures to publicly embrace rock & roll. The *Country Music Reporter*'s November 10, 1956, issue contains an article headlined: "Ken Nelson, With Vincent Success, Says R&R To Stay." This is exactly what the major labels did not want to hear, particularly those with interests in Nashville, while the public at large were sure that rock & roll was naught but a passing fad. Nelson's superior instinct prevailed: "Rock and roll music is a definite type, has a sound all its own and it should stay with us for a long time. . . . It's as easily identifiable as Dixieland jazz and, as in the case of jazz, it will always have people who like it, and artists for whom the field is natural. . . .

"When I take an artist, I feel responsible for him. His whole life may depend on what I arrange for him. That's why I never believe in selling the record—I believe in selling the artist." It was exactly the attitude Rose needed from her producer.

She drove to Hollywood and Vine with high hopes, four songs ("What Makes Me Hang Around?" "Billy Cline," "Gambler's Love," "Lies and Alibis"), and Mama. She felt apprehensive only about how Lula might conduct herself. Once in the studio, Lula wasted no time in making it clear to all that she presumed total control over every aspect of production on her daughter's sessions. Nelson was appalled. Still under Mama's thumb, Rose felt powerless to do anything about it.

"I remember her mother sitting there at the session," Nelson recalled "and she was really taking hold of everything. So I had to tell her, 'Hey, I'm the boss here.' After the first two sessions, I forbade her to come to the studio anymore." Never before had Lula been faced down so forcefully—and this was in front of her daughter and the band.

Imagine Rose's shock at that moment. It was shock, followed by elation, seeing that it could be done. Her heart jumped, realizing that she was not wrong, that Nelson could not function with Lula's "help" either. Not only was this a tremendous boost to Rose's morale, it gave her a sense of appreciation for Nelson's interest in her as an artist, rather than as a part of the Maddox family. It was also the first step towards realizing that a break from Mama must be made.

"I didn't think I was makin' a mistake—I was bound and determined to do this," Rose later remarked, using exactly the same words that Lula had spoken when leaving Boaz. "It was the only way I could see to get out from being dominated by her for the rest of my life, being told what to do, what not to do. After you reach a certain age, especially when one is as dominant as she was, you just get to resenting things, and you get to where you hate the person. And that just don't get it. So I had to slip off to get married, at the age of thirty-four!"

Fortunately, her attentions were not wasted on Brogdon. After receiving Rose's note, he took every possible opportunity to contact her, even though his telephone calls often resulted only in perfunctory chitchat about business with Lula. Finally, hearing that the Maddox trio—Rose, Cal and Mama—were going to be back in Southern California, Brogdon managed to get Rose on the phone.

"One night we was gettin' ready to leave Oregon," Rose recalled. "Me and Cal was appearin' in San Bernardino, and Jimmy called to ask if he could come over and take me out to dinner, and I said, 'Sure!' Well, when we got down there, Mama found it out, and she absolutely refused to let me go—there was just no way.

"And there was no way that I could contact him, she just wouldn't let me. And she made me drive her to Riverside. We stayed there all day long. All she had said was, 'You're not going to have dinner with him—and if you do, I'm going.'" Lula's own dominance and passion for vicarious thrills (being wined and dined by a handsome club owner) finally proved to be her Achilles heel. Still, Rose feared that Brogdon would tire of the pursuit. She was afraid that on finding they were gone for the day, he would just turn back and head to Oceanside. But when they returned to the hotel, he was waiting.

Rose was mortified. "I told him that I couldn't go without Mama, and he just smiled and said, 'That's all right.' So we went to dinner there in the hotel, me and him and her! And afterwards, she forbid me to ever see him again. Mama had found out that he was interested in me, and that did not set well with her. That was the end of that, as far as she was concerned! But he kept callin' me and she would never let me talk to him.

"Two or three nights later, we were workin' in the high desert, at Ridgecrest, California, and someone there at the club told me I had a phone call. I went to answer it, and it was Jim. 'Well, what are we goin' to do about this situation?' he asked. I said, 'The only thing I can see is to get married,' and he says, 'That sounds okay to me.'"

Rose went out and sang one of the greatest shows of her career.

The logistics surrounding their elopement had to be plotted with all the stealth and cunning of an Alcatraz crash out. Fortunately, Rose had her two confederates, Mary and Bev, "the two friends Mama let me have. They came to practically every show we did. Beverly was interested in Cal, so they always sat around and talked to Mama. They both knew Jimmy, and they knew I was interested in him. So, with all this marriage stuff goin' on, if I ever wanted to get a message to Jimmy, it had to go through them—because they were the only ones allowed to be around me."

She laughed. "So we sent messages back and forth between these girls! We finally got the date set. I was workin' in San Francisco, and he was goin' to come get me after work, to go get us married." It was December 7, 1959, Pearl Harbor day—an ideal date for Rose's own sneak attack on unhappiness.

"Mama and I were at the motel there in Frisco when I told her. She had said somethin' about how we were gonna leave that night after the show, and I said, 'I'm not.'"

An instant of silence followed Rose's first-ever note of dissent against her mother—but only an instant. Then Lula responded with a sneer, "What do you mean, 'I'm not?'"

"I said, 'I'm gettin' married.' And she said, 'To who?' And I told her, and that whole roof came off of that room!"

As Rose recalled it, Lula worked herself up into an indignant, self-righteous rage, peppering her attack with vulgarities and wild, sweeping gestures. It was a supremely ugly moment, rivaled only by the second explosion, ignited moments later when Brogdon appeared at their door.

As Rose put it, "He came over to see me and Mama run him off, told him that he was not coming into that room to see me." But Mama had not heard the last of Jimmy Brogdon.

"He and Mary and Bev showed up at the club that night. They didn't come in, just sat out and waited in the car. After the show, I told Mama, 'I am not goin' back home with you. I am going to Las Vegas to get married.' I took my stuff out to Mary and Bev's car. Mama followed me out, looked at me and said, 'I never want to see you again as long as I live.'"

Rose's voice trembled, thirty-six years later, and her eyes filled with tears. "That was the hardest thing I ever had to go through. That hurt, it hurt. And so I said, 'Well, that's up to you.' We left and went to Las Vegas."

Las Vegas? Rose panicked. She had told Lula it would be Vegas because she thought the escape plan specified Reno, and had hoped to throw Cal and Mama off the trail, knowing they'd give chase. Now she dreaded a scene wherein Lula caught up with them and raised hell before a justice of the peace, or railed violently in a crowded casino or hotel lobby.

"But she and Cal went to Reno. She figured that if I said 'Las Vegas,' I was thinkin' Reno. Mama always knew what I was thinkin', before I could even do it. She had this uncanny way of knowin' what I thought. It was a real strong part of her character . . . but anyway, we went to Vegas."

As Lula led Cal from hotel to hotel, fuming and cursing, she quickly sensed the trail was cold. Meanwhile, for Rose what should have been a time of joy and relief became instead a wedding day filled with confusion and disappointment.

"We got there the next day, done went and bought the rings and ever'thing. But we were just wandering around playin' slot machines, and I didn't know why we weren't gettin' married. Finally I said to Jimmy, 'I came up here to get married. We either get married, or I'm goin' home!'

"And Jimmy said, 'Well, I was waitin' for my best man to be here.' A friend of his from Oceanside, who I also knew, and he hadn't showed up yet, and we waited. . . . He hadn't shown up, so we went to the judge.

And Mary and Bev stood up for us, and after it was all over, Cecil, his best man arrived. He had been havin' problems with his wife and couldn't get her up here on time!"

Marriage in the Maddox family was always frowned upon. Each time the brothers wed, the occasion was memorable only for the haste and secrecy in which it was done. Rose's case was no different, and certainly no better. Beside herself with guilt, Rose knew better than to consider turning back. Wandering the casinos that afternoon, her vision blurred with tears, seemed to Rose an endless, absurd pastime, one that poisoned whatever anticipation she had enjoyed. It had been so long since she had been with a man, and the circumstances only combined to make both Rose and Jimmy miserable.

Back in Ashland, Oregon, life was pretty miserable, too. Lula and Cal returned from Reno under a black cloud. They explained to Donnie what had happened and tried to carry on as before. No one was happy. Cal, who had been teaching his nephew to play, took out his guitar and began to show Donnie some more chords. As the boy plunked away, Lula went into a tight-lipped, seething fury. Without Rose, she had no direction. There was no anchor to reality, only the mockery of a normal day-to-day routine, which she hated. Although Cal continued to work with Rose, Mama never went with them again, a situation she hated. Lula never got used to it.

Rose moved into Brogdon's home in Oceanside, a large house near the club, with an upstairs apartment for guest artists. Though she still felt pangs of guilt about the break with Mama, her marriage was improving every day. Her career was in good shape too. The Wheel Club, its reputation bolstered by Rose's regular presence, was hosting some spectacular shows. One night, Rose shared the stage with the Carter Sisters & Mother Maybelle, one of the most potent female combinations imaginable in country music. And that was just one big show of many. On that stage, over the next few years, Rose would duet, guest, and compete with the biggest names in country—and sometimes even bail out a fellow performer.

"We had Johnny Cash, Willie Nelson, Roger Miller, Buck Owens,

Merle Haggard, Bonnie Owens," said Brogdon. "This was before they really hit the top. Once Johnny Cash had booked George Jones with me. Come show time, George still hadn't showed up. I called Johnny. He said, 'George is on his way.' The Jones Boys showed up, drivin' a station wagon. There's George, all dressed up in a thousand-dollar suit, fit to kill, and so drunk he couldn't walk.

"We had a house full of people, and we never did get George onstage. I gave 'em all their money back, and got Rose out of bed. She had just come off of a tour, but she got dressed and came down to entertain 'em, to keep 'em from tearin' the roof off. Rose went back and talked to George in the office, said, 'I know you can do it, and you will do it. You've been drunker than this before, so don't disappoint the people.' She got him out as far as behind the bar, but he wouldn't go any further. So, when she finally went on, I just reached over and handed him a bottle of vodka and said, 'Here, kill yourself, get drunker'n hell, I'm so sick of you.'"

Rose tried to settle in her new lifestyle as best she could. "It was difficult for her, I'm sure," Brogdon said, "to make that break, which she should have made a long time ago, which she had to make. It was very difficult, but Rose has a lot of stamina and when the going gets rough, why, she has always done what she felt she had to do. And I think when it really settled into her, she was very relieved over it, you know?

"We didn't see Lula for a while there, but it wasn't any real period of time that you could say we didn't see her for a year, or six months. Rose would go up there once in a while, because she and Cal were still working, had to work together. It certainly changed things, and Mrs. Maddox complained, but she never really tried to do anything about it."

However, realizing that Rose's Ashland visits were primarily to see Donnie, Lula found her pride injured once more. In early 1960, she finally called Rose and said, "Rose, come get him. I won't have him here."

Lula's motives were not purely selfish, as Rose admitted, because "Donnie had become a very rebellious sixteen year old. So me and Mary went up and got him. To Donnie, it was always just him and I, that was our whole world. Because of that feeling, Donnie was very resentful that I had married. Jim didn't try to be a father to him. He tried to be his friend, and Donnie resented that, too."

For the first time, without Mama's herding and watchful eye, Rose discovered how difficult it was to manage both her escalating career and a complicated personal life. Never before had she dealt with both simultaneously, and she found it an increasingly bothersome drain. Never before had she tried to function as a wife and mother, and the mysteries of domestic life confounded her. Donnie, a surly teenager on a steady diet of rock & roll, became more and more of a problem with each passing day.

Rose's career was now back in full swing, with the potential to take her even higher than the family band had. Country music was becoming an international commodity, and the audience was a huge one. She and Cal worked the road constantly, all over the Western states. When she did get home, though, not all was as she had hoped. Donnie's life of neglect and institutional care had created a dour, often withdrawn teen rebel.

"At the time, Donnie was a spoiled brat," Jimmy Brogdon explained. "I could more or less understand it, in that his mother was gone all the time, his father wasn't there, so he was just left in the military academy, boarding schools. And one of the mistakes a parent makes, Rose tried to give him anything and everything, and of course, it just spoiled him and ruined him.

"I think he was a big comfort to Rose, and they got along fine, except when Donald would pull his little kiddie stuff—you know, taking the car, spending money, stealing money from her, her giving him money hand over fist and him still wanting more, wanting no discipline and not really having no ambition to do or make anything of himself. All the things a mother wants and expects her kid to do, well, he wasn't gonna do any of them things."

As much as she loved him, this was the wrong time for Donnie to be crossing Rose. The situation soon came to a head.

"I brought him down to Oceanside and put him in high school," Rose said. "Of course, I was out on the road and Jim had to oversee him. Donnie started skippin' school, which I didn't know anything about. He and Jim weren't gettin' along, because Jim was tryin' to make him do right and Donnie resented it.

"Finally, Jim told me that he had been skippin' school. I told Donnie that he had to go to school and he said, 'I been skippin' and I am not goin' back.' He only had a half a year to finish, and so I told him, 'You either go back to school, or you are goin' into the service.' Well, he didn't think I'd do it, so he says, 'I'll take the service.' I said, 'You got it,' and went and signed him up for the navy."

"Rose had a lot of tough decisions to make, as far as her personal life goes," Brogdon observed, "and this was probably one of the most difficult. A lot of it was things that, for one reason or another, had built up over a number of years. Both her family situation, as well as with Donald, was just somethin' that got started wrong and was left to go so wrong that finally she had to take a stand. I'm sure it hurt her, forcing him into the service, and a great many other things she has had to do. But time took care of that, and luckily things turned out pretty good."

Raising Donnie had become an ugly mess, far beyond Rose's control. The demands of her career were heavy, and it was simply too late to try and mother Donnie. She hoped that a hitch in the navy would not only mature Donnie but would also take him far away from Oceanside.

"He went through boot camp and finished second in all the tests and things," Rose said, "but he couldn't get the position he wanted because he hadn't finished high school. So instead of sending him somewhere else, they stationed him in San Diego, which was only thirty-five miles from Oceanside—the worst thing they could've done for him!

"And he went AWOL. He was livin' in the lagoon down below where we lived, and he'd sneak up durin' the day to get food and all such as that. I started missin' things out of the house. Jim knew where he was, because bein' a club owner, he knew all the police and they notified him. He told me what was happenin' and said, 'He's got to be turned in or he'll go to prison.'"

The situation deteriorated so rapidly that Rose could scarcely believe her rotten luck. She felt terrible about it, but anger and frustration outstripped the guilt. "So we turned him in, and he got six months in the stockade."

Callous as it may seem, Rose had no choice. Donnie was shipped back to Virginia to serve his time. Although upset, Rose begin concentrating full time on her career, leaving the marriage to take care of itself. During this period she embarked on her first European tour, as part of a package show. She was on a schedule that a fleet of Cadillacs would be hard pressed to keep up with. Free from Lula's domination, Rose was an individual for the first time in her life. She luxuriated in the freedom to satisfy her own whims, to make her own decisions—things she had never been allowed to do. Working the road, away from home and husband, Rose came to recognize her own spirit and came to cherish it. She also began to realize how difficult it was to maintain her relationships with her son and husband while maintaining a singing career. Constant career demands made it easy to ignore the many personal issues and complications that, as Brogdon said, "were left to go wrong." On most days, her attentions were fixed on one spot, center stage, where she was free and in control. The stage was her home, had been for twenty-five years. How could a quiet domestic life possibly compete with the applause and cheers of her extended family, the audience?

CHAPTER SEVENTEEN

Although Jimmy Brogdon helped Rose all he could, without Mama's guidance, life was totally different, a new frontier. The winter of 1959–60 was a turning point, for it brought not only her freedom and second marriage, it was also when Rose finally established herself as a solo singing star.

Even during the worst personal upheavals, Rose maintained her schedule of television and live appearances, never considering taking a break, only adding more bookings to an already heavy work load. Besides the regular Saturday night guest shots on "Hometown Jamboree," dates at the Wheel Club (and numerous Los Angeles area clubs), she and Cal worked Bakersfield's famous BlackBoard Cafe every Wednesday, did Black Jack Wayne's Oakland-based television show, and made regular appearances on the Chester Smith television show in Sacramento. (Smith, former bassist for Al Brown's Alabamans, was an old friend of the Maddoxes, had recorded for Capitol, and had established himself as a radio and television personality in the state capital.)

The contract with Capitol was no small relief. Capitol was one of the best companies a country artist could have behind her, and Rose was friendly with almost everyone on the label's country roster. Ken

Nelson, in particular, had an open perspective. He would let her do as she pleased, seeking only to improve, rather than alter her sound to suit his own notions.

Capitol rushed out her first single, "What Makes Me Hang Around?" backed with "Gambler's Love," releasing the 45 on March 3, 1959. On these wistful heart songs, though Nelson effectively approximated the lush sound that Chet Atkins was popularizing in Nashville, Nelson's approach had none of the emasculated quality so many Nashville Sound productions suffered from. ("People say I brought country music to the middle of the road," Nashville Sound producer Chet Atkins told *Country Music* magazine in a 1974 interview. "Maybe I did and maybe I didn't, but a lot of people seem to like what we're doing.")

The middle of the road was no place for Rose Maddox, and the single lost none of Rose's mournful backwoods power while presenting her with a more sophisticated musical atmosphere, which was exactly what she had been trying to achieve on her Columbia releases. The arrangements and her sweet, traditional tone combined beautifully. "Authentic as the squirrel leaping among the sycamores or the yellow flash of a fox diving into the scrub. The Maddox voice with its strong, bell-like no-nonsense resonance is a pay crop for any handler," read the *Music Reporter*'s "Scoop of the Week," adding: "The 'Gambler's Love' flip is loaded with golden phrasing . . . a four aces holding in any poker game." Two months after its release, "Gambler's Love" became Rose's first recording to hit the *Billboard* national charts, peaking at #22. It was an encouraging start.

Capitol had certainly capitalized on Rose's first single, and Brogdon was doing his best to generate publicity for every disc and date Rose had on her schedule. This was a far cry from the lack of promotion and interest her Columbia sides received. Her next release, on July 6, 1959, consisted of "Custer's Last Stand," a Johnny Horton styled story-song written by Black Jack Wayne, and a rockabilly tune from her brother Henry, "My Little Baby."

Rose flexed her muscles on this disc, shouting tales of historic bloodshed and jet-age rock & roll with all the natural fire of a folk communicator. It was unmistakably California country music, the type she and Cal were laying down every week at the BlackBoard, alongside artists like Bill Woods, Red Simpson, Wynn Stewart, Tommy Collins, Gene Moles, and Buck Owens. The raucous honky-tonk these men played had evolved directly from the roadhouse insanity of the Maddox Brothers & Rose, and was now developing into a distinctive, modern version of that post-war Okie boogie, the sounds favored by Bakersfield's "Beer Can Hill" set.

Essentially codified by Wynn Stewart's band, it was spare yet driving music, laced with stinging Roy Nichols guitar fills and punctuated by the rolling steel guitar comment of Ralph Mooney. The instrumental approach was quickly furthered by the brighter, brasher interpretations of Buck Owens Buckaroos Don Rich and Tom Brumley. Oddly timed vocal phrasing, characterized by idiosyncratic pauses and meter-defying rubato also became associated with the Bakersfield Sound, such as could be heard on Red Simpson's "Party Girl," where he sings: "Partygirl . . . they . . . call . . . her . . . Partygirl." This offbeat phrasing (a convoluted version of Lefty Frizzell's slurred, drawn-out vocal style) became a hall-mark of Bakersfield honky-tonk.

Bakersfield drummer Henry Sharpe, a BlackBoard Cafe stalwart, played on many of Rose's early Capitol sessions and recalled an incident that underscores how important it was to get the Bakersfield feel: "I remember when we went in to do 'Custer's Last Stand,' I had these tom-toms and we kept doin' it over, tryin' to get it right. We wanted that Indi-an type of sound, you know, and finally Rose comes over to me, says, 'Henry, play 'em just like you do at the BlackBoard!' So I did, and it made a good record."

In the next four or five years, San Joaquin Valley rowdies like Owens, Haggard, Stewart, and Simpson, along with some of the best sidemen in the land (Roy Nichols, Don Rich, James Burton) would begin to assault the charts with a vigor and consistency that Nashville could only watch and wonder over. Since Music City U. S. A. had laid claim to the middle-of-the-road, West Coast artists felt free to zoom past on the hard-country shoulder.

Rose was in a prime position to reap the benefits from her countless nights of wild musical experimentation. Whereas many country artists of the time were increasingly touchy and cautious about how they presented themselves (perhaps unsure of themselves after the rock & roll revolution), Rose always felt free to express herself, without inhibition and in any format, pop or traditional folk, that suited her. A perfect illustration of this occurred at the Wheel Club, shortly after Rose and Jimmy had married.

"Patsy Cline had a pretty big record out at the time," Brogdon recalled. "And we booked her in. Now, with country fans, Patsy Cline was all right, but she was more of a pop act. Anyway, Rose showed up and of course she got up and started clappin' her hands and singin', "Sally, Let Your Bangs Hang Down," and everyone went wild. When it came time for Patsy to go on again, we had a bunch of people yellin', 'We want Rose Maddox!' So it was a little embarrassing."

At this point, in 1959, Cline's only national hit had been "Walking After Midnight" in 1957, and though she possessed a powerful voice, Cline was an interloper that night and clearly at a disadvantage on Rose's home turf.

Rose remembers Cline's appearance. "The first and only time I seen her was when my husband booked her in, and she was a person who loved to drink and have a good time, which there is nothing wrong with, nothing at all."

Rose continued, clearly uncomfortable to be on the subject of Cline. "I don't like to talk about things like this, but I guess I should. . . . She had been on and performed and was settin' at the bar, drinkin' beer. Ever'-body was hollerin' for me to get up there, so I sang a couple of numbers. A friend of mine was standin' back there, and Patsy turned to her and said, 'If I got up there and shook like she does, why, I'd be as popular as she is!' And my friend told me what she had said."

Rose still gets mad thinking about this. "I do not get up there and shake; my body keeps time with my singin', is all I do. And that did not set well with me, hearing that she had said that about me."

Several months later, Rose had a far more amicable meeting with another rising talent. In February 1960, a young country singer came to Los Angeles from her home in Custer, Washington, to record her first single for Zero Records, titled "I'm a Honky Tonk Gal." This was Loretta Lynn, who approached Jim Brogdon for a booking at his club.

Loretta and husband Mooney Lynn stopped in one evening, and after Jimmy got her onstage for a few numbers, he immediately agreed to book her. Rose quickly took a liking to the shy, young singer, who squirmed nervously at the thought of performing in front of Rose, one of the idols she had listened to on the radio since moving west from Kentucky in 1950. The Brogdons invited Loretta and Mooney to spend the night in their guest apartment.

"Back before anyone had ever heard of Loretta Lynn, Rose actually sat down and called every place that she usually worked," Jimmy recalled, "and she booked Loretta for two weeks' worth of dates. I think we got her fifty dollars a night, which at the time, she was glad to get. But Rose herself sat down and phoned everyone she knew, and we didn't charge them anything for it, just because we were friends. Why, we boosted, pushed, and worked Loretta every chance we got. I know that Rose helped her, in those early days, and I think it really did help her. She subsequently got to where we couldn't afford her!" Lynn, taking her cue from Rose, stuck to a hard-country style that addressed life's travails with independence and humor. Within several years, she was at the top of the heap.

While Rose's Capitol releases never matched either Cline or Lynn's later sales, they were doing well. Her third single, the mournful ballad "I Lost Today," was released just weeks after her December 1959 elopement. One of her best Capitol sides, it featured a flip side written by Alta, "I'm Happy Every Day I Live," whose title could have been the Maddox family motto. (Or better, as Rose's onstage version goes, "I'm happy every day I live, but these nights are killin' me!"). This disc sold fairly well also, and Capitol released her first LP, *The One Rose,* in January 1960.

Recorded in three sessions, the twelve songs consisted of old favorites from the 4 Star days ("Whoa, Sailor," "Philadelphia Lawyer," "Tramp on the Street"), several Hank Williams tunes, and outstanding versions of "I Want to Live and Love" and "Chocolate Ice Cream Cone." This last song had long been in the Maddox family repertoire. Years earlier, while driving to a dance in separate Cadillacs, Rose and Fred had each heard the daft novelty on their car radios, and upon arriving at the auditorium, each approached the other, saying, "Hey, we ought to learn that 'Ice Cream Cone' song."

Both Cal and Henry played and sang harmony on *The One Rose,* with Henry contributing his trademark muffled mandolin picking to great effect, and Henry Sharpe joined in on drums. This familiar crew made the album a close approximation of Rose's live show. Rose's career, it seemed, was steadily ascending that January; success in the record market, so long almost an afterthought to the Maddoxes, was becoming very important to Rose. She wanted a hit badly. Fred Maddox recalled visiting one of Rose's Capitol sessions where Ken Nelson told him, "If she'd just let me pick her songs, nobody would even remember who Kitty Wells is!" That was all Rose needed to hear.

"The only person who ever picked a song for me was Ken," she said. "4 Star and Columbia had never presented me with any songs. One day, Ken Nelson came to me and said, 'I've got a song here, and we want you to record it. We think it'll be a big hit.' And I said, 'Has anyone else recorded it?' And he said, 'No, they haven't.'

"It was a song by Don Robertson, who was a hot writer at the time, called 'Please Help Me, I'm Falling.' I learned it right there in the studio, recorded it, and made a great record on it."

Recorded January 25, 1960, Rose's rendition, delivered in a tone of honeyed agony and complimented by the tasteful steel of Norm Hamlet and guitar licks of Lee Newman, was solid.

"So I went on the road that weekend, and I got a call from Jim," Rose recalled. "He said, 'Guess what? Hank Locklin just stopped by, and he's got a new record coming out called 'Please Help Me, I'm Falling.' And I said, 'You're kidding me—they told me nobody had recorded that!' And Jimmy says, 'Well, he did, and it's being released next week.' So I got on the phone, called Capitol and told them, 'I know for a fact you can get mine out at the same time his is released. You've got to get it pressed and get it out there.' Well, they were going to have a meeting, you know, discuss it among the biggies. They said they'd meet on Monday, and then Ken Nelson called me back and said, 'Well, we think you've got such a good record on it, that his coming out ahead won't hurt anything.'

"Well, it might not have, if mine had been released maybe a week after his, but they waited over a month, and his had already took off like a bat out of Hades! Mine was just too late. I could have had a hit record there, a big seller, if they had only done what I asked them to. That is the only song a company ever offered me, and they blew it."

It wasn't Nelson's instinct that failed, but the label itself. As Cliffie Stone explained: "That happened quite often at Capitol, where we'd go in and record a song and then they'd sit on it, and some other label would come out and have a hit, and you're dead, you know? It happened a lot of times. Like I cut 'Mule Train' with Tennessee Ernie Ford and the next day Frankie Laine cut it for Columbia, and Columbia rushed it out; Capitol lay on Ernie's for two weeks, and we had a minor hit, but we could've had a major pop hit with it."

Considering that her career has lasted nearly sixty years now, Rose has remarkably few beefs of this sort, and, despite the fact that her version came out just a month after the session, this missed opportunity is one of the few incidents that still rankles her. Locklin's record was #1 on *Billboard*'s country charts for fourteen weeks and also crossed over to become a Top Ten pop hit. Unfortunately, a fine Tommy Collins song, "Down, Down, Down," that was used as Rose's flip side for "Please Help Me" got lost right along with the plug side.

Rose pressed on regardless, and Capitol kept her busy in their Vine Street studio. She spent the rest of January recording material for her next long-player, an all-gospel album called *The Glory Bound Train*. Composed mostly of standards like "The Great Speckled Bird" and "Will the Circle Be Unbroken," it also included an amazing Henry Maddox original, "Smoke, Fire and Brimstone." This rocking gospel song, chockfull of allusions to Satan and the Atomic Age, was a breakneck, red-hot number. More bitingly satiric than anything the Maddox Brothers & Rose had done, its wise-guy, tongue-in-cheek message was so extreme that Capitol's willingness to include the song on an otherwise sober sacred offering strongly suggests that Rose had a free hand in the making of her records.

By the end of 1960, Capitol had released both albums, as well as two other singles, "Shining Silver, Gleaming Gold," and in December "Kissing My Pillow" (with Rose singing double-tracked harmony, à la Patti Page) backed with "I Want to Live Again." Both sides of the latter single were written by Rose's friend and confederate Fuzzy Owen, and both featured the guitar of Roy Nichols, back recording with Rose for the first time in ten years. Some of Fuzzy's golden touch (he, with partner Lewis Talley, later developed Merle Haggard as a recording artist) rubbed off on both sides of the single, for "Kissing My Pillow" lodged at #14 on the charts, with "I Want to Live Again" following closely at #15. Rose was coming into her own professionally, but personally her life was a mess.

New Years Day, 1961. Behind the Cadillac's wheel, Rose tried to reason out the family situation. Her obligation as Mrs. Jimmy Brogdon was her primary concern, but guilt over Lula's rejection followed a close second. She was bound for Kansas City to work her first date as a member of the Johnny Cash road show. Cash, living in Los Angeles at the time, had known Rose both from their days as "Opry" cast members and from numerous appearances on "Hometown Jamboree" and "Town Hall Party." He himself had quit the "Opry" in 1958 expressly so he could relocate to California. Upon his arrival, Fred Maddox greeted him as marshall of an impromptu parade, made up of seventeen Cadillacs loaded with Maddox cronies and Johnny Cash fans. Cash was then approaching the peak of his career, and his invitation to Rose was a welcome offer.

Out on the road, Rose found the time to assess her marriage, her relationship with Donnie, and her own soul. As her car chewed up asphalt, she struggled to put everything into perspective, but her conflicted feelings about her mother could not be easily resolved.

Deeply shaken by her daughter's rebellion, Lula had retired to Ashland. Now more than seventy years old, she was in a dazed condition most of the time and often out of touch with reality. Without her kids to manage, she had little reason to remain in the music business. Whether from a self-inflicted emotional condition or the debilitating spread of Alzheimer's disease, Lula was never the same again. In the coming years, she grew progressively worse.

Rose felt immeasurable guilt. At times, it overwhelmed her. But she so treasured her newfound freedom and independence that the thought brought tears to her eyes. Still, she was a married woman and felt obliged to pursue a domestic life: "I had tried to quit the music business after we were married, and I told Jim, 'I want to be a wife to you.' And he said, 'No, you're too great a talent to deprive the world of your singing.'"

Rose grinned broadly. "Which is true! But at least, I inquired. . . . It was a happy marriage, more or less. Jim is strictly a businessman, and he became my manager. He is the cause of my being so popular on Capitol. He'd send out the promotional records, follow 'em up with letters to all the disc jockeys in the country, like it's supposed to be done." As always, romance and family remained inextricably linked to business. As always, business came first.

Joining the Johnny Cash show was Rose's most strategic, prestigious move since signing with Capitol. Then twenty-nine years old, "The Man in Black" was already one of the biggest artists in country music. He employed the "Tennessee Three" (at the time lead guitarist Luther Perkins, bassist Marshall Grant, and drummer W. S. "Fluke" Holland) on these tours to back the road show cast, which usually consisted of Rose, fiddler Gordon Terry, and Johnny Western. Later that year, Buck Owens & the Buckaroos joined the show.

Rose worked with Cash throughout 1961, averaging twenty-four shows a month. She usually opened, with the Tennessee Three and Gordon Terry backing her. Given the national exposure this afforded her, Brogdon's tireless promotion, and Rose's own intense performances, it was no wonder her career was on an upswing. This was, significantly, the first tour she made without Cal, who stayed home to care for Mama. Rose was completely on her own; she soon realized what a vulnerable position this left her in.

As she sang in the new year in Kansas City, Cash's booking agent, Hap Peebles, stood in the wings. Peebles was an all-around entrepreneurial operator and hillbilly war-horse who had been in the business since 1931, booking everyone from Guy Lombardo to Acuff, Tubb, and Bob Wills (whom he also managed for a time). As Peebles stood there watching Rose sing and keep rhythm with her body, colored lights flashing off her rhinestones, sweat sprang out on his brow.

"He watched me perform, and evidently it set him on fire," Rose said with a laugh. "I had never met the man in my life. I finished and he came up to me and said, 'That's one of the greatest shows I've seen in my life.' I thanked him, and he started in . . . let's see, how did he put it?

"'Why did you marry Jimmy Brogdon?'

"'Because I love him.'

"'You don't know what the word love means. I'm gonna teach you.'

"Now, when this stuff started comin' up, it absolutely scared the livin' daylights out of me, because I knew that a lot of girls in the business, most of 'em who wanted to get to the top, did these kinds of things.

"I was raised in the protection of my family, with four big brothers to look after me, but Cal wasn't with me. I had gone out alone. I thought, 'God, what have I gotten myself into?' Come to find out, after he'd seen me perform, Peebles set it up for me to leave with him that night, supposedly to do some radio promotion for our next appearance."

Cash, at the time, was managed by Stu Carnall, who got his start in the music business with Steve Stebbins, when both had traveled with and booked the Maddox Brothers & Rose in the late forties. Carnall was an eccentric, theatrical character who affected a derby hat and walking stick; on arrival at a hotel, band members Grant and Perkins would often roll out a strip of red carpet and solemnly announce him as "The Baron of Bellflower." An old and trusted friend of the Maddox family, Carnall was well aware of Rose's many frustrated male followers. Knowing this was her first time alone on the road, he anticipated just such an episode. Rose desperately sought him out and explained the situation. Carnall threw his head back and laughed.

"It is not funny, Stu!" Rose fumed.

"I know it's not," he replied, going over mental images he had stored of Lula running off would-be suitors at the countless dances he had accompanied her family to, "but I can't help laughing!"

"It ain't funny, and I ain't goin'!" Rose snapped.

She knew there really was not anything she could do, short of going to Cash himself, which as a new member of the troupe she was loath to do. As Carnall's laughter echoed backstage, Rose found a phone, determined to get out of this jam. She called Jim, who told her, "You can take care of yourself, Rose." In shock, she replied, "I've never been in a situation like this!" All he said was: "Go on. You can take care of yourself, Rose." (What she didn't know at the time was that immediately after Brogdon hung up, he called Stu Carnall, warning him in no uncertain terms of the unhappiness Stu could expect if Peebles had his way.)

Squirming and in a cold sweat, Rose, too afraid to approach Cash, had no choice but to go with Peebles. "So I went with the guy. It was storming bad," she said. "He decided that we should stop and get a hotel room. It was too stormy to go on any further, and I was absolutely petrified." Although the hotel had just one room available, it was a two-bedroom suite. Rose immediately locked herself inside one.

"Well, next mornin', Hap was not happy at all, not at all. But he had this whole tour booked, and he just kept on after me the entire time. Finally Cash couldn't understand why I was off by myself all the time, and so one of the group, Gordon Terry, told him what was goin' on. I was just tryin' to keep out of this guy's way! One night, we were at a big auditorium up in North Dakota, Johnny come and asked me straight out, 'Is Hap botherin' you, Rose?' And he says, 'I'll take care of that.'"

Cash, essentially a gentle poet, was nonetheless the wrong man to cross. He was at his most unpredictable during this period, consuming fists full of pills, going on sprees that often involved such bizarre pastimes as sawing all the legs of his hotel room furniture down to a height of four inches, or painting everything in his room, floor to ceiling, solid black.

He sought Peebles out and backed him into a corner. Hap, pinned to the wall, with Cash's massive frame towering over him, was speechless. Heaving with rage, central nervous system blazing with amphetamines, Cash delivered a tight-lipped warning: "If you ever go near Rose again," he snarled, "I'll kill you."

"And to this day, I have never seen or heard from Hap Peebles," Rose said. "And he had a letter from Jim waitin' for him at his office, when he got back." Brogdon's technique, though it seemed cruel at the time, was in fact a carefully planned scheme. "What he was trying to do was give me the confidence to try and learn to take care of myself; he knew that I had never been out on my own." Stu Carnall, she later discovered, was also made part of this conspiracy to bolster Rose's independence.

While this crash course had taught her a lot about the unchaperoned single girl's position in country music, Rose had other concerns. She needed a big hit, a bona fide Top Ten smash. Around this time, another BlackBoard stalwart, Buck Owens, was beginning to place hits in the Top Ten. (His first, "Second Fiddle," had charted in 1959.) He and Rose were pals, both on the same label, and Buck knew Rose had what he needed. Taking a cue from Jean Shepard and Ferlin Husky's earlier successful duet, "Dear John," Owens had asked Rose, shortly before she joined Cash, if she would care to record a duet or two with him.

On a break from the tour, Rose returned to Los Angeles. She and Owens went into Capitol's studio on January 16, 1961, and cut "Mental Cruelty," an Owens original and one of the sharpest divorce numbers yet to emerge in country music, as well as Freddie Hart's "Loose Talk," a bouncy honky-tonk song about nosy gossips plaguing a happily married couple. She spent the next three days in the studio, recording twelve songs with Cal, Roy Nichols, Norm Hamlet, and Billy Strange. She was booked so heavily that it was necessary to get as many songs in the can as she could.

Capitol held the duets with Buck until *Glory Bound Train* had time to establish itself, releasing the Owens-Maddox single on April 10. Both sides were separate chart entries in *Billboard*, with "Loose Talk" reaching #4, and "Mental Cruelty" hitting #8. Coincidentally, the #2 record on the charts during much of this period was "Foolin' Around" by none other than Buck Owens. Rose, Nelson, and Owens were all delighted.

Rose followed her first Top Ten hits with "Lonely Street," which Carl Belew introduced on 4 Star, where Rose learned it. (Patsy Cline, George Jones, and Andy Williams also recorded it.) Rose was back in a world-weary, blue mood on this recording, and the flip, "Conscience, I'm Guilty" (a remake of a 1956 Hank Snow hit), conjured up an even darker atmosphere. Indeed, it was one of the most desperate cheating songs she ever recorded. The record must have found sympathetic ears, though, for it hit #14 on *Billboard*'s country charts at the end of the summer of 1961.

Both these songs were included on her *Big Bouquet of Roses* album, released in July 1961. The album spotlighted her versatility. It offered weepers; raw, raving rockabilly covers of r&b tunes ("Jim Dandy," "Early in the Morning"); a remake of "Tall Men"; and, last but not least, a version of Johnny Horton's "North to Alaska," which was as much a tribute to her recently deceased suitor as it was part of common practice to round out albums with current hits. Though she jumped from style to style, Rose stood out among her country music contemporaries by consistently coming up with distinct, fresh, and unmistakable interpretations, leaving her mark on each song.

After the gospel sessions at Capitol, Rose still had some time off before the Cash show went out again. She and Jim were organizing a package show of their own, set to tour the Pacific Northwest later in the year when the Cash show had another scheduled break. It was to be headlined by the Maddox Brothers & Rose; Cal, Fred, and even Don would join Rose for these dates, the first of several infrequent reunions. Lonzo & Oscar, and several West Coast acts rounded out the bill.

"We had gone up to Washington and Oregon to book shows and went to spend the night with Mama." Rose said. "She had gotten real bad off, health-wise. And mentally, she was forgettin' things all the time. When we got there, she and Jim got into an argument about somethin'. They really got into it, and finally Jim said he was leavin', and I said, 'I'm goin' with you.' And Mama says, 'No, you're not!'"

A pause. Rose still felt the raw pain of that moment. "And I said, 'Yes, I am.' And I left with him . . . I think that's the straw that broke the camel's back, right there. Just all of a sudden, out of the clear blue, she wasn't competent. . . . Cal stayed with her. I had tore her world apart, and yes, I felt guilty about it, but I had made my decision, and I figured life had to go on."

Life went on as hectic as ever; jumping from auditorium to auditorium throughout the summer of 1961, she also managed a return to Hollywood in July for another three-day studio siege, recording sixteen songs with a band that featured Ralph Mooney, Roy Nichols, and Joe Maphis. Following the Maddoxes' Northwest reunion tour, she worked a date for Black Jack Wayne at Napa, California's Dream Bowl amphitheater and was scheduled to fly out that night and meet the Cash troupe in Boston, Massachusetts, as soon as she finished.

A friend drove her to San Francisco, where she caught a flight east. After changing planes in Chicago Rose fell asleep. The aircraft, coming in on radar, due to heavy fog, approached Boston's Logan International Airport just as dawn broke on Sunday, September 21, 1961. As they touched down on the runway, the landing gear failed and the pilot lost control. The airplane careened down the tarmac, sending up a huge shower of sparks. Panicked passengers shrieked, begging for their lives to be spared. Rose awoke to screams of fear.

With no means to brake, the plane fishtailed and skidded down the entire runway, careened off the landfill, and plunged into the cold waters of Boston Harbor. The sickening impact of the plane's belly flop made drowning seem inevitable to the terrified passengers.

"I credit the pilot with our not going under," Rose said, recalling the incident, "because when he saw we were going into the bay, he lifted the nose of the plane; if it had gone straight in, it would've flipped over, and we'd have been under the water, instead of above it.

"I went out onto the wing, and there was a yacht club sailing by. Of course, they had seen us go in, and they got us all off into their boats and took us to their club, before anyone from the airport ever got out there!

"There was only one guy who died in the accident, and that was from a heart attack. . . . He was in the same boat I was."

Airport officials rushed the passengers back to the terminal. Rose got to a pay phone and immediately called Jim. The press arrived, photographing her in the phone booth, a picture that ran with the story in almost every newspaper in the nation. Back at the hotel, Cash was in bed, only halfway paying attention to the television until a news flash about the accident appeared on the screen.

"The rest of 'em told me," said Rose, "that he had sat straight up and said, 'That's Rose's plane!' He was a nervous wreck by the time I got to the hotel. We were supposed to do a matinee show that afternoon, and I had nothin' but the clothes on my back. Cash canceled the matinee, called some big department store, and had 'em open up, and he took me down there shoppin'. I got one dress for stagewear, and used that dress, with accessories, for the entire tour. We made the show that night, but he refused to do the afternoon one.

"The next day we were doin' a show up in Philadelphia, and the airline called there and said they had had to dismantle the airplane because the tide was out and it had stuck in the mud. They said, 'We've got your luggage. What do you want us to do with it?' And I said, 'Ship it home; it's no good to me.' 'Cause it had been under that water."

The entire troupe, shaken by Rose's brush with death, did whatever they could to put her at ease. Each night, she went to sleep in a somewhat provocative wardrobe: Cash's pajama bottoms and Johnny Western's pajama top. Rose had been lucky. In the early sixties sudden death seemed to stalk country music, claiming in a five-year period Jim Reeves, Patsy Cline, Cowboy Copas, and Hawkshaw Hawkins to plane crashes and Johnny Horton, Ira Louvin, and Jack Anglin to auto accidents. Roy Acuff barely escaped from a 1965 car wreck, coming out of it with a broken collarbone and fractured pelvis.

During the tour, meanwhile, Johnny Cash was undergoing a turbulent, long-distance struggle with his wife, Vivian, who was back in Los Angeles. The demands of the road, an increasing reliance on pills, and serious domestic troubles were besetting him. The worsening tension finally became too much for Stu Carnall, whose wife, entertainer Lorrie Collins had delivered their first child in June 1961. Carnall quit and was replaced by a Canadian, Saul Holiff. Holiff wasted no time in making it clear that he, like Peebles, would not mind instructing Rose in expanded definitions of the word "love."

Cash and Holiff were scheduled to fly to New York City for a meeting at Columbia Records. Johnny himself was very fond of Rose and asked if she would care to accompany them. Not wanting to create any more problems over Holiff's interest in her, especially so soon after Carnall's departure, Rose declined, citing her very real fear of flying, a result of the Boston incident. "I wasn't scared at first, but later it really hit me," she said.

Cash, who had recently adopted a policy of bringing Rose with him on the plane to all road-show dates (while the others drove), was unhappy. He planned to make sure she got over her fear.

"So he said he needed me to fly to Nova Scotia and do advance promotion on our date up there. I said, 'I ain't gettin' on that airplane!' And he said, 'Yes, you are, Rose.' And if he hadn't've pushed me onto that plane, I probably never would've gotten onto another one, because just enough time had passed to really put a scare into me."

Not only did Cash's plan work, his sincere concern for Rose defused Holiff's ardor. She continued to accompany them on flights to their appearances, while below, Luther Perkins, Marshall Grant, and Fluke Holland would race Gordon Terry and Johnny Western to the next town.

Rose became close friends with Cash, though she was completely unaware of Cash's drug problem. Always the Southern gentleman with Rose, Cash certainly would have tried to avoid her whenever his condition and appearance got out of hand. It was not as unlikely a charade as it sounds. Rose was still very naive: "I wouldn't have known a pill if I met one in the middle of the road."

Cash began a destructive pattern of leaving the troupe suddenly and returning to Los Angeles to try and straighten out his marriage. Departing with little or no notice, Cash left the road-show schedule of bookings in an increasingly fouled-up state. As time passed, Cash's escapes became more and more regular. Rose found that the dates Jimmy booked her as a single to take up slack between road-show commitments were now getting overlapped as Cash dates were rescheduled to meet his increasingly erratic behavior. Cash's irresponsibility began to rankle Rose more and more, and it did not help her reputation as a single, but it was still the best gig she had gotten since leaving the brothers. Also, there were other, more personal considerations.

She and Cash enjoyed a boisterous friendship. Cash biographer

Christopher Wren described a typical incident, when the singer wanted a passel of female fans cleared out of his hotel suite. He called Rose down and in an adjoining bedroom the pair began a mock shouting match. At its height, he whipped out an antique cap-and-ball pistol and hollered, "That's it! I'm gonna kill you, bitch!" and discharged the powder load up at the ceiling. The fans quickly dispersed.

One night when they were working in Calgary, Rose had gotten ptomaine poisoning from a hotel meal and was unable to perform. "So Cash got up there onstage and told ever'one gangrene had set in and that I was dyin'."

"He sent a doctor to my room and I got to feelin' a little better. After the show, Johnny came up to my room and he said, 'There's a bunch of girls in my room, Rose, can I stay up here with you?' And I said, 'Why, sure, there's a bed right over there for you.'"

Even at age thirty-five, Rose was unable to decipher the signals Cash was sending her way. Some time passed. Very slowly. "Finally he says, 'I want you to go and clear them girls out of my room.' I didn't know what he wanted, because I was still dumb, just as dumb as they make 'em. So I went on down there, and, sure enough, there was some girls and I ran 'em off, went back to my room and got in my bed. Well, he was real restless over there in his bed, real restless. Finally he got up and said, 'Did you get them girls out of there?' And I said yes. And he says, 'I'm goin' back down to my room. I can't stand bein' this close to you.' And so he left." Lying there in the darkness, it dawned on Rose what had just happened.

They worked their way across Canada and down into Portland, the tour's final show. Rose, flushed and confounded, felt compelled to settle this matter. She called Cash's room: "What do you want of me, John?"

"I want you completely, or not at all."

"I'm married, and you know that, and you can't have me."

Cash would not be put off and tried everything he could think of to persuade Rose to come to him. She finally cut him off: "John, I'm married. I have never cheated on Jimmy, and I have no intention of cheatin' on him."

At the time, this was true. The emotional pressure, combined with the constant rescheduling of tour dates and the effect it had on her own bookings, forced her to quit the Cash show in December 1961, although she was quite welcome to stay on.

"And that's when he hired June Carter," Rose adds tartly. "You know what happened then."

CHAPTER EIGHTEEN

Rose returned to Oceanside, happy to be with Jimmy, who accompanied her to every West Coast date his schedule allowed. She began planning her next recording sessions in Hollywood and tried to come to terms with her damaged family relations. Donnie had served his time back in Virginia, where, it turned out, E. B. Hale made his home. Now remarried, Hale got in touch with Donnie, whereupon the pair began a long overdue relationship. Although he never admitted to being Donnie's natural father (probably in order to preserve his second marriage), Hale's friendship was a boon to Donnie and went a long way towards settling his restless spirit. Though Rose was not overjoyed by the turn of events, she knew Donnie would benefit from contact with his father.

While Rose puzzled over what direction she ought to follow for her career, an unusual opportunity presented itself: a request from bluegrass patriarch Bill Monroe that she record a strictly traditional album. "I done the best I could to help her," Monroe said of his efforts to bring Rose back to the Nashville fold. "She has a good voice to listen to. We've worked some shows together down through the years, and she has always been a good friend."

If the team of Maddox and Monroe seems unlikely, Monroe hardly thought so. "The Maddox Brothers & Rose always had their own style," he said, "but you must remember their home was Alabama, and I always thought they sang a lot of the old Southern style of singin'. So I enjoyed helpin' her on one of her albums. She had some great entertainers workin' on it, and it didn't take long at all."

Rose Maddox Sings Bluegrass was recorded in Nashville with Bill Monroe, the team of Don Reno and Red Smiley, and that duo's Tennessee Cut Ups band. Monroe's contributions were formally unacknowledged, as he was under contract to Decca; Capitol's session details list only Reno, Smiley, and "other personnel unknown." Going through the channels necessary to credit Monroe was too involved, given both Rose's and his own schedule, and the Father of Bluegrass was happy to work anonymously.

She went to Nashville for the sessions on March 19 and 20, 1962. In those two days, the musicians recorded twelve songs, mostly Monroe originals and bluegrass standards. The proceedings were given a Maddox twist by the inclusion of such mainstream country songs as Tommy Collins's "Down Down Down" and "Old Slew Foot" (popularized by Johnny Horton), as well as the presence of a steel guitarist, Wayne "Swamproot' Gailey, a close friend of Rose's. Released in November 1962, the result was a groundbreaking album, the very first bluegrass long-player recorded by a woman, and, at the time, one of the very few attempted by an established mainstream country (rather than bluegrass) singer.

Rose's performances on the album were among her best on record, and her natural affinity for the music created moments of astounding purity. At times she sounds transported, reaching a point of completely unfettered, natural expression. "Cottonfields" rings with authority while "Rollin' in My Sweet Baby's Arms" positively blazes; she matches the mandolin, banjo, and guitar's contributions blow for blow, more like a jazz stylist in a free-form musical dialogue than a country music singer performing a traditional favorite. *Rose Maddox Sings Bluegrass* is her best traditional recording, and her interpretations of Monroe's standards are outstanding.

"Bill Monroe has always told me that I sang bluegrass, and to me, what he was talkin' about is just what I call 'hillbilly,'" Rose later explained. Either way, her bluegrass LP remains one of her most popular. It has been reissued three times in Japan, Britain, and Germany, and an original Capitol LP has gone for as high as three hundred dollars in auction. In early 1996, Capitol Records made the album available for the first time on a domestic compact disc reissue.

While the sessions with Monroe were a soul-satisfying return to her Southern roots, the Maddox career continued to be driven by the up-to-date love songs she was cutting back in Hollywood. The lyrical themes of Rose's records, more often by coincidence than design, have always paralleled her personal life, and at Capitol this pattern held true to a greater degree than ever before. Once again, her material mirrored her personal life, just as "Single Girl" and "Alimony" had during the 1940s. While Rose has insisted these apparent slices of life "are just songs, that's all they were to me," her choice of titles like "Conscience, I'm Guilty" and "You're Kind of Lovin' Won't Do" seemed to anticipate developments in her private life.

Things were not going smoothly for the Brogdons. "I was gone all the time working, and things had gotten slack between Jim and I," Rose quietly explained. "I started getting involved with other musicians. I finally had the ability, and Jim wasn't around. Our sex life had become less and less and, consequently, I turned to others."

This development was not lost on the many hopefuls who had waited more than a decade to pursue Rose. Apparently, there were plenty of them hell-bent on making up for lost time, regardless of how Rose felt. According to her, very few approached the matter with any tact or discretion; Tommy Collins was one of them.

Rose was booked in at an after-hours club in Portland, along with Collins. The club opened at 4 A.M. and Rose went on at 6 A.M. Meanwhile, she killed time at the bar with Collins:

"You comin' back to the motel with me, Rose?"

"You know well enough not to ask me that, Tommy."

"Yeah, I know I do, but there's no harm in askin', is there?"

Between her infrequent visits home and the constant companionship of other men, Rose admitted, she began slipping around with any musician she found attractive, or one who was persistent enough to wear down her resolve.

"None of 'em were serious," Rose insisted. "Like I told my girlfriend, Mary: 'If you're getting what you're supposed to at home, you don't go looking for it somewhere else.' Which is true, I guess. Anyway, that's the way I thought about it."

A typical incident occurred when Rose was working with the Buck Owens road show in the mid-sixties. The show featured Rose, Collins, Wynn Stewart, Freddie Hart, and the Buckaroos—a powerful line-up of West Coast talent. Also traveling with the troupe was a business associate of Buck's, whom Rose had known for almost twenty years.

Rose had been joined on the tour by a girlfriend who was trying to romance a member of Wynn Stewart's band, and the two women, in between man-chasing, were sharing a hotel room. Late one night after the show, there came a pounding on the door. Rose opened it to reveal Buck's associate, flushed with liquor. Without so much as a hello, he grasped Rose's wrist and pulled her down the corridor to his room. Once inside, to her disbelief, he began chasing her around the bed like a Hollywood degenerate, not someone she had known since he was a teenager in Modesto.

Tiring of this foolishness, Rose stood her ground and faced him, flatly refusing any advances. The man, inflamed with years of suppressed yearning, thickly cried, "What's-a matter, Rose, you like girls better'n boys?"

That did it. She hauled off and popped him in the kisser, stalked back to her room, and immediately called Buck's room. Apologetic, he assured her nothing of the sort would happen again. Remembering the incident years later, Owens said he told the guy, "You can't just grab 'em. You got to ask politely first: 'Would you like to come to my room?'" Owens broke up laughing. "But he just couldn't wait!"

Rose and this family friend remained on amicable terms, but she was deeply insulted by his wisecrack. But the man was hardly barking up the wrong tree.

Word of such indiscretions soon filtered back to Oceanside and Jimmy

Brogdon. Rose had put together her own band for use in between Owens's roadshow commitments, package dates, and European tours. She rarely spent more than two or three days at home. The situation between husband and wife inevitably came to a head.

"I came into the house. It was three or four in the morning, and the band was traveling with me at the time," Rose recalled. "I had their costumes that all had to go to the hand cleaners up in Hollywood. At the time I had a little thing goin' on up there anyway. I came in and I thought Jim was asleep. I got something I needed out of the closet and went up to the other apartment, where the drummer was living, 'cause I had to get his uniform. The uniforms all belonged to me; I dressed 'em alike. Well, come to find out, Jim wasn't asleep and he had followed me up there. He grabbed me by the arm, said, 'What the hell is goin' on here?'

"I told him, 'I came to get the uniforms, to take 'em to the cleaners.' 'Cause they were the only ones who did it by hand, and he says, 'You're not goin' anywhere. Get on back down to the house!' And he pushed me towards the landing, caught me unawares. I lost my balance and I went over the railing."

The fall's impact tore open her face below the right eye. Brogdon was horrified. "He immediately seen what happened and grabbed me, carried me out to the car, and took me to the hospital. They sewed it up, and I was in there for a couple of days. When I got out of the hospital, I had a tour to do, and here I had this big black eye! So I wore sunshades, and my hat down to here," she said with a laugh, brushing a hand over her brow.

"Jim never, ever intentionally hit me. That was an accident, and it was my own fault in the first place. But it caused a lot of gossip. It really did."

Rumors of Rose's infidelity, and persistent stories that Brogdon beat her regularly, circulated throughout the music business, damaging an already unstable marriage even further.

Though her marriage was failing, her career was going well. At the time the *Bluegrass* album was released, November 1962, Rose's twelfth Capitol single, "Sing a Little Song of Heartache," with its coolly beguiling vocal and silken pop arrangement, had broken into the country Top Ten and remained on the charts for eighteen weeks. Peaking at #3, this

Del Reeves composition (he had presented it to her when they met on the "Black Jack Wayne" TV show, where Reeves was a regular performer) was the biggest-selling record of her career. With the successes of both the single and the *Bluegrass* album, and the national exposure Rose was starting to get on the road with Buck Owens, her career was fast reaching a peak. With the proper handling, it appeared, Rose could once again vie with Kitty Wells for the coveted title of "Queen of County Music."

1962 drew to a close, and Capitol kept the Maddox releases rolling along, one single every four months, the first release of 1963 appearing while "Sing a Little Song" was still hanging on the charts. The song, "George Carter," had been penned by none other than Lula Maddox. A mordant, dark tale of star-crossed love and funereal woe, it is an old-school folksong that sounds as if Lula had lifted it directly from an ancient ballad. Rose's decision to record it was an affirmation of the love that now seemed spoiled between mother and child. The last verse, where the song's protagonist demands Carter's coffin be opened so she can "kiss his cold, pale lips" was, considering the circumstances, positively chilling.

Rose's next single, "Down to the River," also focused on death, or more specifically, suicide ("Gonna bury my trouble in the river bottom sand"). June 24, 1963 saw the release of yet another pair of Buck Owens-Rose Maddox duets, and this single also contained a song of death and afterlife, one of country music's weirdest, asking will there be "Sweethearts in Heaven?" On her final single of 1963, "Somebody Told Somebody," a sophisticated cheatin' tune, Rose sounded harsh and worn out. No wonder. Her recording dates were being wedged into an intensive schedule of bookings. Rose was not only working her customary six or seven nights a week but was now appearing across the globe, in halls, auditoriums, and U. S. military installations in the Far East, Australia, New Zealand, and Western Europe. (She seemed to cross the international dateline as often as she did the California-Oregon border.) Bookings in Alaska came frequently, too, a lucrative but demanding arrangement.

Given the persistent rumors about Rose's private life, the boys in the band now felt able to approach her as they would any other woman.

When she refused their amorous advances and their wine, she was offered another gift: Benzedrine. This she took, and gladly. While Rose steadfastly maintains that she never used more than a single tablet and then only for the long, grueling drives she had to make (often alone from gig to gig), the specter of drug abuse soon entered the catalogue of rumor that persistently followed her.

"Now, I found out that these bennies would keep me awake. These guys kept sayin', 'Well, you've got a long way to drive, you better take one of these.' And if I had a particularly long siege ahead of me, I would take one, 'cause I drove to practically all my dates."

Though she never used benzedrine to "get up" for a show, she most certainly made them a part of her routine on the road. Nevertheless, the subject of drug use has remained a touchy one for Rose. "I don't call that 'drugs.' I know benzedrine is a form of it, but to me, at least, a bennie wasn't 'taking drugs.' And ever'body has said to me, 'What do you take?' I says, 'Nothin'.' And they'd say, 'Don't tell me that! You can't go up there, and put on a show like you do, unless you're on somethin'.' I know others that go out there, all pilled up. That's the only way they can go onstage and do a show, but I was never one of 'em. All it is, is you've either got it or you ain't got it." End of subject.

Even as her voice began to show the strain, much to Ken Nelson's annoyance, the last few years of work paid off: *Cashbox* magazine named Rose its Top Female Country Vocalist of 1963. This honor had been clinched with the November release of her fifth Capitol long player, *Alone with You,* and was a welcome accomplishment, symbolically trumping Wells, Cline, and every other contender in the field.

Alone With You employed Rose's versatility to great advantage. On this LP she ranged from the playful, sexy title track to a sophisticated cover of a Patsy Cline number ("Stop the World [And Let Me Off]") to the shuffling "When the Sun Goes Down." For good measure, she also tackled traditional hillbilly ("Long Journey Home," and "Let Those Brown Eyes Smile at Me"); covers of Hank Snow, George Jones, and Bob Wills hits ("Beggar to a King [Queen]," "White Lightnin'," and "My Life Has Been a Pleasure"); and what may be the ultimate country dirge,

"Long Black Limousine." Written and originally recorded by Bobby George (whose novelty answer record "Hillbilly Hell," mentions Fred Maddox as the gatekeeper charging twenty five cents admission to the Underworld!), "Long Black Limousine" featured an eerie rhythm guitar pattern and an overwhelmingly dark, melodramatic mood.

In its April 1964 issue, *Stereo Review,* the magazine of hi-fi sophisticates, even took notice of the album. Though the accompanying photo of Rose is condescendingly captioned ("Rose Maddox—fresh corn delivered clean and straight"), the review was largely positive. "Long Black Limousine" in particular came in for special scrutiny. Though derided at one point as a "track you can play to break up your friends at cocktail parties," Rose's performance did prompt the supercilious reviewer to concede that "as amusingly ingenuous as this song and its kind are, they are much more in touch with the daily life and death of Americans than any of the slick songs about effete romantic emotions that you find on, say, a Vic Damone record.

"As for Miss Maddox, some of the more highly touted jazz and pop singers could learn a few things about singing from her. Would that all of them sang with her strong breath support and clean, direct intonation."

Such highfalutin praise notwithstanding, Rose still had worries. By the time that review appeared, Rose and Jimmy were living apart from one another.

"We were two different kinds of people," Jimmy Brogdon explained. "A person in the music business, who has it in their blood, they're a breed all their own. The more time I spent promoting her and the time I would spend out on the road with her, I would feel like I was losing something myself. My business had to take care of itself. I was devoting all my time to her, and I had to choose one or the other. Consequently, I quit going [on the road] altogether. It wasn't in my blood, and it was in hers.

"It really wasn't her family, it wasn't Donnie, it was just a situation where we were traveling two different roads. Mine went around the city of Oceanside, and hers went around the world. Gradually, we could see that it was just not goin' anywhere, and couldn't go anywhere. It didn't come easy for me and it didn't come easy for her. There wasn't any battle.

Nobody was mad at anybody. I think there was just sorrow on both sides that we couldn't make it work—either couldn't or wouldn't, but just not happy about it.

"Probably, too, I was in love with Rose the star, instead of Rose the person. However, the star is about the same as the person. Rose is very genuine. A lot of people, you meet them and they're one thing on stage and something entirely different off. Rose is Rose, no matter where she's at, and I knew that she would never be satisfied unless she just kept doin' what she had done all her life, and that was gettin' on stage in front of an audience and singin' her songs."

The crumbling marriage, coupled with the grueling road schedule, took its toll on Rose. "Whenever she came around, she looked terrible," said Don. "She was emotionally distraught and all that jazz. She and Jimmy had got to where they didn't get along, and he had beat her up, I don't know how many times. . . . Me and Cal was workin' a club at Talent, Oregon, and once in a while, if Rose didn't have anything else to do, we'd book her in with us.

"I was embarrassed for her to be there, because she was in such poor shape. She looked so drained, so emotionally distraught. I'm not sure if she was on dope, or just really upset. She would jump on ever'body in the band."

Rose began to acquire a reputation for being hard to work with, particularly among drummers and bassmen. It was not unheard of for her to stop in midsong and vociferously, as Jack McFadden described it, "chew out their ass" in front of a hushed audience. She took to harassing players on the bandstand, and more than one threatened to quit in the middle of a booked run after Rose began slapping musicians onstage. Whatever the root cause of this unladylike behavior—Lula's authoritarian example, the rough-and-tumble performance style she learned with her brothers, the frustration and unhappiness in her personal life—Rose was becoming a terror to rhythm sections up and down the West Coast.

All this caught up with Rose, to the point where she was hurting herself. When she would show up at Capitol to record, drawn and moody, her voice just was not there, and her attitude was decidedly unpleasant.

As far as Ken Nelson was concerned, this was just another country singer who had concentrated on having a good time and had forgotten to get enough sleep. Roy Nichols, who played on several of her Capitol sessions, recalled Rose appearing at the studio in desperate shape, offering a half-hearted assertion that she was exhausted from "rehearsing her material all the night before."

Whatever the reason, the fact remained that Rose was unable to sing on more than one occasion. Nelson began canceling sessions and sending her home. Years later, a review of Nelson's own index-card file of Rose's recording dates reveals that there were three separate 1963 sessions that yielded completely unsatisfactory material, at least in Nelson's estimation. Moreover, several cards for recordings were emblazoned with an angry scrawl: Do Not Release.

The first of these abortive studio dates, in September 1963, was almost fruitless, with only two songs recorded. Similarly, on January 7, 1964, Rose cut three songs but only had two released. Her next session, the following July, was even more frustrating. Of the five songs recorded, only two were released, and one of these, "Silver Threads and Golden Needles," was a remake of the flubbed version done the prior September.

Despite the rumors of drug abuse, Rose has steadfastly maintained that her problems in the studio were primarily due to her extraordinarily demanding road schedule. In her view, she was simply too exhausted to record properly. Moreover, her marriage was coming apart, just six years after it had begun, a failure she found devastating to accept. Her brother Don grew increasingly concerned over Rose's dreadful appearance and bad temper when she visited Oregon and guested with him and Cal in local clubs.

"I was takin' her to the airport one day," he said, "and I finally told her if she didn't straighten up and get a-hold of herself, that she was goin' to be out of the business, because in my opinion, people wasn't even goin' to let her in their places, much less hire her. I don't know if that had much effect on her, but after that she started pullin' herself together and got on the right track."

Though she had let herself slip pretty far, she knew Don was right.

One day there came a turn of events that brought a strength and joy she was afraid she had lost, and it came from a source she had almost forsaken—her family. In December 1964, she was overseas, working at a military base in West Germany when she got a telephone call from Ashland, Oregon. It was Donnie.

"Rose," he said, "I want to travel with you."

CHAPTER NINETEEN

Rose was elated by her son's request. During most of this trying period, Donnie, now discharged from the navy, was living with his father in Virginia. He returned to Ashland in 1963, but, because of rocky relations with Mama, Rose saw very little of him.

"On Donnie's twenty-first birthday, he decided that he wanted to be a musician," Rose said. "Since he was up in Oregon due to Jim and my separation, Cal had been teachin' him more on the guitar. I was in Europe when he called and told me that he wanted to travel with me. I said, 'My car is in Las Vegas, and when I finish up here on Saturday night, I have to be in Albuquerque on Monday for an appearance.' It was a tight bit of booking, so I told him, 'I will wire you the money to take a bus to Las Vegas and pick up my car so you can meet me in Albuquerque.' I had a long tour booked through New Mexico and Texas."

Since forcing him into the service, Rose had spent scarcely any time at all with Donnie, and she arrived in Albuquerque with no little apprehension. "He met me at the airport, took me to the club where I did my show, and then we headed out for the next town right after I was through. Donnie was talking to me and said that he wanted to play with me. I said, 'When did you learn to play?'"

It was one of Rose's typically barbed confrontational questions. She of course knew that Cal started teaching him guitar in Ashland several years earlier. Donnie, equally tough, shot back: "I'm gettin' pretty good and I want to be your sideman."

"He played rhythm, he didn't play lead," Rose explained. "So I just said, 'Well, let me think about it.'"

Although noncommittal, Rose was nonetheless pleased. She dreaded another endless, lonely tour, killing time in honky-tonks with empty flirtations, long drives, Benzedrine jitters, and the hardest hours, when she thought of Mama, of Jim Brogdon, and of all the love that spoiled between them. With Donnie, she instead found a challenging circumstance. Their reunion was warm though guarded. Getting reacquainted with her son, reassessing her personal life, and scheming on what course to take with her career's future (while Donnie did all the driving) was a decidedly pleasant change.

"Donnie would drive like crazy on that tour, to get to where we were goin' to play so we could arrive in time to practice, to learn all my stuff," says Rose. "I hate to practice, and I sing ever' night anyway—that was my practice. Mama always hated rehearsing. She never let us do it, and I was just like her in that department. But Donnie would make me sing in the car, and when we'd get to the motel he'd make me stay up instead of gettin' a nap before the show. He'd keep me up singing so he could practice the guitar."

At last they were able to use music, which had kept them apart in the past, as a means to unite. The scenes played out in the motel rooms, with son urging mother to sing "just one more," were often affectionate and tender, though laced with the typical Maddox feistiness. There were frequent colorful and high-volume disagreements between the two as Rose, consummate professional, told Donnie exactly what he was doing wrong.

He kept after her to rehearse night after night, but had yet to actually take his place on the bandstand. "We got to Austin, Texas," said Rose, "went down to the club where I was workin', and the band there did not know a single thing I did. I thought, 'Uh-oh, I am in trouble!' So I asked Donnie, 'Do you want to play with me tonight?' He said 'Sure,' went back and got his guitar, walked in there as though he'd been playin' all his life, just so confident. So he went onstage and played with me that night, and after that he would just walk into clubs and take over like he was my number-one picker."

Like his uncles, Donnie essentially learned to play onstage. Even after hundreds of hours of instruction from Cal, the degree of nerve required to lead Rose through a night's work with a band who did not know her songs was certainly not inconsiderable, especially given her reputation for humiliating players onstage.

But it was in his blood. As the inevitable divorce from Jim drew nearer, Donnie's presence was the best possible boost for Rose. She still desperately wanted the marriage to work but knew it was doomed, beyond any hope of salvage. Once more she was cheated out of happiness by the demands of her career. The only difference here was that neither Mama nor her big brothers were involved. It was entirely her own doing.

"Through the years we were married, I grew to respect Jim very highly, and had really fallen in love with him." Rose spoke in a low, saddened tone. "I loved him when I started, but this was a different type of love that developed over those six years, the respect that you've got to have in a marriage. The divorce hurt me very, very badly. He said, 'There just isn't enough of you to go around, for any of you to be left for me.'

"But, as in all my tragedies, I had my music to fall back on." It may sound melodramatic, but she was deadly serious. "If I didn't have that, I think I would just wither up and die, because I can sing out my problems. That is the release for my tragedies."

The marriage was over. Brogdon was understanding and accommodating, even letting Donnie move into the Oceanside residence after Jim and Rose were living in separate quarters. It was an amicable but strained arrangement. Soon mother and son packed up their belongings and took an apartment in Corona, California, a town forty miles southeast of Los Angeles. It was a straight shot from there to Hollywood, east to Vegas, or down to San Diego, cities where Rose worked a great deal. Rose was still unwelcome in Lula's home, even though she and Cal owned it.

Just as it was too late to save her marriage, it was also too late to make any further headway at Capitol. Noting the Beatles', Beach Boys', and Buck Owens's uncanny ability to send records to the top of the charts, and seeking to streamline operations, the label brought their entire country division under X-ray scrutiny. The company still pushed Rose's records throughout 1963, releasing *Alone with You* followed by a six-track EP, and a single. But there was definitely a change in the wind. In 1964, Rose would release only three singles, even though Capitol had decided to exercise the two-year option clause and renew her contract.

A genuine American success story almost from the moment of its founding in 1942, Capitol Records underwent a change in corporate philosophy after being acquired by the English EMI conglomerate in January 1955. In the wake of the Beatles' massive success in 1964, most country artists no longer rated very high in the eyes of the company's British bosses. Hank Thompson, who had been on Capitol since 1947, recalled the changes:

> I was disappointed by the fact that, after they were taken over by EMI, they concentrated more on the British acts, the Beatles. I noticed that country music was not getting the attention it had; Capitol was not getting the job done, as they had before. We weren't getting the publicity, the distribution, the push. Before, I could call the president, say, "Hey, this is Hank Thompson, we'd like to do this." I could get to the head of A&R, the head of promotion, whatever, and tell them what was needed. We could get things done. After the takeover, they'd all say, "Well, uh . . . there'll be a board meeting in a few weeks, and we'll bring that up before the board." Couldn't get anything done! I finally left Capitol on my own. They wanted to renegotiate, but we lost interest in them, because they had apparently lost interest in us. Because, boy, when EMI bought 'em, they became a subsidiary. The British acts over there was all fair-haired babies and over here, it wasn't happening. . . .

While this was the case at Capitol, the factors leading to Rose's departure from the label had little to do with any British Invasion, according to

Cliffie Stone. "I'll tell you what I think happened. I think she got lost on Capitol. They lost her, okay? Capitol just wasn't excited over it, and when that happens, you're dead. That's happened to me a lot at Capitol, where I take an artist, sign 'em, release a record, and then they just don't work on it. But they have say, six hundred artists. They've got to get out Sinatra, they've got to get out the Beatles. Nobody seemed to care anymore, so they [the country artists] all left."

"Rose was one of the top singers," said Buck Owens. "But you know all that means is great radio play. I can tell you exactly why she had to leave Capitol: you have to sell product."

Rose's last Capitol recording session took place on March 10, 1965. Of the four songs recorded, two were doomed to languish in the vault. Despite the apparent anticlimactic conclusion to her stint with the label, Rose's final Capitol release did manage to provide a ringing, defiant coda. The song was a first-rate, raunchy Bakersfield honky-tonk raver, written by Wynn Stewart, and it could not have been more appropriately titled: "Mad at the World."

"I don't know what happened at Capitol," Rose said in retrospect. "They had just taken their option on me, I'd signed a contract with a two-year option, and they renewed. But they decided they needed some new blood on the label and thought they should just eliminate some of the older, established artists. And I was one of 'em. I told 'em, 'You just renewed my contract!' And they just said, 'Well, we can go ahead and record you, but we'll never release any of it.' There was about five or six of us eliminated, me and Wanda Jackson . . . I know they kept Tennessee Ernie and Tex Ritter. I don't really remember. It's one of the things in my life that I've tried to erase from my mind."

Never one to let circumstance slow her down, she remained true to Maddox form and just kept going. Because of Rose's infamous sensitivity over how her rhythm section played, Donnie mastered electric bass guitar and switched to that instrument exclusively. During a stand in Las Vegas, where Rose had some spectacular onstage battles with drummers and bassists, she realized that getting another steady hired hand would save a lot of wear and tear both on her nerves and her reputation. After making inquiries with the local pickers she was given the telephone number of a guitarist named Harold Riley, who was, at the time, living in Louisiana.

"And that boy played lead guitar for me, until he got drafted," she said. "He was, I think, a year younger than Donnie, just the neatest person you'd ever want to be around. He became just like another son to me, spent three years on the road with us, we toured with Buck Owens and Merle Haggard and ever'one of 'em."

It was a fortunate turn of events. Instead of four big brothers, she now had two sharp young 'uns to look after her, keep the music straight, and split the driving. They spent most of 1966 and 1967 with the Buck Owens roadshow.

Donnie's presence helped soothe the acute sense of defeat Capitol's dismissal instilled in her. Donnie had grown into a big, good-looking kid, fully recovered from the resentment and rebellious attitude he had cultivated in the late fifties. Buck Owens recalled him as "a very nice young fella who played bass and sang for Rose while she worked for me." And they were working, after all, in the best and biggest facilities in the country, the fruits of her chart-making stint with Capitol.

In late 1967, Rose joined Merle Haggard's roadshow, and with Hag singing his almost journalistic accounts of Okie life (at the time rivaling Buck in popularity and outstripping him artistically), Rose opening the shows, and Roy Nichols (now a member of Haggard's band) on lead guitar, it was like a happy meeting of two generations of displaced Southerners, vindicated beyond their wildest campfire dreams. After one show in New York state, the promoter only came up with 50 percent of the Haggard guarantee. Merle, who grew up watching the Maddox Brothers & Rose at Bakersfield's Rainbow Gardens, well knew the family's leatherneck attitude regarding finances, and asked Rose to stay behind and make sure the balance due got coughed up. She did, and it was.

Even without a recording contract, Rose was the happiest she had been since splitting with Brogdon. Working with Donnie and Riley was a breeze. Now she could get some sleep while the boys popped bennies and drove all night long. With some breathing space, Rose decided to tend to her image; she had her hair bleached and tinted platinum blonde. Though over forty years old, Rose could play the country glamour queen better than any wet-behind-the-ears Nashville girl singer.

She remained a country music force and was a good draw all over the country. Throughout the early sixties, Maddox Brothers & Rose albums were issued by half a dozen independent companies; even Columbia compiled a best-of LP, released on their Harmony label, when Rose was at her peak, in 1963. Live, she sounded as good as ever. Don Pierce, still a partner in Nashville's Starday Records, took notice.

Perhaps out of vestigial guilt pangs left from his association with the unscrupulous Bill McCall—but more likely out of sound commercial sense—Pierce signed Rose to record for Starday. He had recently done the same for T. Texas Tyler, and Starday, in fact, was one of the only labels still recording artists like Tyler, Cowboy Copas, and similar old-school hillbilly performers.

"I heard that she had problems with the tranquilizers and all that at Capitol," Pierce recalled, "and that Nelson had gotten kind of pissed off at her and didn't feel that he could—well, that she was just not able to do it. I don't know if the problem was with her marriage or what, but she was fine when she came back here.

"She was okay, and she sang like a bird. I don't think anybody could outsing that girl. I don't think any of 'em could. Rose is just absolutely . . ." (He searched for a description.) ". . . a Kay Starr, and she's got balls!"

Titled *Rosie,* the Starday album included a dramatic four-minute version of the Bob Wills standard "Faded Love" and a rollicking "The Key's in the Mailbox." The sound was contemporary honky-tonk, heavy on the steel. Even though both sides of the single—"Faded Love," and "The Bigger the Pride"—got a respectable amount of airplay, the album sold only moderately. There were no plans for a follow-up, though tracks from the album would subsequently turn up on several Starday compilations.

Still, recording was a welcome break from the road, and the album's release also kept the Maddox name in the press—so much so that in 1967 the newly opened Country Music Hall of Fame gave Rose some small recognition, a square on their Walkway of Stars. She continued to enjoy top bookings as a guest star and worked her typically relentless schedule but found it increasingly difficult to make any real in-roads with the reigning country gate keepers. As the unspoken rivalry between Southern California and Nashville reached critical intensity, new alliances between camps were difficult to establish, and many of long and good standing cooled suddenly.

Country music was giddy with the unparalleled popularity that television brought it in the mid-sixties. After the TV shows of Roger Miller and Jimmy Dean drew more national notice than any previous airwave country music personalities had, it seemed like all the networks jumped aboard. By May and June of 1969, the networks debuted "Hee-Haw," "The Johnny Cash Show" (a surprise hit summer replacement series), and the even more popular "Glen Campbell Goodtime Hour." With its pop-tinged musical slant, slick presentation, and well-groomed country-politan image, the "Goodtime Hour" was the most telling example of how country music perceived itself and its new audience.

This broad national acceptance, something almost entirely new to the field, wrought great changes throughout country music. Both Nashville and Hollywood successfully manufactured hordes of commercial country-pop acts, typified by Campbell and Bobby Goldsboro. Established stars like Rose, clinging to her tradition-based art form, were forced to contend with green performers and their often snide attitudes.

In 1967, Rose was appearing on a package show at San Francisco's Cow Palace. Topping the bill were George Jones and Tammy Wynette, then riding high with "I Don't Wanna Play House." After the show, Jones saw Rose standing in the wings. They had been friends long before he began recording for Pappy Daily, but they had not seen each other since Jones's disastrous Wheel Club booking. He gave her a friendly, pleased greeting and was eager to introduce her to Tammy. Excusing himself at Tammy's approach, Jones scampered over to announce there was someone she had to meet, "the greatest gal singer ever." Wynette cast a cold eye in Rose's direction, wordlessly shook her arm from George's grasp and stalked off to her dressing room.

To Rose Maddox, who blazed the trail that enabled virtually every other girl singer in the business to get a start, this was a rude awakening. Without her, not only Tammy Wynette but also Kitty Wells, Skeeter Davis, Jean Shepard, Patsy Cline, and Loretta Lynn would have been hard pressed to get a foot in the door of the male dominated Southeastern music hierarchy.

The situation was difficult for Rose to accept and was exacerbated by the overall change the business had undergone. Gone were the Jim Dennys and A. V. Bamfords, talent brokers with national connections and influence. By the same token, regional scene bosses like D.C.'s Connie B. Gay, Dallas's Big Ed McLemore, and California's Black Jack Wayne and Bill Woods commanded only a ghost of the clout they had wielded for years. The course of country music was increasingly being determined by corporations, lawyers, and agencies, entities which by and large had never played a large part in the way Rose had done business.

Her career slowed, tapering off to appearances in lounges and honky-tonks; she now played showrooms only as a guest star, not as a headliner. To make matters worse, that year she underwent major surgery following increasingly unbearable bouts of stomach pain. Diagnosed initially as cancer (a fact that the doctors kept from Rose), the problem turned out to be several ulcers that had healed, ruptured, and then healed again, creating a mass of scar tissue. Over the course of two surgeries half of her stomach was removed, and Rose was laid up in a hospital bed for weeks. To compound her woes, guitarist Harold Riley was drafted.

After her recovery, she went straight back to work, but now the range of bookings she got was limited. She and Donnie worked innumerable one-nighters in small clubs, playing to the hard-core devotees who had heard Maddox Brothers & Rose music all their lives. The adoration remained, but the glory was elsewhere.

She was in exactly the same spot that the Maddox Brothers & Retta had found themselves in ten years before, still a popular "name" act, but one that the winds of commerce had swept past. Most of the brothers had given up their dreams of stardom and stepped out of the limelight. Don was immersed in life as a cattle rancher. Although he worked occasional local club dates with Cal, he did so only when the financial need arose or as a favor to his brother. What little desire Don may once have had to perform was long since battered to inconsequence by Mama's demands and domineering attitude.

Cal, too duty bound to Lula to feel cheated out of a career, looked after Mama and contentedly worked clubs throughout the area. He performed regularly, recorded for Fred's Flat Git It label, and spent his free time as any rural bachelor might: hunting, fishing, and helping Don on the ranch.

Henry continued appearing in Southern California clubs, and in the mid-sixties made the most unlikely move of all the brothers, relocating to a small town near Oklahoma City to open a pizza parlor. Along the way, he and Loretta divorced. Henry eventually returned to California, settled in San Diego, and married again. By 1968, the new couple moved to Oregon, and Henry resumed performing with Cal and, often, with Don.

Fred Maddox, naturally, was a different story entirely. He stayed in the business as long and as actively as he could, continually burnishing his reputation as a local legend with fresh conquests and tomfoolery. After the brothers stopped working as a unit, he opened, concurrently, three nightclubs in the Southern California area (Fred Maddox's Playhouse in Ontario, the Mozart Club in Carpinteria, and the Copa Club in Pomona), and held three radio DJ jobs as well.

He continued performing all over the state and worked with some of the wildest acts in rock & roll. One tour featured Fred, the Fendermen (who toured in a converted hearse and are best remembered for their howling 1960 Soma Records version of "New Muleskinner Blues," which owed a good deal to the Maddoxes' 4 Star recording), and faded rockabilly star Gene Vincent.

Fred's style remained a droll, brilliant hillbilly tangent, typified by songs like his own "Who's Gonna Chop My Baby's Kindling (When I'm Gone?)" and Dub Dickerson's "I Must Have Drove My Mules Too Hard," both of which he cut for Flat Git It. His hard, rocking country growl perfectly fit in with the style of Glen Glenn (who still frequently worked with Fred) and Wynn Stewart, the great country singer who sang rockabilly as passionately as anyone. At his nightclubs, Fred would book

Glenn, Stewart, the entire Bakersfield crew (Tommy Collins, Red Simpson, Merle Haggard, and Buck Owens, as long he could afford them), and also top out-of-state talent like Johnny Cash and George Jones (who included "Who's Gonna Chop" on a 1985 live Epic album).

Buck Owens, who regularly played the Mozart, Copa, and Playhouse before his Capitol singles began hitting the charts, recalled an incident typical of Fred's wily style: "I went to work for Fred one time, at the Copa Club, and he had me booked at one of his other places that same night—only he didn't tell me! I had taken Roy Nichols with me, because he wasn't doin' anything else at the time, so I had him playin' for me. This was '57 or '58, I only had one little record out." (Presumably he's referring to "Hot Dog," another California rockabilly specialty, cut as "Corky Jones" for the Pep label.)

"Went into the first place and it was just packed, so we played and then Fred took me out to his Cadillac. He said, 'Come on over here with me.' And he took me over to his other place, got inside, and just jumped onstage and announced me! I don't know if he'd announced before that I would appear, but I do know that he got two shows out of me for the price of one!" (Owens recalled that at the time his price was thirty-five dollars.)

"I remember another story about Fred," Owens said, clearly relishing an opportunity to tell yet another colorful Maddox tale. "This was in '62 and I was playin' a little place called the Five High club in Salinas. Had my little group with me, and about midnight this guy who had the local band there, he really wanted to get up and sing with Buck & the Buckaroos. So I finally let him up, and he was a pretty good singer. Now, he's right in the middle of his first song when the back door flies open—this just a little club, 200 people—and in came Fred Maddox with John McDonald, a guy who helped him out all the time, and he was carryin' Fred's bass.

"Fred climbed right up on the bandstand. He don't say anything, not a word, and just as the song finishes he grabs the mike and says, 'Boy, ain't that great, folks? Give this boy a big hand!' And Fred don't know this guy from Adam. By this time he's got his bass up onstage, and he just turns to the band and says, 'Key of G, boys!' and starts slappin' that bass and sin-gin' 'Truck Drivin' Man.'"

Owens laughed so hard at the memory that he had to pause and catch his breath. "And we all just looked at him in awe. Fred is the kind of guy who can do things like that and never offend anybody. The crowd loved it, but that young man didn't think so much of it. Oh, there's a million stories like that."

As ever, Fred's capacity to cut up and do whatever struck his fancy matched his unbelievable drive. At the height of his career as a nightclub operator he had three full bands working for him at the same time. "It was a big headache, really," Fred later remarked with a sigh. "Then when I finally got used to the headache, I got rid of the clubs."

After the sixties, though, Fred found virtually no opportunity to work. By 1970, apart from annual European tours where hundreds of slack-jawed teddy boys marveled at his slap-bass style, Fred found himself in a state of semi-retirement, even though he was not yet fifty years old. He went from 1971 to 1975 without performing once, happily spend-ing those years at home with Kitty, when he was not raising hell with buddies like Red Simpson. Perhaps California's greatest songwriter, af-ter Haggard and Tommy Collins, Red Simpson composed approximate-ly thirty-five songs recorded by Buck Owens, wrote "You Don't Have Very Far to Go" for Haggard, and scored his own #1 hit in 1971 with "I'm a Truck," a talking novelty which he originally recorded for Gene Breeden's independent Portland label. Capitol promptly leased it and it raced up the charts. Known around Bakersfield as "Suitcase Simpson," because he always toted a valise crammed with songs, Simp-son still performs regularly throughout the San Joaquin Valley and ranks as one of the greatest purveyors of the Bakersfield sound. "I remember one time Fred asked me if I wanted to drive to San Bernardino and back with him to pick somethin' up," Simpson said. "We were gone for four days!"

Another trip, this one to Mexico, climaxed with a lovely young señori-ta dancing on the hood of Fred's Cadillac. The high jinks got out of hand, and Fred and Simpson were literally chased across the border by machete-brandishing Federales. Returning into California, they were recognized by an American border guard.

"Aren't you Fred Maddox?" he asked.

"Oh, Lord," Fred groaned, pushing his hat back. "What have I done now?"

Meanwhile, Rose, fully recovered from her stomach surgery, found good bookings increasingly difficult to come by. Although still based in Corona, she and Donnie were spending more and more time in Ashland with Cal and Mama. Lula's condition steadily worsened and she became more irascible each day.

Rose continued to send Cal half her earnings, as if he were still working with her, but the money all went to support Lula. Even though every Saturday night found Cal and Henry and sometimes Don working the dance in Talent, a nearby small town, the money they made was not enough for Mama's needs. Rose worried more and more about her oldest brother, and the way he was pushing himself to take care of Mama. Early in 1968 Cal, almost sixty years of age, suffered a heart attack.

"He had a heart problem," said Rose. "And when he was in the hospital he had me come up and get an attorney, because the land was in both our names, to fix it up so that if anything happened to one of us, the other would automatically get the place, so we wouldn't have to deal with the probate and inheritance tax, all that stuff. So we fixed it up, and Donnie and I had to go to Washington; we were working throughout there and Oregon. One Friday night we were appearing in Newport, on the coast, and Saturday we came and worked in Talent with Don, Henry, and Cal over at the city hall."

It was the first time in several years they had worked together as the Maddox Brothers & Rose. Despite Fred's absence, Rose recalls that the old family chemistry was still there and that they worked the crowd masterfully. The old combination show-and-dance could still mesmerize a crowd. Reunited onstage, the family was ecstatic.

The next day, Rose and Donnie hit the road early, headed for Corona. Cal woke, made sure Mama was quiet and content, then stepped outside.

Standing in the yard, he may have gazed out across the valley at Ashland, up to the mountain range that ringed the town in, and then up to the vast western sky. It was hot and still, like so many other days the family had known. He probably thought of the previous night's dance and smiled. Then suddenly, Cal fell to the ground. He died right there, on July 3, 1968.

"We got back to Corona on Monday," Rose recalled. "And I got a phone call from Don, saying that Cal had had a heart attack and died in the front yard that morning. I was opening in Las Vegas that week, so Don and Mama made the funeral arrangements while I opened the show in Vegas, and then left the band there to go up for the funeral. I flew back right after and was onstage the next night—I only missed one show.

"It was very hard . . . but that's where my music comes in. It's my way of releasing everything inside me. Without that, I don't know what I would do."

Lula, with no such recourse, was staggered. "Mama just fell apart after Cal died," Rose said. "Somebody had to take care of her, so Donnie and I loaded everything up, took all our stuff out of the apartment in Corona after we finished in Vegas, and moved up to Ashland."

It was up to Rose to support all three of them. She continued working every night she could, now with a strict policy of flying to all her dates, to minimize the amount of time spent away from home and Mama. This development did not do much to boost her earning power, but she maintained steady bookings in various Las Vegas lounges, all over California, Oregon, and Washington, and often north to Alaska.

Even so, when Buck Owens offered her and Donnie a place on his next roadshow outing, they could not resist. With Don and Nila living on the adjoining parcel of land, Mama would be looked after. Rose and Donnie worked with Buck for several weeks in the spring of 1969, then returned home to rest up before his next tour kicked off. In the meantime, Rose continued working dates, as a single, whenever she could.

"I was being booked by Buck's agency, out of Bakersfield, and I had to fly to Tucson, Arizona," she recalled. "And Mama was beggin' me not to go, because Donnie had started playin' around the area with various local groups. I was gettin' ready to go to the airport, and Mama was still beggin' me not to go, to stay there, but I said 'I have to go.'"

Rose stood in the living room, bags packed and ready at the door. Lula came out of the kitchen, pleading with her to remain, still trying to make her daughter follow her wishes. "I was standin' there talkin' to her when she just went down into my arms . . . and she died right there." It was July 2, 1969, a year minus one day since Cal's death. Grief and panic washed over Rose as she struggled with her mother's lifeless body. It was Mama who had gotten the family everything. Without her, who knows what dreary fate might have befallen them. Even after the bad blood that developed after the elopement, Rose never lost her love and respect for Mama. It is as Alta has said, "If Mama was still here today, I'd do exactly what she told me."

Lula made the Maddox Brothers & Rose. It was she who insisted on hiring Nathan Turk to costume them; she who kept tabs on every recording session; she who gave orders to record companies, booking agents, and radio executives without pause. She held and guarded her children's earnings, urged them to assemble the fleet of Cadillacs. She created their stage act and the colorful sense of style that brought them fame. She had chased down Fred every time she knew that he slipped out, and had spanked, censured, and disciplined each of them whenever she thought necessary. If she was an abrasive, and at times abusive, mother, she was also one who loved her children above all else. For all her faults, Lula Maddox was a visionary. Her unstoppable drive enabled the Maddox Brothers & Rose to become a potent and influential musical force.

After pulling herself together, Rose laid her mother's body out and started calling the brothers, and she canceled her show in Tucson. (That night, in a bizarre twist, a woman claiming to be Rose's sister appeared at the Arizona club and went on in her place, which infuriated Rose when she later heard about it.)

As the funeral arrangements took shape, word of Mama Maddox's death spread along the coast. Artists and club operators all swapped tales of Lula's eagle-eyed protection of Rose's chastity, of her crude manner and tough business sense. Perhaps the best example of Lula's drive and character, the single most symbolic tableau of her amazing life, is this one told by Cliffie Stone: "You've heard the famous Cadillac story of Mama Maddox? Well, she walked in and bought seven Cadillacs at once. Went into the showroom, walked through there and said, 'I want one of those and one of those, a white one and a black one and one of them there.' And the salesman just couldn't believe it, and he asks, 'How are you going to pay for these?' She said, 'Cash.' And she pulled out a paper bag and laid out about thirty grand, okay? And they all got into those Cadillacs and drove away." (Although she always bought one Cadillac expressly for herself, she never learned to drive. Other versions of this tale have Lula pulling all the money from inside her bib overalls. Either way, one can easily imagine Lula stalking the dealership showroom like a drill instructor on an inspection tour.)

Not long after Mama was laid to rest, Rose returned to hell-raising and wild living with a vengeance. The catalyst, reportedly, was Lula's safety deposit box. Rose opened it to discover the rat-holed proceeds from years of selling key-fobs, eight-by-ten glossies, and recordings: one hundred thousand dollars in cash.

Rose cleaned out the entire stash, went to Las Vegas, and willfully squandered it all during a supercharged streak of carousing with Jerry Lee Lewis, only recently welcomed back onto the charts with 1968's "Another Place, Another Time." Always a fan of the Killer, Rose has admitted that his reputation as a wild man "turned me on," and also that she "fell hard for Jerry Lee," but she insisted that their relationship in Vegas during this period was limited to visiting Lewis's dressing room after both had finished working, then going out for breakfast the next morning. One can only imagine at what time Lewis took breakfast and can assume that the menu would be as likely to include plenty of pills and whiskey straight from the bottle as it would eggs Benedict and freshly squeezed orange juice.

In Rose's Ashland home, her mantel's centerpiece is a series of framed photographs taken in Lewis's dressing room at the International Hotel, showing the two in a decidedly friendly embrace. Indeed, Lewis's open shirt is falling from his shoulders. Asked specifically about her relationship with Lewis, Rose offered nothing more, save for a Cheshire Cat grin that lingered on her face long after the subject was changed.

By the late sixties, Las Vegas and Reno had become the working playground for many West Coast-based country artists, including Hank Penny, Joe & Rose Lee Maphis, Hank Thompson, and dozens of others, all of whom were experiencing a decline in their commercial viability with the coming of the new order in country music. Most were struggling just to keep working, and many would go crazy with drink after finishing their shows.

More and more, Rose's name surfaced in the bawdy gossip that circulated back and forth between Nevada and Hollywood. One musician, a former member of George Jones's band, recalled a typical tale: "I was workin' with Tom T. Hall in Reno, it was '68 or '69, and that Rose Maddox calls up at the hotel, yellin', 'Where in the hell is that goddamn Tom T. at?' She would not be put off, and she was usin' language that would make a sailor blush!"

Rose bristled when confronted with such claims and said she never even met Hall until he made an appearance in Medford, Oregon, during the late seventies. "People will tell me these stories and swear till they are blue in the face that it's the truth," she said.

Whether the stories are based on actions by individuals (like the woman who passed herself off as Rose's sister following Lula's death) or incidents that occurred and are now erased from Rose's memory is a matter of opinion. All these stories can be dated to periods when she was contending with the blackest of personal tragedies. Though it is difficult to picture Rose at the center of wild parties, raising hell and guzzling booze following the death of her mother and brother, it is just as difficult to accept her hot denial, "I never drank in my life!"

Yet in that strange isolation of life on the road, while enjoying the company of avowed bingers like Johnny Cash and Jerry Lee Lewis and all the bored boys in the band, to have slipped occasionally into their hedonistic ways would have been perfectly natural; to have so chastely and totally avoided them, as Rose said she did, would have been remarkably unnatural. Playboys like Wynn Stewart and Tommy Collins, gifted performers and exceedingly charming fellows, certainly would have tempted most women.

With both Mama and Cal gone, Rose lost much of the drive that had already taken her so far. More and more often she found herself at home between bookings, where she walked the floor and stared out the window. Yet though she was no longer sure how to get there, she still craved the spotlight badly, more than anything else in life.

CHAPTER TWENTY

Throughout the 1970s, Rose's days and nights were much the same: driving, arriving, waiting through dusk, then taking the stage to unleash the frustrations and energy that lay dormant within. The value of her songs as an emotional release became increasingly important to Rose, the only definition in an otherwise repetitive blur. Work was steady, pay was decent, the bands not so good. Her friends and fans always came out, and many a routine night became one of brilliance, as Rose sang away the dreary circumstances; but great performances alone could not pull her back up the ladder at this stage in her career.

Playing the folk-festival circuit, Rose eventually became more a revered pioneer than a singing star. Although not particularly lucrative, these dates guaranteed large, enthusiastic audiences. Alaska remained one of Rose's mainstay bookings, and she often flew there to work for weeks at a stretch. While there in 1970, a friend showed her a pup he had just gotten, a young Norwegian elk hound. Rose, engrossed in playing puppy games, did not pay much attention as her pal explained that he knew of a litter on the way, and that he would be happy to send one down just as soon as the pup was weaned. Rose went to the club and forgot the incident entirely.

Several months later, she got a message from Alaska: "Your dog will arrive in Medford tomorrow." An exasperating piece of news: Rose was due to leave for an appearance in Washington state. She arranged to have Donnie drive out and get the animal.

By the time she returned several days later, Donnie had fallen in love with the pup—another Norwegian elk hound, a dead ringer for the one Rose saw in Alaska. Reluctant to take on the responsibility of caring for such a huge animal, she balked at first. Shortly thereafter, Rose, too, fell for the pup and wrested him from Donnie in another high-volume Maddox brawl.

She named the hound Rattler. He was a constant companion from then on, everywhere she went. If a motel would not allow him, she kept him out in the Cadillac, around the premises of the club, anywhere but at home. She loved Rattler and was happy for his company.

Donnie was no longer accompanying her on the road, being more involved with his new bride. In a 1987 letter, Rose described her son's marriage: "He married on December 7, 1969, to Barbara Jones from Sacramento. He made her Barbara Hale, not Maddox. I absolutely hated it! I was in Reno for the wedding but not of my choosing, because of Donnie. I flew in from a date in Colorado. We, her and I, never got along, and still don't. We tolerate each other because of the kids."

During this period, Rose went back to her natural hair color, worn in a very plain pageboy cut, and eschewed any make up or flashy stagewear. A promotional photo from the early seventies still touts her as the "Most Colorful Entertainer in America," but the tired, almost haunted looking eyes and careworn expression seem more like the countenance of the Dust Bowl emigré she had been back in the 1930s.

Rose spent countless lost afternoons, waiting with Rattler for the sun to go down and the club to fill up, waiting for the moment when her name was called and the applause washed over her. Only then was Rose really at home, finally content and joyful. She had no other home, no other life. Donnie worked with her as often as he could. He also presented her with three grandchildren: Donnie, Rose, and Kelli. Rose made them a part of her life as much as she could, though she had by no means ceased to pursue her career. The road was her sole means of support and much more.

Unable to land any major-label record deals, she continued to record for independent companies, but never on a long-term basis. She would not tie herself down, as promise of a big break always hovered just beyond the range of her mind's eye. She kept working, pushing, hoping to get her name back up in the strata where it belonged, right alongside all her old friends, the "living legends" of country, artists like Ernest Tubb, Johnny Cash, Merle Haggard, all of whom she had known for years.

Even for the best of them, times were difficult. Rose went to see Lefty Frizzell perform at a Medford baseball diamond, just weeks before his death in July 1975. His last few records had been excellent, among his best work ever, yet Frizzell was reduced to working small-time fairs and package shows, often with backing bands unfit to share the stage with him. Despite the fact that Frizzell introduced a vocal style that still dominates contemporary country music, he died virtually forgotten by the general public.

Rose's career would never regain the degree of activity and success she had known for so long; the persistent rumors about her taste for amphetamines, her capacity for alcohol, and her quick temper worked against her. Considering, too, that half her stomach had been surgically removed, many people during this period viewed Rose as a risky booking.

She had given the bookers little reason to look beyond the rumors. Her stubborn, prideful demeanor, which carried her to the top, was now more of an impediment than a benefit. Rose maintained her pride and faith in the fans. Slowly, she became accustomed to the less demanding, less prestigious turn her career took. She never complained; perhaps she grumbled some, but she was too wise to let bitterness replace the joy her songs provided. She spent longer stretches of time at home, watching her grandchildren play, enjoying Donnie's company and trying to stay on good terms with her daughter-in-law, Barbara. Rose seemed to have inherited her mother's pervasive distrust of in-laws, and relations were often rocky between Rose and Barbara.

Rose suffered another blow in June of 1974, when her brother Henry passed away from kidney failure and a weak heart. What remained of the family gathered for the funeral, and once again they sang away their grief. In an eerie coincidence, as Fred was driving to the funeral, his car radio began playing Merle Haggard's latest release, the Maddox-styled tune "Old Man from the Mountain."

"When I heard Merle call Friendly Henry's name in the song," Fred later said, "I nearly drove into a ditch."

With only Fred and Don left, Rose felt that it was up to her to get the family the recognition rightfully due them and, more importantly, to fight for her place in the acknowledged hierarchy of country artists. By this time, Don had completely retired from performing, and Fred had gone four years without appearing onstage.

In an interesting turn of events, Rose recorded several sides for Portland Records, an Oregon-based company headed by none other than Gene Breeden, the hired hand who replaced Roy Nichols in 1950. Having left the music business for more than a decade, Breeden was back in operation. Unfortunately, the collaboration of Rose and Gene was only partially successful. One of the singles, "I'll Fly Away," found Rose in excellent voice, and Breeden's guitar and arrangement were wonderful approximations of the Okie gospel they performed together some twenty-four years earlier.

"I really enjoyed doin' them, because she had been my legal guardian when I was with them," Breeden said. "It was kind of like the old group, even though I was the producer, had selected and recorded the songs. But when things got goin' for her again, all of a sudden she was sayin': 'Here's what we're goin' to do, Gene.' So I really wasn't interested after that began."

There is a lot of Lula in Rose, and the resemblance became more pronounced in the years following Mama's death. In a working musical situation, Rose's word is incontrovertible law: you do just as she says, or you do nothing. Never before was she forced to contend with inadequate players, but it now became a common problem for her.

As Rose struggled to keep her career moving forward under strict Maddox control, a different type of support was coming into play. In

1976, Rose appeared on the Western Regional Folklife Festival, where she was approached by Chris Strachwitz, a German immigrant who grew up hearing the Maddox Brothers & Rose over KTRB and who never forgot the force and liveliness of their music. Owner and operator of Arhoolie Records, Strachwitz specialized in both recording and reissuing material by classic hillbilly and blues artists.

"I was interested in reissuing old Maddox Brothers & Rose," he explained. "So I made a contract with her to reissue her family's earliest records. I had all the discs. The few that weren't originally issued [such as "Blue Eyes Cryin' in the Rain" with Jimmy Winkle singing] I got out of the stash at KTRB. I was lucky enough to get in there before they threw all that stuff away. We sort of 'liberated' all those. But it is totally hazy as to which of these discs were made for release, and it's so hard to know what's what. They are on acetate, and you couldn't tell if they were on 4 Star or if they had just cut them there. There was very little indication; it was usually scribbled on with crayon, 'Theme Song' or, if a song had bad words in it, 'Do Not Play,' and even the title was scribbled with crayon on the acetates. The station apparently played them on good equipment, so they are all in pretty good shape. Of course most of the first [Arhoolie compilation] LP was commercial 4 Star 78s, and I had pretty much mint copies that I had collected over the years."

He released two albums that year, with photos from Rose's collection and excellent liner notes. It was the first time many of these songs were available in twenty years and also the first time that the band was accorded their place in country music history. Arhoolie had a loyal following, a thriving mail-order business, and the respect of folklorists and fans throughout the nation. The albums slowly built up interest and support for Rose, not only for her talent but also for her considerable contributions and influences on the music as a whole.

Soon *The Maddox Bros. & Rose, 1946–51, Volumes One and Two* were among Arhoolie's top selling LPs. Rose was elated; she found Strachwitz to be a completely reliable business associate, and the two became close friends. Now she had tangible evidence of her legacy and carried the albums in her Cadillac to every show, just as Lula had once peddled the family's 4 Star 78s. This revived interest worked to her advantage, too, as the folk festivals brought her into contact with musicians who had long idolized her. They were able to see past the numerous horror stories they heard about her, and instead viewed her as the significant artist she is, rather than as a crotchety throwback. Rose played her new part happily, trying to stay as gracious as possible in vexing situations.

In 1977, she began work on a new LP for West Coast independent Takoma Records. The sleeve showed her looking healthy and happy, and back to her glamorous Las Vegas platinum blond coiffure. She was joined on the record by some fine California musicians: fiddler Byron Berline and steel player Wayne "Swamp Root" Gailey, both of whom often worked with Rose. Gailey, one of her closest friends, was soon to pass away, which was another emotional blow for her. The LP did not set the charts ablaze, but with the Arhoolie set available, each complemented the other. Titled *Reckless Love and Bold Adventure,* it featured three songs by sister Alta, including the title track, a new song "Dancing Shoes," and her anthem "I'm Happy Every Day I Live," which Rose originally recorded for Capitol in 1959.

While Rose was working on the album in a Venice, California recording studio, she proved herself to be as feisty as ever. An old fan, who had followed the Maddoxes' career from the 1940s on, dropped by the studio to visit and began offering some extremely pointed suggestions as to how a certain song should be arranged. Rose responded by first hollering, then running him out of the studio, chasing him down sunny streets, bellowing and shaking her fist after his swiftly disappearing form. Nobody tells Rose how to sing.

After seven years of struggling and battling obscurity, Rose became more confident and was able to secure better, steady bookings than she had only a few years before. With his three children now in school, Donnie was able to work more regularly with Rose, a situation that pleased her. They worked fairs, clubs, festivals, lounges in Reno, anywhere they could.

In the late seventies, two trends in American music and popular culture combined to affect Rose's career, charging it up considerably, and in very unexpected ways. One of these was the shock of punk rock, which redefined rock & roll in many ways and indirectly sparked a renewed interest in roots-music styles like rockabilly. The other trend centered around the 1980 release of the film *Urban Cowboy* and the huge boost in national popularity that it imparted to country music.

Unlikely as it seems, the large homosexual community on the West Coast embraced the *Urban Cowboy* movement, began redesigning their clubs along western lines and booking country performers to appear. Foremost among these was Rose Maddox, whose rollicking, ballsy brand of song thrilled this new constituency. She was soon appearing regularly in several San Francisco gay bars and worked the newly established gay rodeo in Reno every year. The first several bookings invariably found Rose and Donnie sitting at the bar, warily eyeing the clientele and wondering, often aloud, why there were no women in any of these joints. On at least one occasion, when a good looking "woman" did appear, Donnie was quick to clue Rose in as to the actual nature of the glamorous creature.

These bookings raised many an eyebrow among old acquaintances, especially those back in Nashville, who could scarcely deal with headlines in Reno newspapers trumpeting Rose Maddox as Queen of the Gay Rodeo. But to Rose, "people is just people, and they always treated us great and paid us well. I don't care what they do, or what anyone does, as long as they're civil and friendly."

The *Urban Cowboy* craze, which held America's attention rapt for a few short years, soon fizzled, and bookings at gay bars tapered off completely. At the other end of the cultural spectrum, punk rock, which had flared into life in 1977, had now splintered off into a series of musical movements, one of which was a neo-rockabilly cult.

These young kids were exploring the roots of rock & roll with an intensity that elevated obscure recording artists like Glen Glenn to a position almost equaling that of undisputed stars like Gene Vincent and Carl Perkins. In short order, the young rockabilly fans discovered the Arhoolie LPs, with tracks like "George's Playhouse Boogie," "Mean and Wicked Boogie," "Shimmy Shakin' Daddy," and others, and Rose's name soon became one of the most talked about in these circles. In Europe, where rockabilly music has always maintained a fanatical following, Maddox Brothers & Rose records were well known and much sought after. A West German label, Bear Family, began reissuing classic Maddox Columbia sides. Along with the Arhoolie LPs and two by Bear Family, tracks by the Maddox Brothers & Rose started turning up on numerous rockabilly compilation albums released both by European and American companies (even Columbia released a series of these records), and the sounds of the Maddoxes became familiar in nightclubs from London to Los Angeles.

This rockabilly revival opened up a whole new audience to Rose, and she was soon being booked into trend-conscious Hollywood nightclubs that catered to the punk rock and neo-rockabilly movements. In the wake of Rose's appearances, several bands formed that featured girl singers who covered Rose's songs. (Blood on the Saddle recorded "Single Girl" replete with buzz saw guitars and thrashing drums, and the Screamin' Sirens waxed a version of "Ugly & Slouchy.") Even after singing to drunken transvestites, Rose was hardly prepared for the garishly costumed, adoring crowds who attended these shows, but she took it all in stride, coping with the often inadequate bands who backed her with as much patience as she could muster.

In 1981, Rose was approached by a San Francisco Bay Area folklorist, Gail Waldron, who wanted to put together a video documentary on the Maddox Brothers & Rose. Strachwitz introduced her to Rose, and though she felt reticent at first to open up to Waldron, the two became well acquainted. Rose allowed Waldron to go through her collections of photos and closets full of Turk uniforms, and helped arrange interviews for her with Don, Fred, and Kitty. Completed in 1984, the documentary is an enjoyable, standard history of their career, albeit a facile and too brief effort.

Yet even with her career now on a definite upswing, Rose's family life was spiraling downward. Donnie and Barbara, after thirteen years of marriage, were at increasingly bitter odds with one another. They separated, and Barbara took all three children to live with her in Sacramento. Even as this confirmed her suspicions and distaste for the "in-law," Rose hated to see Donnie suffering from loss of contact with his children, and she too missed them. Now nearing forty years of age, Donnie remained the one constant source of joy in Rose's life. He had worked innumerable shows with her and had been her friend, driver, confidante, bass player and, above all else, her son. She loved him fiercely.

During the late seventies, Donnie suffered a heart attack and required open-heart surgery; shortly afterward, Rose was stricken by the same condition. The Maddox frailty of the heart seems a peculiar weakness for a family of such natural intensity. It is almost as if Charlie and Lula did not have enough life force between them to spread around. Both Cliff and Henry had health problems at an early age, and Fred underwent open-heart surgery and several by-pass operations. Rose herself suffered from throat trouble, had stomach surgery, and had the same spinal cyst as Henry. "Apparently, it runs in the family, or seems to," Rose said of their many health problems. "Donnie had five by-passes and Fred needed three, but we also inherited that strong will from Mama, that dominant, strong will."

That she would need: in late December 1981, Rose had a heart attack while at home. In her hospital bed at Ashland on New Year's Eve, with one of the most severe local blizzards in decades raging outside, she lay there thinking bitterly of the bookings she canceled. Disgusted, she wished more than anything to be at the club, preparing to sing, when a second heart attack gripped her, much worse than the first. She summoned a nurse, who realized that Rose's heart was failing.

"I was so close to death. I was dying and I knew it, but they brought me back . . . and what they used to bring me back was terrible; some kind of drug that just didn't go well with my system." As she recounted this, Rose was tense, almost angry. "And as soon as they got me stabilized, they realized they did not have the facilities to support me, and so I had to be transferred to a hospital in Medford."

Grim and furious, she hung on to life, refusing to let herself go. She still had plenty of work to do. The twelve-mile drive seemed to take hours over the snow-bound road. Once at the hospital, a specialist tried to probe her system by inserting a tube through a vein in her chest; in the process he punctured and collapsed her left lung. This was turning into one hell of a New Year's Eve.

"It was so scary, and I kept tellin' him not to do it, that it wouldn't work on me. But he said, 'Oh, it's the only way to go, the latest development.' They got me on a lung machine, fixed it up right away."

She recovered well but had to return to Medford in February, "to have them do a heart catheter, see if I needed open-heart surgery. Donnie was trying to make me feel confident by telling me it wouldn't hurt at all." Rose paused to laugh. "And when they wheeled me back out afterwards, he was there, and I yelled, 'You lied to me, Donnie!' It was awful, and the doctors said there had been a lot of damage to my heart, but they didn't feel I was a candidate for heart surgery, that they could heal it with medication . . . and I take that medication ever' day that comes."

It was an appropriate start to what turned out to be the most painful year of Rose's already troubled life. She busied herself helping Gail Waldron on the documentary and worked the gay bars, new wave clubs, and folkie joints a good deal, usually with Donnie by her side, more often with the Vern Williams Band, a bluegrass group based in Northeastern California's Motherlode, where Charlie and Lula had panned for gold forty years earlier. Originally from Arkansas, Williams was a fine mandolinist and harmony singer. He assembled a band who worked well together, managing to avoid the self-indulgent banjo banging that typifies so many latter-day bluegrass outfits. The Vern Williams Band became the closest Rose had come to finding a steady backup group since the early sixties, and she recorded an LP with them for Arhoolie, *This Is Rose Maddox*. It featured remakes of "Single Girl" and "Sally Let Your Bangs Hang Down," and it showed that her voice and delivery had only gotten better with time.

In July, Rose was at home, killing time before leaving to work a rodeo in Reno. Donnie telephoned from Sacramento, where he was trying to make a reconciliation with Barbara, "for the kids' sake." Donnie was upset not only by that situation but also because he was troubled with intense shooting pains, "going from his eyes to the back of his skull," as Rose recalled.

Worried, Rose urged him to see a doctor immediately. But Donnie, reluctant to leave the kids, said he would wait and see. That night, he took Barbara and the children to a drive-in movie. Rose went into Ashland with Gail Waldron to see zydeco performer Queen Ida. At the dance, she ran into her doctor and described Donnie's symptoms. Knowing Donnie's medical history, the doctor urged immediate medical attention. Disturbed even more, Rose went home to try telephoning Donnie and Barbara.

Meanwhile, at the drive-in, Donnie's headaches had become more intense. He and his family left the drive-in and went home. Rose telephoned the house and told Barbara what the doctor had said. Yet somehow, it was not until early morning that an ambulance was summoned. The couple wanted to believe everything would be all right, but when Donnie cried out in agony and his eyes rolled up into his head Barbara knew any further delay was impossible. She called Rose after they took him to a hospital and told her Donnie had suffered a stroke.

Rose clenched the receiver tight in her hand and asked, "Are we talkin' death here, Barbara?" Both her daughter-in-law and the doctors assured her this was not the case, but Rose knew in her heart it was his end. She got into the Cadillac and drove straight to Sacramento. She found Donnie in his hospital bed, looking pale and in great pain. He spoke his last words to her: "You're goin' to have to get someone else to play bass for you in Reno, Rose. . . ." (Donnie had never called her anything except Rose: "Even when he'd introduce me to his friends as his mom," she said, "it'd sound so funny, 'cause he never called me that.")

"It's already been taken care of," she replied and made what she knew would be her final good-bye.

One of Vern Williams's band members recalled getting a hastily scrawled note from Rose, sent that afternoon, which said, "I have just come from a hospital in Sacramento where Donnie is dying. I have to go to Reno and work."

She had to stop and do her wash before continuing, and there she penned this grim note, alone in a Laundromat, closing with, "Pray for me." She drove to Reno and was there when Donnie died the next day,

August 1, 1982. "It was the worst thing that ever happened to me," she said.

Four years later, Rose stood in her living room as she told the story, tears streaming from her eyes. In front of her stone fireplace, she stood three paces from the spot where Lula died, a stone's throw from where Cal had lain in death. It was a winter morning and the house was silent. She stood alone, shaking off the very real sense of lost family, and continued with her own life.

She was almost unable to handle the logistics but finally arranged a funeral. A friend rented an air-conditioned van and drove Donnie's remains back to Oregon. Rose wanted music at the service but was unsure, fretful, and confused. She telephoned Vern Williams and told him what had happened, asked if he and the boys would come play at the funeral. They rushed to Ashland and played during the service as Rose tenderly and mournfully sang "Gathering Flowers for the Master's Bouquet."

Vern's band accompanied her home. After an uncomfortable, silent interval, someone grabbed a guitar and they spent all afternoon in the backyard, singing spirituals beneath Rose's favorite weeping willow tree, the same one under which she would lay Rattler to rest, when he died one year later.

Appearing in San Francisco two months after Donnie's death, she approached Strachwitz and asked if he would produce an album of gospel songs, with the Vern Williams band backing her. He agreed instantly, booked studio time, and three days later they all went in to record. The resulting album was dedicated to her son's memory. Donnie's death was a terrible counterpoint to the burst of activity her career was enjoying. Not only had she made the alliance with Vern Williams and released an LP of their work together, she was also at work on an album with none other than Merle Haggard.

It so happened that a couple of staunch Rose Maddox fans out of Bangor, California, were ready, willing, and able to fund, organize, and arrange for release of a record. Rose took the idea to Haggard, and he readily agreed. Hag had always remained in close touch with Rose and

Fred, both of whom entertained at his 1978 marriage to Leona Williams. The resulting album, *Queen of the West*, featured Rose at the peak of her abilities. With Haggard's band, the Strangers (at that time one of the best bands in their field) backing her, Rose delivered an album of spectacular California country music.

Haggard and Roy Nichols supplied hot, twin guitar work; Tiny Moore and Gordon Terry provided glorious, sweeping fiddles; and both Leona Williams and Emmylou Harris chipped in harmony vocals. Merle narrated an introduction to one track and wrote two of the songs chosen: "Shelley's Winter Love," which Rose had recorded on the *Reckless Love* LP, and a new one that Leona suggested they cut, "Downtown Modesto." On Fred Rose's "Foggy River," Rose sang so sweetly, with such forlorn tenderness, that the cut surely qualifies as one of the very best sides she ever made in nearly forty years of recording. Haggard worked for free on this project, the Strangers for union scale. It was done in several sessions and released in 1983 on the Varrick label. The album was dedicated to Donnie.

Within several weeks of *Queen of the West*'s hitting record stores, Arhoolie released two more Maddox LPs, *A Beautiful Bouquet* and *On the Air, Volume One*, a collection of transcribed KGDM and KFBK radio shows from 1940 and 1945. The Maddox Brothers & Rose had established themselves as the second best-seller in the esoteric Arhoolie catalogue. (A klezmer band held down the number-one spot.)

So, with three new releases available, Rose's career was going better than it had for over ten years. Fred began joining her on dates in the San Joaquin Valley and also appeared in San Francisco for Waldron's documentary. During this period, usually together (but often separately), Rose and Fred were guests on the shows of Willie Nelson, Waylon Jennings, Merle Haggard, and Loretta Lynn. They inevitably drove audiences into a frenzy with their lightning-quick, razor-sharp cornball gags and singular interpretations of traditional hillbilly music. The bandstand reunion of Rose and Fred, both still outrageous as ever, was soon the talk of many country artists.

Haggard often booked Fred into his now-defunct Silverthorn resort, a nightclub where the Strangers, when not touring, acted as house band, and many a night saw both Fred and Merle onstage, playing to small crowds of local fans and vacationers from Lake Shasta. On one occasion, when both Rose and Fred were there, Merle requested Fred's "I Must've Drove My Mules Too Hard." Fred, eager to sing, thrust the bass into Rose's hands but Hag quickly intervened, forced the battered instrument on Fred, saying, "I've got to hear that bass. Ain't nobody plays like you, Fred."

These Silverthorn shows were among the best latter-day Maddox appearances. The combination of Fred, Rose, and old hired hand Roy Nichols came as close to recreating the glory days of the Maddox Brothers & Rose as any fan could hope for. They perfectly duplicated their "Whoa, Sailor" routine, and only Nichols could manage to propel forgotten Maddox standards like "Shimmy Shakin' Daddy."

In 1983, it seemed as if the tide was turning. Columbia released a Maddox Brothers & Rose album as part of its Historic Edition series, beautifully remastered in mono. (Unfortunately, Rose, Don, and Fred received not so much as a promo copy of the album, let alone any royalty payment.) That year Rose was a guest on Garrison Keillor's nationally broadcast "Prairie Home Companion" on National Public Radio, with fiddler Johnny Gimble and Chet Atkins backing her. (It was her second appearance on the show; Rose and Donnie had previously appeared in 1981.)

Meanwhile, on any given night, Rose could still be found in a suburban honky-tonk, singing to happy but small audiences. This was hard work and, to a degree, frustrating for Rose. "I don't mind working the nightclubs, I do it all the time," she said. "But dealing with drunks—now, I'm not saying that all people who go to nightclubs are drunks. They're not. I draw an awful lot of people who don't even go to nightclubs in the first place. Because I'm one of the older ones in the business, I get older people who don't frequent nightclubs, like younger ones do.

"But mixed up among them are the people who go there to drink, period. They enjoy your show, but along toward the end of the evening they're drunk, and they can't talk to you without putting their hands all over you . . . I'd rather work more stage shows, auditoriums, or festivals."

There was always a distinct difference in watching Rose Maddox perform at anonymous neighborhood joints rather than at Bakersfield or Porterville honky-tonks. There, surrounded by friends and colleagues who grew up with them, Rose and Fred (who lived just up Highway 99 in Delano and invariably joined her onstage) radiated a joy and strength peculiar to their San Joaquin Valley appearances. It was a spontaneous fun-house atmosphere that grabbed listeners and pulled them in. If it did not, and Fred detected aimless conversation from the bandstand, he would snarl: "I hear a lot of chitchat out there, and you're a-gonna have-ta cut some of that CHIT out!"

In the Valley, long-term fans approached them, warmly reminiscing about long lost nights at the Pumpkin Center, Riverbank Clubhouse, George's Playhouse, or the Rainbow Gardens. Rose and Fred responded with a delighted sense of connection to these memories and their fans. The San Joaquin Valley has not forgotten the Maddoxes. When the daily *Bakersfield Californian* ran a poll to determine who played the area's best country show of 1986, George Strait's appearance at the county fair took first place, while Rose and Fred's at Julie's Saloon held down the number-two spot. Considering that Strait was one of the top-drawing acts in the nation, the near tie was impressive.

In 1987, Delano radio station KCHJ had just started broadcasting a live Saturday morning barn dance program, featuring Fred as a regular performer. After a few weeks, they invited Rose to appear as a guest on the show. It was a sight to behold.

KCHJ was housed in an old Quonset hut, lost amongst the cotton fields west of Delano. By 9:30 A.M., the parking lot was jammed with cars and trucks. There were twenty-five or so fans, young and old, stamping on the frozen gravel. Despite a 48-degree temperature on this gray morning, they stood around happily, drinking cold beer and waiting for the Maddoxes. The two Cadillacs pulled in and were immediately swamped by the enthusiastic crowd. It was the same scene, on a less grand scale, that Rose and Fred were accustomed to on their arrival at dance halls in their heyday, forty years before. The fans' enthusiasm, it seemed, had only intensified.

Among the gray-haired couples were several younger pickers, ready to accompany Fred and Rose, all of whom were raised on Maddox music. One talked enthusiastically to Fred about his favorite, "Kiss Me Quick (And Go Away)." He knew all the lyrics, and the two sang a verse, breath steamy in the frosty Delano air. The Barn Dance kicked off at 10 A.M., with Fred, Rose, several guitarists, and a toothless old fiddler who once played with the Arkansas Travellers. (Despite a crushed left arm, he still drew a fine bow.) They stood in a semicircle before a 1950s vintage mike on a huge boom. All of KCHJ's equipment was pre-1970s, much of it still run by tubes. Turntables were rusted with age, and the walls were lined with an incredible array of old, autographed photographs and records. In their Hank Williams section, all the records were original-issue MGM sides. KCHJ, reputedly haunted, had an almost eerie atmosphere, like a window to the past.

Rose and Fred sang with a spirit and bite that filled the studio. At one point, Fred, eager to concentrate on his vocals, thrust the doghouse bass into Rose's hands. Not missing a beat, she played it flawlessly, eyes flashing. Fred sang, Rose played, and the crowded studio became a party, an event, as it must have back in 1937, or '47, or '57.

What was most amazing about this performance was that just one week earlier Fred had been hospitalized, in very serious condition. His weak heart had become so sluggish that one ankle had swollen to the same circumference as the thigh it supported. Rose had spoken to him on Friday night and was worried at how low he sounded. Yet the following morning, Fred stood on his front porch, waiting for Rose with eyes glinting wicked as ever, looking for all the world in perfect health. Yet the condition was not one to be ignored. On doctor's orders he was forced to pull out of a European tour that Glen Glenn had already booked. Kitty was beside herself with worry; Fred simply relied on his humor to get through it all. Rose, asked if the prospect of doing the broadcast had brought him around, quietly replied, "Yes, I'm sure it has."

As Fred recovered from his circulatory problems, Rose replaced him on Glen Glenn's European tour. She played every night for two weeks to sell-out crowds of fanatic teenagers, usually at halls with a capacity of two thousand. In each country the tour reached, she was met at airports and train stations by hordes of fans, all toting stacks of albums, singles, reissues, and original 4 Star 78s, all clamoring for autographs. Rose made a big splash in the press, with headlines that invariably tagged her as a "Rockabilly Grandmother." She relearned all her old ravers ("Wild, Wild Young Men," "My Little Baby," "Hangover Blues," and a dozen more) generally singing an all-rockabilly set, except during one bluegrass date that she did to promote the reissue in Britain of her *Rose Maddox Sings Bluegrass* LP. Within a few weeks of her return from Europe, she traveled to Sacramento and met up with Fred and Kitty to attend a Fiftieth Anniversary tribute to them, hosted by the California Western Swing Society.

They had come a long way from being fruit tramps from the class of '37, and 1987 found them still full of hard-nosed Maddox drive. Arriving at the club in a white stretch limo, Rose, Fred, and Kitty were greeted first by the blazing lights of a television news crew, then by old friends they had not seen for decades. Gene LeMasters was there, Truitt Cunningham, Al Brown Jr., even Bud Duncan. Both Rose and Fred were elated; the atmosphere was amplified, exciting. There were folks from KTRB, KFBK, dozens of musicians who had sat in with the Maddoxes over the years. People came from as far as Redding, Reno, and Los Angeles.

Everyone in the joint was swapping stories about the Maddox Brothers & Rose, many of these tales dating back to the 1940s. Before they took the stage to perform, Rose and Fred were presented with congratulatory plaques and letters from the President of the United States, the governor of California, the California State Legislature, the state of Nevada, and the city of Sacramento, and they were inducted in the California Western Swing Society Hall of Fame.

The Maddoxes kicked off the show with a perfect "I Want to Live and Love" and Fred went into his standard introduction: "Yes sir and howdy folks, how're y'all today? Give us a gre't big smile, wontcha? Thanks a million, folks. Now let's smile and dance with . . ." he paused, as if wishing he could call his brothers' names, ". . . Fred Maddox and my sister Rose!"

Midway through their set, Rose invited Bud Duncan to come up and "sing one." After their short-lived fling in the late forties, the moment was almost a confrontation. Bud and the Maddoxes sparred verbally for a moment, then Rose looked him in the eye and asked what song were they doing.

"Let's do that one: 'We met downtown in a barroom,'" Duncan suggested.

"We certainly did! In downtown Modesto!" Rose shouted, adding, "But I don't know which one you mean," as if she did not recognize the opening line from a recent Merle Haggard hit, "We Had a Beautiful Time."

Bud kicked it off anyway, and she fell right in, singing harmony and injecting some tart comments between his lines. "I had a beautiful time, holdin' your body close to mine," Duncan sang as if he meant every word of it, and one could almost imagine the words were a confession from Bud to Rose. What had been a tense moment became a warm reunion: a beautiful, emotionally charged scene that settled the old score between them. The audience, well aware of the circumstances, roared its collective approval.

Two weeks later, Rose and Fred were working a stand at Bakersfield's Executive Lounge. It was a Saturday morning, as Fred wound down his barn dance broadcast and Rose sat alone in her motel room. Several miles away, Roy Nichols climbed onto his motorcycle, kicked it into life, and set out to find her. Merle Haggard had promised Roy a "job for life" with the Strangers back in 1966, but Nichols, recently retired from the band, was killing time at home in Bakersfield and knew that Rose would be at one of several motels in town. He decided to stop at each one until he found her. Nichols's first stop was the Rodeway Inn, the place where Red Simpson regularly appeared and that was usually first choice among visiting country artists, Rose included. He knocked at her door.

"Roy came out to the motel and he was so sincere." Rose recalled. "He said, 'I'm not comin' out to the club tonight [because of his distaste for some of the musicians playing there] but I wanted to come out and personally give you my respects, and I want you to pass this along to Fred.

"'I want to tell you how much it meant to me, for you guys to hire me when I was so young.'

"'You was sixteen!'

"'I know, and the way you treated me, just like I was one of the family, with no jealousy there, no nothin', and the way you taught me, I just had to thank you personally, because I never have before. I want to tell you how much I respect you, and the whole family. Now, Mama never got on me but a couple of times, and I deserved it when she did!'"

Rose cleared her throat, and continued recounting Nichols's speech. "He says, 'I've been with Merle for twenty-one years, and I'm the senior in the group now. These young guys come in, and they look at me like they'd rather I wasn't there. I didn't have to learn to cope with jealousy in your group. . . . There was none of that and you treated me just like family. I can't take that, the jealousy and back-stabbin' of other musicians, because it wasn't in your group, and you guys are the ones who taught me. I had to tell you that I will never forget it, and for that, I respect you guys the fullest.'

"That's what he said, and then he got on his motorcycle, offered me a ride, but I said, 'No thanks!' and so he left."

Roy Nichols, the most talented and influential guitarist to come out of the West Coast country clan, found himself an anomaly in the field he had pioneered and developed, just as Rose and Fred had before him. When he rode off into the Bakersfield afternoon, Rose smiled.

CHAPTER TWENTY-ONE

Following the year of fiftieth-anniversary tributes that 1987 brought, Rose kept on working as often as possible, but her calendar still had far too many off days. She played San Joaquin Valley honky-tonks and Los Angeles nightclubs mostly, making an occasional guest appearance with Loretta Lynn, Merle Haggard, and newer artists like the Desert Rose Band and Marty Stuart. In 1988 Rose recorded an album's worth of material, backed by the Desert Rose Band (without leader Chris Hillman). Featuring some new material, remakes of her Capitol hits, and several duets with guitarist John Jorgenson, it was a fine piece of work. To Rose's great disappointment, though, no label—from Desert Rose's own MCA Records and Curb Records to small independents like Rhino, Rounder, and High-Tone—would touch it. (In 1996, the independent Country Town label finally issued the album under the title *The Moon Is Rising*.)

On a more positive note, Rose returned that year to Europe with Glen Glenn and even started receiving small artist royalty checks from Capitol for a series of reissues of her solo albums on the British Stetson label. In sad contrast, no such royalties have been forthcoming from Columbia Records for the domestic Historic Edition LP. Likewise, despite Bear Family Records in Germany having released a lavish CD box set of Rose's Capitol material as well as earlier Maddox Brothers & Rose compilation LPs, Rose has yet to see so much as a pfennig in royalties from the label. According to Bear Family president Richard Weize, Bear Family's licensing agreement includes a specific artist royalty payment, yet somehow, through the intricacies of foreign licensing administration, Rose's royalties from over a decade of steady Bear Family sales have yet to reach her own pocket.

In early June 1989, Rose, accompanied by her teenage granddaughter Rosie, was driving to work a job in Bakersfield when she suffered the first of a new series of heart attacks. Although Rose blacked out momentarily, she shook it off, rallied herself, and somehow continued driving. By the time they reached the city, she was in great pain and checked into Bakersfield Community Hospital. Her heart condition rapidly worsened and Rose sank into a coma.

For the next three months, Rose remained unconscious, lying deathly still, wasting away. When peritonitis set in, her rib cage was wrenched apart to enable staff to clean the waste from her chest cavity, and it was kept open for weeks. Her chances for recovery seemed nonexistent. No one expected Rose, now sixty-four, to live, but family, friends, and fans refused to abandon hope. Fred and wife Kitty visited Rose at the intensive care unit regularly. Daughter-in-law Barbara took an apartment in town and brought grandchildren Donnie, Rosie, and Kelli to live there with her. Gradually, word of Rose's plight spread among country musicians on the coast and elsewhere.

On one day alone, approximately thirty separate benefits were held all over the country to defray Rose's hospital costs. In Nashville, Johnny Russell helped organize several benefits, one of which was staged at Opryland. Rose's condition did not improve. In desperation, Fred and Kitty brought in a portable cassette deck and played the old 4 Star recordings over and over, hoping to break through Rose's coma. Finally, at the close of a song, Rose lifted her fist and waved it in the familiar circular motion she had always used to signal a number's finish. It was the first outward sign of life in her for twelve weeks. Shortly afterward, Fred sat at her side pleading with her to "wake up so's we can go back to work." Incredibly, she did just that. When she came around, Rose thought she had just slept a single night, not the last three months.

Released from the hospital in September 1989, she moved in with Barbara and the kids, finally reconciling the differences that had troubled relations with her daughter-in-law for so long. Barbara singlemindedly devoted herself to Rose's recovery, and by January of 1990 Rose was singing again, first from a wheelchair, at a tribute held in a San Juan Capistrano club, and then at a special benefit show held at North Hollywood's Palomino club. She looked ravaged, immobile, and frail but took the stage, stood on her feet, and sang away the pain of her ordeal. It was an electric, deeply emotional moment. Virtually everyone in the packed room was in tears.

Rose's recovery was slow but steady, and grandson Donnie played a crucial role, staying by her side as much as he could and offering the support and encouragement that enabled her to progress. By November of that year she had put together her own group, fronted by Donnie and dubbed, in typical Maddox style, the Foggy Notion Band. They began working up and down the West Coast, and the onstage chemistry between Donnie and Rose drew out the best from each of them. The only thing that kept her alive was an almost mystical belief that her career had not run its course. Rose, never one to give up midway through the job, poured everything she had into each performance.

Ironically, a brush with mortality always seems to drive up a country music veteran's stock. In mid-1990 Rose was invited to appear on The Nashville Network's "Nashville Now" with Emmylou Harris and Desert Rose Band's John Jorgenson, and also participated in the taping of a Harris television special that apparently will never air. A second "Nashville Now" appearance, this one featuring Donnie, soon followed.

Still operating out of Ashland, Rose began dropping by Merle Haggard's Tally Studio near Redding, California, whenever she was on her way out or coming back in from a personal appearance. Soon she was singing back-up on various Haggard demos and gratefully took him up on his offer for free studio time to cut demos. She recorded fourteen songs there with the Foggy Notion Band. Haggard was so enthusiastic over the quality of Rose's voice and the interplay between her and the musicians that he brought Fred up from Delano to participate. All three recorded a new Haggard song, "Dusty Memories," a typically grim, image-laden Haggard look at the Dust Bowl. Rose sang lead, Merle added ghostly harmony, and Fred reeled off a gloomy recitation. At Haggard's urging, Fred also remade "Ugly & Slouchy" and just about improved on his original 1957 Columbia version. Although her recent surgery made it necessary for her to sing everything one key lower, Rose lost none of the fire, drive, and spirit she has always had.

Rose had always hated being at home between jobs, and there were never enough of them to keep her happy. Finances had become extremely tight, and Rose raised extra cash any way she could. In 1990, she was forced to sell her entire collection of Nathan Turk uniforms—all her outfits and all of Henry and Cal's; dozens of suits, enough to fill two walk-in closets—to young country performer Marty Stuart for $5,000. Considering that a single men's-dress-shirt from Nathan Turk cost only $45 in 1946, Rose had certainly seen an increase on her investment. Sadly, though, she might have seen even more money if she had held on just a little longer. A year later, a private collector, unaware of Stuart's purchase, contacted Rose and offered roughly the same amount for one uniform.

The five grand did not last long, and Rose was compelled to dissolve her band. But she continued working in Oregon and Reno with country singer Marty Davis, who has been instrumental in keeping Rose's schedule as full as he can. In 1992, they toured Austria, where a proposed recording project fell through. To this day, Rose is constantly courted by well-intentioned but financially strapped individuals proposing albums, tours, and movies. So far, there has been more frustration than substance to any of these offers.

In the meantime, country music underwent its biggest boom since the *Urban Cowboy* craze of the early eighties. As the "hat acts" redefined and broadened the country music audience, it seemed as if there would be little room left for the originating performers. Then Branson, Missouri, long a stop off for middle-class family vacationers to get a little country music along with their recreation, exploded in the press as the new Promised Land for older country artists. Rose made two trips to Missouri, but by the time she finished her second visit she realized that no performer in Branson makes much money except those who actually own their own theaters. So she returned West and kept plugging away.

Both Rose and Fred were prominently featured in a 1991 PBS television documentary called "Bakersfield Country!," that also included Buck Owens, Merle Haggard, Red Simpson, Roy Nichols, and Henry Sharpe. The show resulted in a higher profile for Rose and Fred, and also a Los Angeles local-market Emmy nomination for best performance. Fred, Kitty, and Henry Sharpe traveled to Los Angeles for the ceremony. (Comedian Tim Conway won the award.) Later that night Fred suffered a minor heart attack and was briefly hospitalized in Pasadena.

On October 29, 1992, the heart trouble that had plagued Fred for decades finally took his life. Rose was distraught, all the more so because she had committed to three shows in Idaho with Marty Davis and could not afford to travel to Delano for the funeral. Even if she canceled the dates, grandson Donnie was working in Branson, and without him to handle the driving she was stuck. It was a Friday, with the funeral scheduled for Monday. Half an hour before she had to leave, her phone rang. It was Merle Haggard.

"Rose," he said, "what do you need?"

"I need a plane ticket."

"You got it."

She was able to make two of the Idaho shows and flew out from Boise with just enough time to spare. At the Delano mortuary, a somber crowd spilled over into the lobby. Fred lay in an open casket, with an American flag draped over it. His bass fiddle, covered with flowers, stood beside him. Merle Haggard, Stu Carnall, Roy Nichols, and Henry Sharpe were among the pallbearers. The mortuary's public address system played the Maddox Brothers & Rose's sacred songs. Fred could be heard singing "When I Lay My Burden Down."

At the cemetery, Rose joined with Fred's neighbors Richard and Linda Thompson to sing "Will the Circle Be Unbroken," as the late afternoon Delano air swirled with tiny motes of airborne cotton, each wisp a reminder of why Fred chose the music business as a means of survival. There was more wistful laughter than tears among the mourners, as befitted this gathering of an extended family that had been formed decades earlier, each sustained by memories of Fred's singular wit. Throughout the formal mortuary and graveside services, and later at the Delano V.F.W. Hall, Rose appeared composed, dignified, and resolute. Despite her terrible personal loss, she thought only of Kitty's well-being.

Rose is, as Henry Sharpe recently said, "a walking miracle," who continues to live her life as she always has, biding her time until the sun sets and the nightclub fills, when she can once more take the stage and sing away the struggle, pain and sacrifice that have been such a dominant part of her recent years.

The single girl, long parted from her four big brothers, continues moving forward. Her music is the only constant in an ever shifting, often discouraging, but soul-sustaining pursuit of expression. She lives solely to articulate and satisfy her own personal, artistic needs and to maintain the neglected line of cultural expression that first produced her and was then reshaped by her. It is a rare, emotional process that sustains her, one that occurs only upon the bandstand. It is there, onstage, that Rose Maddox is at ease, surrounded by the audience, the best friends she has known, relying on the strongest guiding force in her life: the songs she has always sung.

Although they made innumerable television appearances, the only known film-footage of the Maddox Brothers & Rose is a color eight-millimeter home movie of a performance in Malibu around 1955. Despite its brevity and lack of a soundtrack, it is an absolutely electrifying piece of film. Clad in a scarlet Turk uniform, hair short and dark, Rose is beautiful, compelling. She becomes even more so when Fred, singing lead, suddenly thrusts the bass fiddle at Rose; she takes it from him, slapping it like a veteran, a smile on her lips.

An all-too-brief blaze of color and motion against the blue Malibu sky, it is an image of a performer with a natural, guileless affinity for her art. That celluloid instant expresses everything, conjuring all the pioneering, vibrant power that made Rose Maddox one of country music's key forces, a woman whose independence and passion had such impact that it still rings out, loud and clear, on recordings and radio today.

She has never demanded, taken, or expected to be given anything. Rose simply does what she must, and has always done that better than just about anyone else. Coming as much from the gut as from the heart, Rose delivers her songs as simply and forcefully as she can. There is such common, soulful wisdom within her, despite the lean and frustrating circumstances she has endured, that her music's vivid, untamed purity transcends her historic role. Rose Maddox gave everything she had to the public, a gift that will live on. Hear her and cherish that gift. There will never be another like it.

NOTES

Preface: All material drawn from author visits to Rose Maddox home and interviews with Rose Maddox, October 5, 1983, February 18–23, 1985, February 2, 1987, April 26, 1987, and December 8, 1995.

Chapter 1: Interview with Alta Troxel, June 25, 1985; interviews with Rose Maddox, October 10, 1983, February 19, 1985; interview with Fred Maddox, February 3, 1986; interview with Don Maddox, February 5, 1986; for information on cotton price jump, see W. J. Cash, *The Mind of the South*, 360, 366; photo of Lula in Rose Maddox personal collection.

Chapter 2: Material in this chapter drawn from previously cited interviews with Rose, Don, and Fred Maddox and Alta Troxel; also interview with Rose Maddox, April 26, 1987; interview with Gordie Maddox, April 3, 1985; earthquake information courtesy of California Polytechnic Institute Seismological Laboratory; "Family Roams U.S. for Work," *Oakland Tribune,* April 11, 1933, p. 1.

Chapter 3: Previously cited interviews with Rose, Gordie, and Fred Maddox and Alta Troxel; also interview with Fred Maddox, March 22, 1987; Depression-era quotes from *Down and Out in the Great Depression: Letters from the "Forgotten Man,"* ed. Robert S. McElvaine (Chapel Hill: University of North Carolina Press, 1983), 34, 68, 72; Gene Fowler and Bill Crawford, *Border Radio* (Austin: Texas Monthly Press, 1987).

Chapter 4: 1937 population figure courtesy Modesto Chamber of Commerce; previously cited interviews with Rose Maddox as well as interviews on October 10, 1982, and December 8, 1995; interview with Wesley Tuttle, July 9, 1989; previously cited interviews with Don Maddox, Alta Troxel, Fred Maddox; Roy Rogers and Dale Evans, *Happy Trails.* (New York: Bantam Books, 1980), 39–42; Rich Nevins, *Pioneers of Country Music* (Yazoo Records card set, 1985); *Definitive Country,* ed. Barry McCloud (New York: Perigee, 1995); Bakersfield 1937 Frontier Days program, author's collection.

Chapter 5: Previously cited interviews with Rose, Fred, and Don Maddox; interview with Roy Nichols, January 8, 1986; interview with Chester Smith, Nevada City, California, 1987; interview with "Jolly" Joe Nixon, March 11, 1990.

Chapter 6: Previously cited interviews with Rose and Don Maddox and Wesley Tuttle; also Rose Maddox interview, February 2, 1987; Jonny Whiteside, "Hillbilly Hollywood," *L.A. Style* 5, no. 5 (October 1989): 132–37; interview with Tiny Moore, February 24, 1985.

Chapter 7: Previously cited interviews with Rose and Fred Maddox; interview with Gene Albright, April 5, 1987; for information about and quotes from Bud Duncan, see Bud Duncan, "Profiles in Music: Bud Duncan," *California Western Swing Society Music News* 2, no. 12 (December 1987) (Bud Duncan declined numerous requests to be interviewed for this book); interview with Jimmy Winkle, February 26, 1987; Hugh Cherry described to author the audience's amazement at the price of Wills's footwear; interview with Bobbie "Mrs. Nudie" Cohen, September 1, 1994; for Bill McCall information, see Margaret Jones, *Patsy: The Life and Times of Patsy Cline* (New York: HarperCollins, 1994), 52–60, 70, 75; interview with Don Pierce, December 7, 1986; for Cecil Gant information, see Arnold Shaw, *Honkers & Shouters: The Golden Age of Rhythm and Blues* (New York: Collier, 1978), 89–92.

Chapter 8: Previously cited interviews with Rose and Fred Maddox, Don Pierce, and Jimmy Winkle; interview with Wesley Tuttle, July 9, 1989; interview with Cliffie Stone, April 8, 1985; interview with Jackie Lee Waukeen Cochran, January 10, 1991; Jonny Whiteside, "Untold Stories: Wesley Tuttle," *Journal of Country Music* 13, no. 2 (1990): 4–5; interview with Hank Thompson, April 6, 1985; interview with Cliffie Stone, April 8, 1985; interview with Jack McFadden, December 31, 1986; interview with Ray Campi, December 31, 1982.

Chapter 9: Previously cited interviews with Jack McFadden, Jimmy Winkle, Gordie Maddox, Don Maddox, and Rose Maddox; interview with Fred Maddox, April 15, 1987.

Chapter 10: Previously cited interviews with Don Pierce, Cliffie Stone, Wesley Tuttle, Tiny Moore, Rose Maddox; interview with Jack McFadden, January 22, 1987; interview with "Jolly Joe" Nixon, May 4, 1990; interview with Buck Owens, January 24, 1986; Marty Landau obituary, Academy of Country Music newsletter (Los Angeles, February, 1973); interview with Wesley Tuttle, September 28, 1989.

Chapter 11: For information on Webb Pierce quitting Opry, see Albert Cunniff, "Jim Denny: Muscle Behind the Music," Part 2, *Journal of Country Music* 11, no. 2 (1986): 56; previously cited interviews with Rose, Fred, Don, and Gordie Maddox, Cliffie Stone; interview with Roy Nichols, January 8, 1986; interview with Jim Brogdon, January 23, 1986; *Billboard*, February 12, 1949; interview with Bill Monroe, August 30, 1985; Steve Hall, "Kings of the Roadshow," *Bakersfield Californian*, September 24, 1986, Section D, p. 1; Paul Groah, letter to author.

Chapter 12: Previously cited interviews with Rose, Fred, and Don Maddox and Roy Nichols, Cliffie Stone; interview with Gene Breeden, January 2, 1987; interview with Webb Pierce, January 6, 1987.

Chapter 13: Live recording of Compton dance from Glen Mueller collection; previously cited interviews with Rose and Fred Maddox, Gene Breeden; interview with Webb Pierce, January 6, 1987; Charles K. Wolfe, LP notes to *Lefty Frizzell: His Life, His Music* (Bremen, Germany: Bear Family, 1984), 20–21.

Chapter 14: Previously cited interviews with Alta Troxel, Gene Breeden, and Rose, Don, and Fred Maddox; interview with Tommy Collins, January 5, 1987; interview with Glen Glenn, April 9, 1986.

Chapter 15: "Cracker Barrel" column, *Country Music Reporter,* October 6, 1956; Albert Cunniff, "Jim Denny: Muscle Behind the Music," Part 2, *Journal of Country Music* 11, no. 2 (1986): 54–55, 58; previously cited interviews with Rose Maddox.

Chapter 16: Previously cited interviews with Rose Maddox, Jim Brogdon; interview with Ken Nelson, May 9, 1987.

Chapter 17: Previously cited interviews with Rose Maddox, Jimmy Brogdon, Cliffie Stone; *The Music Reporter,* April 13, 1959; interview with Henry Sharpe, January 12, 1987; background information on Hap Peebles, who died on January 8, 1993, in Kansas City, Missouri, from *Definitive Country,* ed. Barry McCloud (New York: Perigee, 1995), 628; the late Bill Boyd, who traveled with Cash in the late 1950s, described many of these stunts to the author in a January 1988 interview; see also Christopher Wren, *Winners Got Scars Too: The Life of Johnny Cash* (New York: Dial, 1971), 128, 131, 143.

Chapter 18: Previously cited interviews with Rose, Don, and Fred Maddox, Bill Monroe, Ken Nelson, Hank Thompson; Capitol release information courtesy of Loretta DiBasio, Capitol A&R Library; Ken Nelson's index-card file for most of the Capitol sessions he supervised between 1951 and 1968 is housed at the Country Music Foundation Library & Media Center in Nashville, Tennessee.

Chapter 19: Previously cited interviews with Rose Maddox, Hank Thompson, Buck Owens, Cliffie Stone, Don Pierce; interview with Red Simpson, January 12, 1987; interview with Murrell Counts, February 24, 1985.

Chapter 20: Rose Maddox letter to author dated March 8, 1987; previously cited interviews with Rose Maddox; interview with Chris Strachwitz; interview with J. D. Rhynes, August 15, 1987.

Chapter 21: All material drawn from contemporary conversations with Rose, Fred, and Kitty Maddox or experienced firsthand by author.

BIBLIOGRAPHY

Cantwell, Robert. *Bluegrass Breakdown: The Making of the Old Southern Sound.* Urbana: University of Illinois Press, 1984.

Cash, Johnny. *Man in Black.* Grand Rapids, Mich.: Zondervan, 1975.

Cash, W. J. *The Mind of the South.* New York: Simon & Schuster, 1940.

Clark, Alan. "The Glenn Glenn Story." *Legends of Rock and Roll.* Los Angeles: 1983.

Cooper, Daniel. *Lefty Frizzell: The Honky Tonk Life of Country Music's Greatest Singer.* Boston: Little, Brown, 1995.

Cunniff, Albert. "The Muscle Behind the Music: The Life and Times of Jim Denny," Part 2. *Journal of Country Music* 11, no. 2 (1986): 26–59.

Duncan, Bud. "Profiles in Music: Bud Duncan." *California Western Swing Society Music News* newsletter 2, no. 12 (December 1987): 1, 3, 5.

Fowler, Gene, and Bill Crawford. *Border Radio.* Austin: Texas Monthly Press, 1987.

Gentry, Linnell. *A History and Encyclopedia of Country, Western and Gospel Music.* Nashville: McQuiddy, 1961.

Guralnick, Peter. *Lost Highway: Journeys and Arrivals of American Musicians.* New York: Vintage, 1982.

Haggard, Merle, and Peggy Russell. *Sing Me Back Home.* New York: Simon & Schuster, 1981.

Hall, Steve. "Kings of the Roadshow," *Bakersfield Californian,* September 24, 1986, D, p.1.

Hemphill, Paul. *The Nashville Sound: Bright Lights and Country Music.* New York: Simon & Schuster, 1970.

Jones, Margaret. *Patsy: The Life and Times of Patsy Cline.* New York: HarperCollins, 1994.

McElvaine, Robert S., ed. *Down and Out in the Great Depression: Letters from the Forgotten Man.* Chapel Hill: University of North Carolina Press, 1983.

Malone, Bill C. *Country Music U.S.A.,* revised edition. Austin: University of Texas Press, 1985.

Malone, Bill C., and Judith McCulloh, eds. *Stars of Country Music.* Urbana: University of Illinois Press, 1975.

McCloud, Barry, ed. *Definitive Country.* New York: Perigee, 1995.

Morthland, John. *Best of Country Music.* New York: Doubleday/Dolphin, 1984.

Nathan, Hans. *Blackface Minstrelsy in the Nineteenth Century*. Urbana: University of Illinois Press, 1950.

Oleson, Keith. LP notes to T*he Maddox Bros. & Rose: 1946–51*, Volumes 1 & 2. El Cerrito, Calif.: Arhoolie Records, 1980.

Rogers, Roy, and Dale Evans. *Happy Trails*. New York: Bantam Books, 1980.

Shaw, Arnold. *Honkers and Shouters: The Golden Age of Rhythm & Blues*. New York: Collier, 1978.

———. *The Rockin' 50s*. New York: Hawthorn, 1974.

Steinbeck, John. *The Grapes of Wrath*. New York: Viking, 1939.

Strachwitz, Chris. LP notes to *The Maddox Bros & Rose: On The Air*, Volumes 1 & 2 . El Cerrito, California: Arhoolie Records, 1983 and 1985.

Stricklin, Al, with Jon McConal. *My Years with Bob Wills*. San Antonio, Tex.: Naylor, 1976.

Tosches, Nick. *Country: The Biggest Music in America*. New York: Stein & Day, 1977.

———. *Hellfire: The Jerry Lee Lewis Story*. New York: Delacorte, 1982.

Townsend, Charles R. *San Antonio Rose: The Life and Music of Bob Wills*. Urbana: University of Illinois Press, 1976.

Whiteside, Jonny. "The Manifest Destiny of the Maddox Brothers & Rose." *Journal of Country Music* 11, no. 2 (1986): 6–15.

———. "Untold Stories: Wesley Tuttle," *Journal of Country Music* 13, no. 2 (1990): 4–5.

Williams, Roger. *Sing a Sad Song: The Life of Hank Williams*. New York: Doubleday, 1970.

———. LP notes to *Hank Williams: Country & Western Classics*. Alexandria, Va.: Time-Life Music, 1981.

Wolfe, Charles K. LP notes to *Lefty Frizzell: His Life, His Music*. Bremen, Germany: Bear Family, 1984.

Wren, Christopher. *Winners Got Scars Too: The Life of Johnny Cash*. New York: Dial, 1971.

Author Interviews

Gene Albright, April 5, 1987, Sacramento.

Gene Breeden, January 2, 1987, Nashville.

Jim Brogdon, January 23, 1986, Oceanside, California.

Tommy Collins, January 5, 1987, Ashland City, Tennessee; also letter to author.

Paul Groah, letter to author, March 5, 1987.

Ben Maddox, April 3, 1985, Anaheim, California.

Don Maddox, February 5, 1986, Ashland, Oregon.

Fred Maddox, October 5, 1985, Redding, California; February 3, 1986, March 22 and April 15, 1987, Delano, California.

Gordie Maddox, April 3, 1985, Anaheim, California.

Rose Maddox, October 5, 1983, San Francisco; February 18–23, 1985, Ashland, Oregon; February 2, 1987, Hollywood; April 26, 1987, Bakersfield, California; December 8, 1995, Ashland, Oregon.

Jack McFadden, December 31, 1986; January 22, 1987, Nashville.

Bill Monroe, August 30, 1985, San Francisco.

Patsy Montana, February 23, 1985, San Francisco.

Tiny Moore, February 24, 1985, Redwood City, California.

Ken Nelson, May 9, 1987, Somis, California.

Roy Nichols, February 24, 1985, Redwood City, California; January 8, 1986, Bakersfield, California.

"Jolly" Joe Nixon, March 11, 1990

Buck Owens, January 24, 1986, Oildale, California.

Don Pierce, December 7, 1986, Hendersonville, Tennessee.

Webb Pierce, January 6, 1987, Nashville.

Henry Sharpe, January 12, 1987, Bakersfield, California.

Red Simpson, January 12, 1987, Bakersfield, California.
Chester Smith, 1987, Nevada City, California.
Cliffie Stone, April 8, 1985, Hollywood.
Hank Thompson, April 6, 1985, Torrance, California.
Alta Troxel, June 21, September 19, 1985, Ceres, California.
Wesley Tuttle, July 9, September 28, 1989, San Fernando, California.
Jimmy Winkle, February 26, 1987, Twin Falls, Idaho.

DISCOGRAPHY

This discography encompasses the commercially released recordings of the Maddox Brothers & Rose on 4 Star and Columbia, as well as Rose's solo Columbia releases, and her complete Capitol, Takoma, Starday, Varrick, and Arhoolie recordings; it also includes a listing of reissued 4 Star material that appeared on Decca and King.

Because of the different types and sources of information available, depending on the record company, this is basically a compendium of the most significant commercial releases, presented in as consistent and logical a format as possible. In many cases, information is limited to release numbers and title. This discography is sequenced more or less chronologically by record company. Reissue information is included to give a better sense of the availability of Maddox recordings during their career. Personnel listings have been reconstructed through interviews, study of the recordings themselves, and Musician Union Local 47 records.

I wish to extend sincere gratitude to Chris Strachwitz of Arhoolie Records for supplying much information and to the Country Music Foundation and Patrick Milligan for personnel listings on Rose's Capitol sessions.

Maddox Brothers & Rose on 4 Star Records, 1946–1950

This list is by no means complete, compiled as it is primarily from Strachwitz's personal collection; release dates for the 4 Star records are approximate, drawn from the issue date of *Billboard* reviews. Thus, this serves more as an overview of their body of work on 4 Star, rather than a complete list of songs, dates, personnel, etc.

Recordings made in Hollywood, California, at various studios (Electro-Vox, Radio Recorders etc.). Personnel: Rose Maddox, lead vocal. Fred Maddox, bass, vocal. Cal Maddox, rhythm guitar, harmonica, vocal. Henry Maddox, mandolin, guitar, vocal. Don Maddox, fiddle, vocal. Jimmy Winkle, lead guitar, vocal on "Blue Eyes Crying in the Rain." (1946–48) Bud Duncan, steel guitar (1946–49). Gene LeMasters, lead guitar (1948). Roy Nichols, lead guitar (1949–50). Gene Breeden, lead guitar (1950–53).

Master	Song Title	Release Number	Approximate Release Date
1587	Midnight Train	1184*	September 1947
1588	Careless Driver	1184*	September 1947
1589	I Couldn't Believe It Was True	1185*	September 1947
1590	Milk Cow Blues	1185*	
1624	Mean and Wicked Boogie	1210*	December 1947
1625	Sweet Little You	1210	
1626	Whoa, Sailor	1209*	May 1948
1627	Last Night I Heard You	1322*	July 1949
1628	Navajo Maiden	1209	
1683	Honky Tonkin'	1238*	
1684	Mama Says It's Naughty	1657*	April 1954
1687	Tramp on the Street	1239	July 1948
1688	Flowers for the Masters Bouquet	1239*	July 1948
1691	Time nor Tide	1271*	October 1948
1692	Old Pal of Yesterday	1657	April 1954
1695	I'll Never Do It Again	1664	August 1954
1697	I've Stopped My Dreamin' About You	1664*	August 1954
1698	On the Banks of the Old Ponchartrain	1328	
1702	Move It on Over	1209, 1240*	
1703	New Muleskinner Blues	1288, 1240*	January 1949
1732	Brown Eyes	1238, 1288*	
1734	Rosalie by the Rio	1633	
1883	Dear Lord Take My Hand	1326*	December 1949
1885	He Will Set Your Fields on Fire	1473	
1886	Who at My Door Is Standing?	1301	June 1949
1890	Meanest Man in Town	1633*	
1893	Gosh, I Miss You All the Time	1271	
1909	Oklahoma Sweetheart Sally Ann	1527*	November 1950

(* denotes a song's availability today on an Arhoolie compact disc.)

Master	Song Title	Release Number	Approximate Release Date
19101	I Want to Live and Love	1586*	November 1951
1913	Sally Let Your Bangs Hang Down	1398*	December 1949
1914	Baby You Should Live So Long	1671	
1916	I Wish I Was a Single Girl Again	1586*	November 1951
1918	It's Only Human Nature	1527*	November 1950
2003	When God Dips His Pen of Love in My Heart	1301	June 1949
2004	Garden in the Sky	1326	December 1949
2005	Philadelphia Lawyer	1289*	
2006	Sunset Trail Waltz	1289	
2056	We Are Climbing Jacob's Ladder	1473	
2059	At the First Fall of Snow	1328	
2062	Eight Thirty Blues	1596*	January 1952
2063	Honky Tonkin' [remake?]	1322	July 1949
3315	Why Don't You Haul Off and Love Me?	1369	October 1949
3316	George's Playhouse Boogie	1369*	October 1949
3318	Chill in My Heart	1507	August 1950
3324	Detour #2	1604*	April 1952
3418	I'm Sending Daffydills	1399*	November 1949
3419	Jingle Bells	1400	October 1950
3420	Silent Night	1400	October 1950
3421	Mule Train	1399*	November 1949
3425	I Just Steal Away and Pray	1626	
3428	You've Been Talkin' in Your Sleep	1398*	December 1949
3457	I'll Fly Away	1639	
3510	I'll Still Write Your Name in the Sand	1604*	April 1952
3515	The Land Where We'll Never Grow Old	1639	
3516	I Love the Women	1440*	March 1950
3517	Water Baby Blues (Boogie)	1507*	August 1950
3519	Shimmy Shakin' Daddy	1570*	August 1951
3522	Red Ball to Natchez [?]		
3526	Just One Little Kiss	1440*	March 1950
3534	I'd Rather Have Jesus	1626*	
3539	Your Love Light Never Shone	1596*	
3541	No One Is Sweeter than You	1570*	August 1951
3542	You Will Have to Pay [?]		
3543	My Sweet Love Ain't Around?		
3544	I'm Gonna Change or He's Gonna Leave [?]		
3545	Rocking Chair Money [?]		
3546	You'll Never Have My Love Anymore?		
3547	(Pay Me) Alimony (Blues)	1549*	March 1951
3605	A Rose from the Brides Bouquet [?]		
3606	Choc'late Ice Cream Cone	1458	April 1950
3890	Dark As a Dungeon	1540*	
3891	South	1577*	September 1951

(* denotes a song's availability today on an Arhoolie compact disc.)

Master	Song Title	Release Number	Approximate Release Date
3892	(New) Step It Up and Go	1549*	March 1951
3895	How Can You Refuse Him Now?	1553	May 1951
3897	If We Never Meet Again	1553	May 1951
3899	Rock All Our Babies to Sleep	1577	September 1951
3903	Faded Love	1540*	
3906	Cowboy Bugle Boy	1618	October 1952
3908	Texas Guitar Stomp	1618	October 1952

(* denotes a song's availability today on an Arhoolie compact disc.)

Maddox Brothers & Rose on Decca

4 Star masters, licensed from the label and issued as singles during the mid-fifties after the family had signed with Columbia

Master	Song title	Release Number
83549	Jingle Bells	DE 28478
83550	Silent Night	DE 28478
83735	Why Not Confess	DE 28551
83736	Hangover Blues	DE 28551
84383	I'll Be No Stranger There	DE 28784
84384	The Unclouded Day	DE 28784
86721	Gonna Lay My Burden Down	DE 29279
86722	Yes, He Set Me Free	DE 29279

Maddox Brothers & Rose on Columbia, 1952–1958

Note: when the catalogue number appears with the 4 at the end, it means the song was released as both a 78 and a 45 r.p.m. disk.

Master	Song Title	Release Date	Release Number
	1-29-52 rec. date		
RHCO-10099-1N	I'll Make Sweet Love to You	6-13-52	20955-4
RHCO-10104-1N	Cocquita of Laredo	9-19-52	21016-4
RHCO-10105-1N	Wedding Blues	6-13-52	20955-4
RHCO-10106-1N	Take These Shackles from My Heart	9-19-52	21016-4
	10-26-52 rec. date		
CO-48525	Empty Mansions	4-24-53	21099-4
CO-48526	Little Willie Waltz	1-9-53	21062-4
CO-48527	Green Grow the Lilacs	4-24-53	21099-4
CO-48528	The Hiccough Song	1-9-53	21062-4

Master	Song Title	Release Date	Release Number
	12-13-52 rec. date		
CO-48646	No Help Wanted	1-23-53	21065-4
CO-48647	Hearts And Flowers	1-23-53	21065-4
CO-48648	Will There Be Any Stars in My Crown?	7-18-55	21426-S-4
CO-48649	Just Over the Stars	7-18-55	21426-S-4
	6-3-53 rec. date		
CO-49493	I Won't Stand in Your Way	11-9-53	21181-4
CO-49494	On Mexico's Beautiful Shores	8-3-53	21146-4
CO-49495	Kiss Me Quick and Go	11-9-53	21181-4
CO-49496	A Wooin' We Will Go	8-3-53	21146-5
	12-9-53 rec. date		
RHCO-10659-1N	A Kiss from Your Lips	6-28-54	21270-4
RHCO-10663-1N	Beautiful Bouquet	2-22-54	21217-4
RHCO-10664-1	The Time Is Spring	2-22-54	21217-4
RHCO-10665-1N	My Child Has a Billy Goat	6-28-54	21270-4
	3-22-54 rec. date		
CO-51169	Forever Yours	9-20-54	21306-4
CO-51170	You Won't Believe This	9-20-54	21306-4
CO-51171	I Could Never Stop Lovin' You	12-27-54	21345-4
CO-51172	Fountain of Youth	12-27-54	21345-4
	2-7-55 rec. date		
CO-53133	A Rusty Old Halo	2-21-55	21375-4
CO-53134	I Gotta Go Get My Baby	2-21-55	21375-4
CO-53135	No More Time	6-6-55	21405-4
CO-53136	I've Got Four Big Brothers (To Look After Me)	6-6-55	21405-4
	10-1-55 rec. date		
RHCO-33526-1N	I'll Find Her	8-6-56	421546
RHCO-33550-1N	It's a Dark, Dark Place	4-9-56	21513-S-4
RHCO-33551-1N	Away This Side of Heaven	4-9-56	21513-S-4
RHCO-3352-1N	Wish You Would	8-6-56	421546
RHCO-33556-1N	Let This Be the Last Time	11-7-55	21466-4
RHCO-33560-1N	Old Black Choo-Choo	11-7-55	21466-4
	8-16-56 rec. date		
RHCO-33920	Ugly & Slouchy	1-28-57	4-40836-C
RHCO-33921	By the Sweat of My Brow	1-28-57	4-40836-C
RHCO-33922	Paul Bunyan Love	9-10-56	4-21559
RHCO-33923	The Death of Rock & Roll	9-10-56	4-21559

Master	Song Title	Release Date	Release Number
	3-12-57 rec. date		
RHCO-40143	Love Is Strange	3-25-57	4-40895-C
RHCO-40144	My Life with You	3-25-57	4-40895-C
RHCO-41045	A Short Life and Its Troubles		
RHCO-41046	Dig a Hole		
	8-30-57 rec. date		
RHCO-40354	Let Me Love You	9-30-57	4-41020-C
RHCO-40355	Stop Whistlin' Wolf	9-30-57	4-41020-C
RHCO-40356	The Way with God Is So Beautiful		
RHCO-40357	Tell Him Everything		

Rose Maddox on Columbia, 1953–58

Master	Song Title	Date	Number
	5-19-53 rec. date		
CO-49425	I'd Rather Die Young*	6-1-53	21127-4
CO-49426	The Nightingale Song*	6-1-53	21127-4
CO-49427	These Wasted Years	8-24-53	21155-4
CO-49428	Little Red Caboose	8-24-53	21155-4
	9-1-53 rec. date		
CO-49903	Just One More Time	10-12-53	21171-4
CO-49904	Kiss Me like Crazy	10-12-53	21171-4
CO-49905	The Life That You've Led	8-16-54	21297-4
CO-49906	Second Choice	5-9-55	21394-4
	12-10-53 rec. date		
RHCO-10666-1N	The Birthday Card Song	2-8-54	21215-4
RHCO-10667-1N	Breathless Love	2-8-54	21254-4
RHCO-10668-1N	There's No Right Way To do Me Wrong*	11-22-54	21333-4
RHCO-10669-1N	Hasty Baby*	10-3-55	21453-4
	3-22-54 rec. date		
CO-51173	Marry Me Again	5-17-54	21253-4
CO-51174	Poor Little Heartbroken Rose	5-17-54	21253-4
CO-51175	Waltz of the Pines*	8-16-54	21297-4
CO-52276	I Wonder If I Can Lose the Blues This Way	11-22-54	21333-4

+ denotes Rosie & Retta duets; * denotes *Best of Rose Maddox* Harmony LP HL-7312 reissue, released 4-13-64

Master	Song Title	Date	Number
	2-24-55 rec. date		
RHCO-33354-1N	The Hoot-Owl Melody+	*4-11-55	21385-4
RHCO-33355-1N	Was There a Teardrop+	9-12-55	21447-4
RHCO-33356-1N	I'm Gonna Be Loved Tonight+	4-11-55	21385-4
RHCO-33357-1N	Wild Wild Young Men*	5-9-55	21394-4
	6-6-55 rec. date		
RHCO-33460-1N	Hummingbird*	6-13-55	21419-4
RHCO-33461-1N	Wild Wind+*	9-12-55	21447-4
RHCO-33462-1N	When the Sun Goes Down	10-3-55	21453-4
RHCO-33463-1N	Words Are So Easy to Say	6-13-55	21419-4
	12-21-55 rec. date		
RHCO-33649	Tall Men*	1-9-56	21490-4
RHCO-33650	Hey Little Dreamboat	1-9-56	21490-4
RHCO-33651	Burrito Joe	6-25-56	421533
RHCO-33652	False Hearted	6-25-56	412533
	11-21-56 rec. date		
CO-56996	Did You Ever Come Home		
CO-56997	Looky There Over There	12-17-56	4-40814-C
CO-56998	Let Those Brown Eyes Smile at Me*	11-11-57	4-41047-C
CO-56999	I'll Go Steppin' Too	11-11-57	4-41047-C
CO-57000	Your Sweet Mean Heart	12-17-56	4-40814-C
	2-20-57 rec. date		
RHCO-40135	Take a Gamble on Me	3-18-57	4-40873-C
RHCO-40136	1-2-3-4 Anyplace Road	3-18-57	4-40873-C
RHCO-40137	Tomorrow Land	6-17-57	4-40948-C
RHCO-40138	Old Man Blues	6-17-57	4-40948-C
	8-30-57 rec. date		
RHCO-40356	The Donkey Song		

+ denotes Rosie & Retta duets; * denotes *Best of Rose Maddox* Harmony LP HL-7312 reissue, released 4-13-64

Both 2-25-58 and 2-26-58 were *Precious Memories* Columbia LP CL-1159 sessions, released 6-2-58; the Hank Williams compositions "I Saw the Light" and "How Can You Refuse Him Now" were also released on Harmony HL-7265 on 7-25-60; "Precious Memories," "I Saw the Light," "Take My Hand Precious Lord," and "Bringing in the Sheaves" were also released as B-11591 sometime in 1958 or 1959, no release date available.

Recording Date	Master	Song Title	Release Date	Release Number
2-25-58	RHCO-40695	Precious Memories	6-2-58	CL-1159
	RHCO-40696	I Saw the Light	same	same
	RHCO-40697	Someone to Care	same	same
	RHCO-40698	Dear Lord Take My Hand	same	same
	RHCO-40699	He Leadeth Me	same	same
	RHCO-40700	Keep on Talking	same	same
2-26-58	RHCO-40701	How Can You Refuse Him Now	same	same
	RHCO-40702	Take My Hand Precious Lord	same	same
	RHCO-40703	No One Knows What Faith Can Do	same	same
	RHCO-40704	Swing Low Sweet Chariot	same	same
	RHCO-40705	Just Over the Stars	same	same
	RHCO-40706	Bringing in the Sheaves	same	same

Maddox Brothers & Rose 4 Star titles reissued on King Records during mid 1950s

A Collection of Standard Sacred Songs (King 669)

Tramp on the Street / When God Dips His Pen of Love in My Heart / Dust on the Bible / I'll Be No Stranger There / Farther Along / I Just Steal Away and Pray / Gathering Flowers for the Master's Bouquet / The Land Where We'll Never Grow Old / The Unclouded Day / He Set Me Free / I'd Rather Have Jesus / I'll Fly Away.

Maddox Bros. & Rose (King 677)

Whoa, Sailor / You've Been Talkin' in Your Sleep / I'm Sending Daffydils / Water Baby Blues / No One Is Sweeter Than You / Gosh, I Miss You All the Time / Why Don't You Haul Off and Love Me / Sally Let Your Bangs Hang Down / Choc'late Ice Cream Cone / (New) Step It Up and Go / I Wish I Was a Single Girl Again / Philadelphia Lawyer.

I Still Write Your Name in the Sand (King 752)

Careless Driver / New Muleskinner Blues / I Want to Live and Love / Meanest Man in Town / Hangover Blues / Kiss Me Quick and Go / Brown Eyes / Shimmy Shakin' Daddy/ I'll Still Write Your Name in the Sand / Mama Says it's Naughty / May You Never Be Alone / Old Pal of Yesterday.

Rose Maddox on Black Jack Records, 1958

Produced by Black Jack Wayne.

Personnel: Rose Maddox, vocal. Cal Maddox, vocal, guitar. Others unknown

Black Jack single 104: Gotta Travel On b/w What Makes Me Hang Around

Rose Maddox on Uni Records, 1958

Produced by Cliffie Stone; recorded in Hollywood, California.

Personnel: Rose Maddox, vocal. Cal Maddox, vocal, guitar. Others unknown.

Uni single 55040: (Don't the World Look Better) Through the Bottom of a Glass b/w Step Right In

Rose Maddox on Capitol Records, 1959–65

Producer on all sessions: Ken Nelson. Note: four-digit release number denotes 45 configuration; T and four digits denotes LP, SXA and four digits denotes EP, S denotes stereo; personnel info courtesy of Patrick Milligan and Musicians Union Local 47. All 111 of Rose's Capitol recordings, including the unissued material, appeared on Bear Family four disc 1993 CD box set, BCD 15743.

Hollywood, February 25, 1959. Session # 7608. Personnel: Rose Maddox vocal; Cal Maddox, guitar, vocal; Henry Maddox, mandolin, vocal; Joe Billy Hodges, Fred Henry Marciel, J. Lee Newman, guitars; Charles T. Shults, drums.

Master	Song Title	Release Number
31225	What Makes Me Hang Around	4177
31226	Billy Cline	4432
31227	Gambler's Love	4177
31228	Lies and Alibis	unissued

Hollywood, June 8, 1959. Session # 7794. Personnel same as Feb. 25, except add Allen J. Williams, bass; Henry Sharpe replaces C. Shults

Master	Song Title	Release Number
31845	Custer's Last Stand	4241
31846	I Lost Today	4296
31847	Live and Let Live	(S)T 1312

Hollywood, June 9, 1959. Session # 7796. Personnel same as June 8.

Master	Song Title	Release Number
31854	My Little Baby	4241
31855	Philadelphia Lawyer	(S)T 1312
31856	Tramp on the Street	(S)T 1312
31857	Gathering Flowers for the Master's Bouquet	(S)T 1312

Hollywood, June 10, 1959. Session # 7798. Personnel same as June 8.

Master	Song Title	Release Number
31862	I'm Happy Every Day I Live	4296
31863	Sally Let Your Bangs Hang Down	(S)T 1312
31864	Whoa, Sailor	(S)T 1312
31865	On the Banks of the Old Ponchartrain	(S)T 1312
31866	Honky Tonkin'	(S)T 1312
31871[?]	At the First Fall of Snow	(S)T 1312

Hollywood, June 11, 1959. Session # 7801. Personnel same as June 8.

Master	Song Title	Release Number
31876	Why Don't You Haul Off and Love Me	(S)T 1312
31877	Chocolate Ice Cream Cone	(S)T 1312
31878	Move It on Over	(S)T 1312

Hollywood, January 25, 1960. Session # 9226. Personnel same as June 8, 1959, except add Norm Hamlet, steel guitar.

Master	Song Title	Release Number
33111	Shining Silver, Gleaming Gold	4432
33112	Down, Down, Down	4347
33113	Please Help Me, I'm Falling	4347
33114	Johnny's Last Kiss	(S)T 1993

Hollywood, January 26, 1960. Session # 9228. Personnel same as Jan. 25.

Master	Song Title	Release Number
33119	Wait a Little Longer	
	Please Jesus	(S)T 1437
33120	An Empty Mansion	(S)T 1437
33121	The Great Speckled Bird	(S)T 1437
33122	This World Is Not My Home	(S)T 1437

Hollywood, January 27, 1960. Session # 9232. Personnel same as Jan. 25.

Master	Song Title	Release Number
33137	That Glory Bound Train	(S)T 1437
33138	Drifting Too Far from the Shore	(S)T 1437
33139	When I Take My Vacation in Heaven	(S)T 1437
33140	How Beautiful Heaven Must Be	(S)T 1437

Hollywood, January 28, 1960. Session # 9236. Personnel same as Jan. 25.

Master	Song Title	Release Number
33148	I'll Reap My Harvest in Heaven	(S)T 1437
33149	Smoke, Fire & Brimstone	(S)T 1437
33150	Will the Circle Be Unbroken	(S)T 1437
33151	Kneel at the Cross	(S)T 1437

Hollywood, September 6, 1960. Session # 9648. Personnel: Rose Maddox, vocal;. Billy Strange, guitar; Roy Nichols, guitar; Henry Maddox, mandolin, vocal; Allen J. Williams, bass; Lionel "Les" Taylor, Harold Hensley, fiddles; Cal Maddox, guitar, vocal; Marion Z. "Pee Wee" Adams, drums.

Master	Song Title	Release Number
34421	There's Better Times a-Comin'	(S)T 1548
34422	I Want to Live Again	4487
34423	Kissing My Pillow	4487

Hollywood, January 16, 1961. Session # 9885. Personnel: Rose Maddox, vocal; Buck Owens, vocal, guitar; Don Rich, guitar, fiddle; Marion Z. "Pee Wee" Adams, drums; George French Jr., piano; Ralph Mooney, steel guitar; Allen J. Williams, bass.

Master	Song Title	Release Number
35214	Loose Talk	4550
35215	Mental Cruelty	4550

Hollywood, January 17, 1961. Session # 9887. Personnel same as September 6, 1960, except delete Les Taylor, Harold Hensley; add "Gentleman" Jim Pierce, piano

Master	Song Title	Release Number
35232	Conscience, I'm Guilty	4598/(S)T 1548
35232	Read My Letter Once Again	(S)T 1548
35233	Tall Men	(S)T 1548
35235	Early in the Morning	(S)T 1548

Hollywood, January 18, 1961. Session # 9890. Personnel same as Jan. 17.

Master	Song Title	Release Number
35244	There Ain't No Love	4651
35245	What Am I Living For	(S)T 1548
35246	Stop the World (And Let Me Off)	(S)T 1993
35247	Jim Dandy	(S)T 1548
35248	North to Alaska	(S)T 1548

Hollywood, January 19, 1961. Session # 9892. Personnel same as Jan. 17.

Master	Song Title	Release Number
35249	Lonely Street	4598, (S)T 1548; JS 6163[?]
35250	Gotta Travel On	(S)T 1548
35251	Just One More Time	(S)T 1548
35257	Don't Tell Me Your Troubles	(S)T 1548

Hollywood, July 10 & 11, 1961, Session # 10182 & 10184. Personnel: Rose Maddox, vocal. Cal Maddox, guitar, vocal. Ralph Mooney, steel guitar. "Gentleman" Jim Pierce, piano. Roy Nichols, guitar. Allen Williams, bass. Marion Z. "Pee Wee" Adams, drums. Joe Maphis, fiddle, guitar.

(Note: There is an apparent discrepancy in Ken Nelson's session details between master and session numbers, in conjunction with break in master # sequence, making it difficult to determine at which session "Take Me Back Again," "Your Kind of Lovin' Won't Do," and "Fool Me Again" were actually recorded. Likely this was an overtime situation.)

Master	Song Title	Release Number
36142	Long Journey Home	(S)T 1993
36143	From a Beggar to a Queen	(S)T 1993
36144	Let's Pretend We're Strangers	4771
36145	If You See My Baby	(S)T 1993
36146	You're Kind of Lovin' Won't Do	4651
36147	Take Me Back Again	4771
36148	Fool Me Again	4709
36152	Let Those Brown Eyes Smile at Me	(S)T 1993, SXA 1993
36153	When the Sun Goes Down	5110, (S)T 1993
36154	Alone with You	5110, (S)T 1993, SXA 1993; JS 6163[?]
36155	My Life Has Been a Pleasure	SXA 1993, (S)T 1993

Hollywood, July 12, 1961. Session # 10185. Personnel same as July 10.

36156	Curley Joe	(S)T 1993, SXA 1993
36157	Here We Go Again	4709
36158	Long Black Limousine	(S)T 1993
36159	White Lightnin'	(S)T 1993

Nashville, Tennessee, March 19, 1962. Session # 10552. Personnel: Rose Maddox, vocal; Bill Monroe, mandolin; Don Reno, banjo; Red Smiley, guitar; Mack McGaha and Tommy Jackson, fiddles; John Palmer, bass; Wayne Gailey, steel guitar.

Master	Song Title	Release Number
37317	My Rose of Old Kentucky	(S)T 1799
37318	Uncle Pen	(S)T 1799
37319	Footprints in the Snow	(S)T 1799
37320	Blue Moon of Kentucky	(S)T 1799
37321	Molly and Tenbrooks	(S)T 1799

Nashville, Tennessee, March 20, 1962. Session 10553. Personnel same as March 19, except Donna Stoneman, mandolin, replaces Bill Monroe.

Master	Song Title	Release Number
37322	Rollin' in My Sweet Baby's Arms	(S)T 1799
37323	Cotton Fields	(S)T 1799
37324	Each Season Changes You	(S)T 1799
37325	The Old Crossroad Is Waitin'	(S)T 1799
37326	I'll Meet You in Church Sunday Mornin'	(S)T 1799
37327	Down, Down, Down	(S)T 1799
37828	Ole Slew Foot	(S)T 1799

Hollywood, California, August 6, 1962. Session # 10737. Personnel same as July 10, 1961.

Master	Song Title	Release Number
38057	Lonely Teardrops	4905
38058	Sing a Little Song of Heartache	4845
38059	Tie a Ribbon in the Apple Tree	4845
38060	George Carter	4905

Hollywood, California, March 18, 1963. Session # 11807. Personnel: Rose Maddox, vocal; Cal Maddox, guitar, vocal; Lawrence B. Wooten, Ralph Mooney, steel guitar; Henry K. Vernon, Joe Maphis, fiddle, guitar; Gwynn M. Nichols, "Gentleman" Jim Pierce, piano; Roy Nichols, guitar.

Master	Song Title	Release Number
39344	Let Me Kiss You for Old Times	5038
39345	I Don't Hear You	4975
39346	Down to the River	4975
39347	Somebody Told Somebody	5038

Hollywood, California, March 19, 1963. Personnel: Rose Maddox, vocal, Buck Owens, vocal., guitar; Don Rich, guitar; Jay McDonald, steel guitar; "Gentleman" Jim Pierce, piano; Cal Maddox, guitar, vocal; Kenny Pierce, bass; Ken Presley, drums.

Master	Song Title	Release Number
39382	Sweethearts in Heaven	4992
39383	We're the Talk of the Town	4992
39384	Back Street Affair	unissued
39385	No Fool Like an Old Fool	unissued

Bakersfield Civic Auditorium, September 12, 1963. Session # 11426. Personnel: Rose Maddox, vocal; other personnel unknown. Live recording produced by Ken Nelson: *Country Music Hootenanny* LP, featuring Buck Owens, Joe & Rose Lee Maphis, Johnny Bond, Tommy Collins, Merle Travis, Glen Campbell, Roy Clark.

Master	Song Title	Release Number
50748	Down to the River	(S)T 2009

Hollywood, California, September 30, 1963. Session # 11486. Personnel: Rose Maddox, vocal; Cal Maddox, guitar, vocal; Glen Campbell, guitar, vocal; Gwyn Nichols, Ralph Mooney, steel guitar; Roy Nichols, guitar; Robert Morris, bass; "Gentleman" Jim Pierce, piano.

Master	Song Title	Release Number
50615	I Won't Come in While She's There	unissued
50616	Silver Threads and Golden Needles	unissued

Hollywood, California, January 7, 1964. Session # 11634. Personnel same as September 30, 1963, except add Lawrence Wooten, piano.

Master	Song Title	Release Number
51095	Blue Bird Let Me Tag Along	5186
51096	That's a Mighty Long Way to Fall	unissued
51097	Stand Up Fool	5186

Hollywood, California, July 13, 1964. Session # 11977 & 11978. Personnel same as January 7, 1964.

Master	Song Title	Release Number
52426	Silver Threads and Golden Needles	5263
52428	Tia Lisa Lynn	5263
52429	Lonely One	unissued
52430	Big Balls In Cowtown	unissued
52431	Wabash Cannonball	unissued

Hollywood, California, March 10, 1965. Session # 12286. Personnel same as January 7, 1964, except delete Glen Campbell, Roy Nichols, add Phillip Baugh, Roy Lanham, guitar.

Master	Song Title	Release Number
53471	I'll Always be Loving You	5439
53472	Mad at the World	5439
53473	Big Big Day Tomorrow	unissued
53474	Cottonwood Road	unissued

Maddox Brothers & Rose reissues from 4 Star masters, ca. 1963

Maddox Brothers And Rose (Wrangler LP WR-1003)

Baby, You Should Live So Long / That'll Learn Ya, Durn Ya / Just When I Needed You / Don't Let Your Sweet Love Die / Sugar Pie / I've Stopped My Dreaming about You// Move It on Over / Why Not Confess / Bring It Down to My House Honey / Honky Tonkin' / Molly Darlin' / Small Town Mama (Note: tracks 1–5 on side A were remastered at wrong pitch)

Maddox Bros. & Rose Go Honky Tonkin' (Hilltop Records LP JS-6007)

I Wish I Was a Single Girl Again / Gosh, I Miss You all the Time / Hangover Blues / Meanest Man in Town / Kiss Me Quick and Go / Philadelphia Lawyer// Honky Tonkin'/ Sally Let Your Bangs Hang Down / Water Baby Blues / No One Is Sweeter Than You / Mama Says It's Naughty/ Shimmy Shakin' Daddy

Rose Maddox on Starday Records, 1967

Produced by Darrel Glenn; recorded in Nashville, Tennessee, 1967.

Personnel: Rose Maddox, vocal; Tom Brumley, steel guitar; Jerry Rivers, fiddle; others unknown.

Rosie! (Starday SLP 463)

Faded Love / The Bigger the Pride / Get It Over / I Still Believe in Tomorrow / Goodbye on Your Mind / Rocky Top / All I Have to Offer You Is Me / The Key's in the Mailbox / I'm Happy Every Day I Live / Philadelphia Lawyer.

Starday single 895: Faded Love b/w The Bigger the Pride
Starday single 921: Get It Over b/w The Two of Us

Rose Maddox on Cathay Records, ca. 1971

Cathay single 1149: As Long as I Live b/w One Day at a Time
Cathay single 1150: Wouldn't You b/w One Day at a Time
Cathay single 1153: House of the Rising Sun b/w What Good Will it Do
Cathay single 1156: I Really Don't Want to Know b/w There's a Time and a Place

Rose Maddox on Portland Records, 1974

Produced by Gene Breeden, recorded in Portland, Oregon.
Personnel: Rose Maddox, vocal; Gene Breeden, guitar; others unknown.

Portland single 032: Lord It's Been a Long Time b/w I'll Fly Away
Portland single 1011: Mr. Jackson b/w Baby Hang On
Portland single 1020: Weekend Widow b/w If I Stopped Loving You

Rose Maddox on Takoma Records, 1977

Produced by Charlie Mitchell & Doug Decker, recorded in Venice, California.
Personnel: Rose Maddox, vocal; Byron Berline, fiddle, mandolin; Wayne "Swamp Root" Gailey, pedal steel guitar; John Hickman, banjo; Frank Reckard, guitar; Jim Hobson, John Herron, piano.

Reckless Love & Bold Adventure (Takoma D-1055)
Reckless Love & Bold Adventure / Heart of a Country Song (Rose's Song) / It's Been a Long, Long Time / Lion in the Winter / My Tennessee Mountain Home / Tramp on the Street//Mr. Jackson / Willie's Winter Love / I'm Happy Everyday I Live / Pass Me By (If You're Only Passing Through) / Dancing Shoes

Takoma single 5055: Reckless Love & Bold Adventure b/w Mr. Jackson

Rose Maddox on Varrick Records, 1984

Produced by Don Reich & Charles Johnson, recorded in Modesto, California.
Personnel: Rose Maddox, vocal; Merle Haggard, guitar, fiddle; Roy Nichols, guitar; Tiny Moore, fiddle, mandolin; Dennis Hromek, bass; Eldon Shamblin, guitar; Gordon Terry, fiddle; Biff Adams, drums; Don Markham, trumpet; Mark Yeary, piano; Norm Hamlet, steel guitar; Emmylou Harris, Leona Williams, vocals.

Rose Maddox, Queen of the West (Varrick LP 010)
Down, Down, Down / Downtown Modesto / Cold in California / Oklahoma Sweetheart / Alone with You//Foggy River / Mr. Jackson / Shelly's Winter Love / Somebody's Looking for Gold / My Love Is Too Hot for You

Bear Family Records (reissues of Maddox Brothers & Rose on Columbia)

Rockin' Rollin' Maddox Bros. & Rose (Bear Family LP BFX 15076)
Paul Bunyan Love / I Gotta Go Get My Baby / Let Me Love You / No More Time / I've Got Four Big Brothers (To Look after Me) / Old Black Choo-Choo / Ugly and Slouchy / The Death of Rock and Roll // Stop Whistlin' Wolf / Love Is

Strange / A Short Life of It's Troubles / Empty Mansions / Looky There (Over There) / You Won't Believe This / I'll Find Her / No Help Wanted

Maddox Bros. & Rose, Family Folks (Bear Family LP BFX 15083)
Tall Men / I'll Go Steppin' Too / One-Two-Three-Four / Did You Ever Come Home / I Wonder If I Can Lose the Blues This Way / Marry Me Again / Burrito Joe / I'm a Little Red Caboose// Cocquita of Laredo / On Mexico's Beautiful Shores / I'll Make Sweet Love to You /Kiss Me Quick and Go Away / Little Willie Waltz / Let This Be the Last Time / Wish You Would / A Beautiful Bouquet//

Maddox Brothers & Rose, Columbia reissue

Maddox Bros. and Rose. Columbia Historic Edition (Columbia Records FC 39997). LP released in 1985.
I've Got Four Big Brothers (To Look After Me) / Dig a Hole / A Rusty Old Halo / Ugly and Slouchy / I'm Cocquita of Laredo / Green Grow the Lilacs / Bringing in the Sheaves //Old Black Choo Choo / Tall Men / The Death of Rock & Roll / The Hiccough Song / Will There Be Any Stars in My Crown / Love Is Strange

Maddox Brothers & Rose on Arhoolie Records (4 Star reissues)

Maddox Brothers And Rose, 1946–51 Vol. I (Arhoolie LP 5016), released 1976.
Midnight Train / Move It on Over / Careless Driver / Whoa Sailor / Milk Cow Blues / Mean and Wicked Boogie / Brown Eyes / Honky Tonkin'// New Mule Skinner Blues / Time nor Tide / Philadelphia Lawyer / George's Playhouse Boogie / Blue Eyes Cryin' in the Rain / Sally Let Your Bangs Hang Down / I've Stopped My Dreamin about You / Gonna Lay My Burden Down / Water Baby Boogie

Maddox Brothers & Rose, 1946–1951 Vol. II (Arhoolie LP 5017), released 1976.
Oklahoma Sweetheart Sally Ann / I'm Sending Daffydills / Mule Train / It's Only Human Nature / Step It Up and Go / Dark as a Dungeon / Pay Me (Alimony) / Don't Bother to Cry / I Want to Live and Love//Shimmy Shakin' Daddy / I Wish I Was a Single Girl / South / Eight Thirty Blues / Your Love Light Never Shone / Texas Guitar Stomp / Detour #2 / Hangover Blues / I'd Rather Have Jesus / I Still Write Your Name in the Sand

The Maddox Brothers And Rose - On The Air: 1940 and 1945 (Arhoolie LP 5028). Released 1984. Tracks 1–6 recorded at KFBK, Sacramento, California on February 19, 1940; tracks 7–8, and all of side B recorded at KGDM, Stockton, California on December 29, 1945.

Theme & A Cowboy Has to Yell / Let Me Ride My Pony Down the Sunset Trail / Once I Had a Darling Mother / Hold that Critter Down / I'm Talking about You / I'm Going to the Hoedown & theme / Theme & Small Town Mama / Mama, Please Stay Home With Me // If You Ain't Got the Do-Re-Mi / I Might Have Known / I'll Reap My Harvest in Heaven / Don't Hang Around Me Any More / A Sinner's Prayer Is Never Answered / The Girl I Love Don't Pay Me No Mind / Write Me, Sweetheart, I'm a Handy Man to Have Around / I've Rambled Around & theme

The Maddox Brothers & Rose On The Air Vol. 2 (Arhoolie LP 5033). Released 1987. Tracks 1 & 2 recorded from WSM Grand Ole Opry broadcast of February 19, 1949; the rest are KTRB and/or demo acetate recordings.

Gathering Flowers for the Master's Bouquet / I Couldn't Believe It Was True / KTRB Theme & Regal Pale Beer ad / The Goldrush Is Over / Almost / Too Old Too Cut the Mustard / Breathless Love / Lord Take My Hand / KTRB theme out// Walkin' in My Sleep / Fred's Boogie woogie / Introduction by Fred & Rose / Nobody's Love Is Like Mine / Texas Playboy Rag / Lost John Boogie / Meanest Man in Town / Freight Train Boogie / Kiss Me Quick / Fried Potatoes / KTRB theme out

Rose & Fred Maddox Talk About 50 Years in Country Music (Arhoolie C-277, cassette only) An interview with Rose and Fred conducted by KTRB's Bob Smith; recorded at KTRB, Modesto, California, July 29, 1987, released that same year.

The Maddox Brothers & Rose, America's Most Colorful Hillbilly Band, 1946–51 Vol. 1 (Arhoolie CD 391). Released 1994. Compact disc compilation of remastered 4 Star recordings (featuring the first ever reissue of their 4 Star Faded Love)

George's Playhouse Boogie / Midnight Train /Shimmy Shakin' Daddy / Careless Driver / Move It on Over / Whoa Sailor / Milk Cow Blues / Mean & Wicked Boogie / Brown Eyes / Honky Tonkin' / Time nor Tide / New Mule Skinner Blues / Philadelphia Lawyer / Sally Let Your Bangs Hang Down / When I Lay My Burden Down / Hangover Blues / Water Baby Boogie / Dark as a Dungeon / Mule Train / Oklahoma Sweetheart Sally Ann / Faded Love / New Step It Up and Go / (Pay Me) Alimony / I Wish I Was a Single Girl Again / Your Love Light Never Shone / Meanest Man in Town / I Want to Live and Love// (note: track 12 listed as New Mule Skinner Blues is actually I Want to Live and Love)

The Maddox Brothers & Rose, America's Most Colorful Hillbilly Band, 1946–51 Vol. 2 (Arhoolie CD 437). Released 1995. Compact disc compilation of remastered 4 Star recordings and previously unissued radio acetates.

New Mule Skinner Blues / I Couldn't Believe It Was True / You've Been Talking in Your Sleep / Gosh, I Miss You All the Time / I'm Sending Daffydills / South / Chill in My Heart / Texas Guitar Stomp / Eight Thirty Blues / It's Only Human

Nature / Why Not Confess / I'll Never Do It Again / Just One Little Kiss / I Love the Women / I Still Write Your Name in the Sand / Last Night I Heard You Crying in Your Sleep / You're Gonna Be Sorry Some of These Days / No One Is Sweeter Than You / Detour #2 / Mama Says It's Naughty / I've Stopped My Dreaming About You / Kiss Me Quick & Go / Freight Train Boogie / Lonesome Hearted Blues / Cherokee Maiden / Okie Boogie / No One Will Ever Know / Red Silk Stockings and Green Perfume / Garden in the Sky / Dear Lord Take My Hand

Maddox Bros. & Rose On the Air (Arhoolie CD 447). Released 1996. Collection of radio acetates, same as Arhoolie releases 5028 and 5033.

Rose Maddox on Arhoolie Records, 1981–1994

This Is Rose Maddox (Arhoolie LP 5024). Released 1981. Rose Maddox; Vern Williams, vocal, mandolin; Delbert Williams, vocal, rhythm guitar; Keith Little, vocal., banjo; J.D. Rhynes, Ray Park, fiddle; Kraig Hutchins, lead guitar. Recorded September 20–21, Berkeley, California, 1980.

Philadelphia Lawyer / Let Those Brown Eyes Smile at Me / Old Black Choo Choo / Single Girl / Dark as a Dungeon / This Old House / Sally Let Your Bangs Hang Down //Rusty Old Halo / Dream of the Miner's Child / Ashes of Love / Silver Threads and Golden Needles / Foggy Mountain Top / Amazing Grace / Rocky Top

A Beautiful Bouquet (Arhoolie LP 5034). Released 1983. Rose Maddox with the Vern Williams Band; Hutchins, Park, Rhynes out, add Ed Neff, fiddle, Kevin Thompson, bass. Recorded November 20–21, Alameda, California, 1982.

We are Climbing Jacob's Ladder / Life's Evening Sun / Church in the Wilderness/ When God Dips His Love in My Heart / I Can't Feel at Home Anymore / Farther Along / I'll Fly Away // In the Sweet Bye and Bye/ Kneel at the Cross / Turn Your Radio On / Beautiful Bouquet / Take Me in the Lifeboat / If We Never Meet Again / Swing Low Sweet Chariot

Rose Maddox: Rose Of the West Coast Country (Arhoolie CD 314) compact disc compilation of tracks from *This is Rose Maddox* and *A Beautiful Bouquet.*

Philadelphia Lawyer / Let Those Brown Eyes Smile at Me / Old Black Choo-Choo / Single Girl / Dark as a Dungeon / This Old House / Sally Let Your Bangs Hang Down / Rusty Old Halo / Dream of the Miner's Child / Ashes of Love / Silver Threads & Golden Needles / Foggy Mountain Top / Amazing Grace / Rocky Top / When God Dips His Pen of Love in My Heart / I Can't Feel at Home Anymore / Farther Along / I'll Fly Away / Kneel at the Cross / Turn Your Radio On / Beautiful Bouquet / Take Me in The Lifeboat / Swing Low Sweet Chariot

Rose Maddox: "$35 and a Dream," (Arhoolie CD 428). Released 1994. Produced by Chris Strachwitz. Rose Maddox, vocals; Byron Berline, fiddle, mandolin; John Jorgenson, guitar, mandolin; Herb Pedersen, guitar, banjo; Jay Dee

Maness, steel guitar; Bill Bryson, bass; Steve Duncan, drums. Recorded Van Nuys, California, July 17–18, 1994. Tracks 13–14 were recorded at Tally Studios, Palo Cedro, California, 1990. Rose Maddox, vocals; Merle Haggard, vocal (13 only); Fred Maddox, recitation (13 only); Tim Howard, guitar; Larry White, drums; Donny Maddox, bass; Norman Hamlet, dobro; Steven Grahn, mandolin, guitar.

Fried Potatoes / I Wonder Where You Are Tonight / Falling for You / Sin City / We're Gonna Let the Good Times Roll / Blood Stained Hands of Jesus / Blueridge Mountain Blues / $35 and a Dream / Cajun Lady / Where No One Stands Alone / The Place Where Love Comes From / Old Train / Dusty Memories / I Wonder Where I'll Find You at Tonight / Tonight I'm on Stage / a comment from Johnny Cash.

INDEX

"Long Black Limousine," 213
"Long Journey Home," 212
Lonzo & Oscar, 200
"Looky There Over There," 167, 169
"Loose Talk," 199
"Louisiana Hayride," xix, 90, 144,
    145–146, 149, 151; appearances on,
    138–140, 142–143, 166
Louvin, Ira, 202
Louvin Brothers, 3, 166, 178
"Lovesick Blues," 8, 103
Lulu Belle & Scotty, 138
Lupino, Ida, 120
Lynn, Loretta, 192, 225; appearance with,
    247, 254
Lynn, Mooney, 192

McCall, Bill, 64, 65, 87, 131–132, 170,
    223; exploitative nature of, 70; 4 Star
    Music and, 133; signing with, 68–69
McClatchy Broadcast Network, 42, 44,
    47, 69, 89
McDonald, John, 227
McDonald, Skeets, 70
McDonald Ballroom, 137
McFadden, Jack, 81; booking by, 93; on
    Cliff, 116, 117; hiring, 92; on Rose,
    142, 214
McLemore, Big Ed, 225
McMichen, Clayton, 40
Macon, Uncle Dave, 103
Maddox, Benny, 115, 118
Maddox, Charlie, 7, 10–12, 14, 18–20,
    26, 31, 34, 39, 43, 172, 243; and
    divorce, 85–86, 124; Donnie and, 78;
    family role of, 5; house for, 79; mar-
    riage of, 3–4; Rose's marriage and, 50;
    and separation, 45, 85
Maddox, Clifton R. E. (Cliff), 9, 10, 13,
    15, 17, 27, 29, 31–33, 36, 42–44, 48,
    55, 104, 110, 159; birth of, 4; death
    of, 117–118, 123, 124; and health
    problems, 47, 105, 115, 243; legacy of,
    118; musicianship of, 41, 47, 116;
    playing by, 34, 75, 116–117; and
    poverty, 26, 115; songs by, 40–41
Maddox, Clotha Reynolds (Kitty), 228,
    242, 250, 251, 258; Fred's death and,
    259; marriage of, 110; Rose's illness
    and, 255
Maddox, Foncy, 7, 9, 10, 32, 118; black
    musicians and, 8; blues and, 41
Maddox, Fred Roscoe, xx, 11–13, 19, 21,
    29, 31, 33, 36, 43, 55, 57, 120, 195,
    213, 242, 248; on band competition,

42; barn dance program and, 249;
    birth of, 4; bookings by, 92, 125, 154;
    on bouncers, 82; on brakemen, 18; and
    cars, 61–62, 105; and comedy, 45, 73,
    74, 94, 112–113; death of, 258–259;
    deejay jobs of, 177, 226; on fan mail,
    40; Fifieth Anniversary and, 251, 252;
    and health problems, 250–251; leader-
    ship by, 32–33, 39, 48, 56, 110, 123,
    161, 162; on Lula, 17, 23, 110–111,
    145; marriage of, 110; and military
    service, 47, 48, 56; musicianship of,
    130; music lessons for, 39, 44; and
    nightclubs, 226–227; on Pipe City, 20;
    playing by, 34, 58, 73, 75, 96, 131,
    134–135, 157, 162; on Presley, 156;
    recollections of, 5, 8–9, 27–28, 48,
    141; recording and, 69, 72, 144;
    reunion tour and, 200; on rock & roll,
    155; Rose's illness and, 255; singing by,
    71–72, 81, 250, 257; style of, 160,
    226; on work camps, 25
Maddox, Gertrude Alta May, 6, 12–15,
    26, 33, 39, 41, 43, 45, 153; birth of, 4;
    on Cliff, 10; on Don/Fred, 151; Donnie
    and, 78; on Lula, 27, 231; recollections
    of, 7–8, 30; songwriting by, 192, 240
Maddox, Gordie Whissenant, 9, 10, 15,
    27, 39, 41, 43, 45, 48, 153; Cliff's
    death and, 118; performing by,
    116–117; poverty for, 26, 115
Maddox, Henry Ford, xx, 16, 19, 30, 31,
    47, 49, 55, 60, 63, 98, 105, 109, 130,
    131, 134, 141, 153, 157, 161, 177,
    229; birth of, 4; death of, 237–238;
    and divorce, 226; and health problems,
    148, 151, 243; marriage of, 123; play-
    ing by, 56, 57, 71, 73, 75, 96, 111,
    126, 148, 162, 193, 226; rock & roll
    and, 155; songwriting by, 189, 194
Maddox, John Calvin (Cal), xx, 10, 11,
    12, 18, 19, 29, 31, 33, 36, 42–44, 111,
    131, 140, 153, 175, 184, 197, 199,
    214, 225–226; birth of, 4; boogie style
    and, 41, 61; car for, 105; death of,
    229–230; Donnie and, 183, 217, 218,
    219; "Grand Ole Opry" and,
    164–165, 166, 167; and health prob-
    lems, 229; Lula and, 171, 172, 173,
    196, 200, 219, 226; and military ser-
    vice, 47, 48, 56; music lessons for, 39;
    playing by, 29, 34, 57, 58, 73, 75, 92,
    96, 101, 134, 135, 148, 157, 177, 193;
    recording by, 72, 169–170; reunion
    tour and, 200; rock & roll and, 155;

Rose-Lula break and, 180, 182, 183; songwriting by, 40, 41

Maddox, Kenneth Chalmer (Don), xx, 12, 14, 16, 19, 27, 28, 31, 49, 55, 58, 111, 131, 146, 177, 229, 230, 242; birth of, 4; cattle ranching by, 225–226; Donnie and, 171; on Foncy, 9; gags and, 74, 112–113; on Hale, 48; Lula and, 21, 110–111; marriage of, 123; military service by, 56; musicianship of, 47, 130; on Pipe City, 20; playing by, 43, 73, 74–75, 96, 134, 160, 162; on Presley, 157; problems for, 115; recollections of, 34, 48; Rose's marriage and, 49, 50, 51; on Rose-Jimmy break, 214; on Rose-Winkle romance, 79; Maddox, Loretta Graham (Retta), 141, 153; contract for, 154; divorce for, 226; marriage of, 123; singing by, 162

Maddox, Lula, 10, 16, 17, 19, 20, 21, 23, 26, 32, 34, 55, 101, 134, 153, 175; and Alzheimer's disease, 196, 200, 229; break with, 177–178, 180, 181–184, 187, 195, 219; Cal's death and, 230; and buying cars, 232; control by, 36–38, 40, 43, 45, 47, 75–76, 77, 80, 82, 85–87, 93–95, 109, 110–115, 120, 123–128, 130, 140–142, 146–148, 150, 154, 172, 173, 179, 180–182, 226, 231–232, 238; death of, 231–232; and divorce, 85–86, 124; Donnie and, 171; 4 Star and, 131, 145; house for, 79; marriage of, 3–4; outsiders and, 147–148; recording contract and, 69; reputation of, 5, 11–12, 15–16, 27, 54, 94–95, 145, 169, 173, 243; Rose's marriage and, 50; Rose-Winkle romance and, 82, 84–85; separation for, 24, 45, 85; songwriting by, 211

Maddox, Nila Bussey, 230; Donnie and, 171; marriage of, 123

Maddox, R. E., 5–7

Maddox, Roselea Arbana, xiv, xvii, 11, 14, 16, 19, 27, 30, 31, 44, 60; auditions for, 52–53; band competition and, 42; birth of, 4; on brakemen, 17–18; on Cal's death, 230; on Charlie, 25; contract for, 148–149, 152, 154; and drug problems, 212, 218, 223, 237; Fiftieth Anniversary and, 252, 253; on 4 Star, 88; gags and, 81, 112–113; "Grand Ole Opry" and, 163, 164–166, 168–169; and health problems, 215–216, 229, 243–244, 255–256; on hobos, 18; influence of, xviii,

xx–xxi, 160, 224–225, 239–240, 259; on Lula, 13, 15, 21, 28, 29, 36–37, 39, 123, 141–142, 145, 218; marriages of, 49–51, 181–183; motherhood and, 55, 78–79, 124, 149–150, 170–172, 184–187; on musicianship, 130, 151; and plane accident, 201–202; playing by, 35, 57, 58, 73, 75, 77, 91, 164, 166, 173, 177, 188, 254; recording by, 69, 144, 149, 154, 169–170, 178, 189–190, 194–195, 200, 201, 215, 238, 240; reputation of, 211–214, 232–233, 237; and school, 23, 39, 119; singing by, xii, 33–34, 36, 40, 47, 71, 135, 250, 260

Maddox, Tom, 115, 118

Maddox Bros. & Rose, 1946–51, Volumes One and Two, The, xvii,; 239–240

Maddox Brothers & Her, 159

Maddox Brothers & Retta, 162, 163, 225

Maddox Brothers & Rose, xi–xii, xiii, xiv; and changes, 37, 44, 59, 60–61; comedy by, 73–74, 160; documentary about, 242, 244; end for, 158–159, 177; and exposure, 42–43; film footage of, 259; influence of, xix–xx, 95–96, 190, 231; modus operandi of, 36–37; recording by, 70–71, 152–153, 170; and rereleases, 223, 248; and reunion, 200, 201, 229; style of, 56–57, 75, 159–160, 207

Mae, Daisy, 120

Mandrell, Barbara, 160

Manners, Zeke, 35

Manuel. *See* Cuevas, Manuel

Maphis, Joe, 120, 134, 162, 201, 233; recording by, 169; Riverside Rancho and, 97

Maphis, Rose Lee, 120, 233; Riverside Rancho and, 97

Mary (friend), 181, 182, 183, 209

"Matthew Twenty-Four," 100

"Mean and Wicked Boogie," 241

"Mental Cruelty," 199

Mercer, Johnny, 67

"Midnight Jamboree," 106, 108

"Midnight Train, The," 71

Mike & the Skillet Lickers, 96

"Milk Cow Blues, The," xii–xiii, 122, 152

Miller, Emmett, 8

Miller, Roger, 183, 224

Modern, 64

Modesto: home in, 26, 28, 30, 32, 45, 79, 87

Modesto Bee, 31

Modesto Police Department, deputization by, 81–82
Moles, Gene, 190
Monroe, Bill, 103, 105, 166; & the Bluegrass Boys, 106; bluegrass and, 208; "Opry" and, 106–107; recording with, 206–207
Montana, Patsy, 29, 34, 38, 119
Mooney, Ralph, 190, 201
Moore, Tiny, 94, 247
Morgan, Lorrie, xix
Morse, Ella Mae, 67
Moten, Bennie, 109
"Move It on Over," 91
Mozart Club, 226, 227
"Mule Skinner Blues," 122
Mullican, Moon, 166
Murieta, Joaquin, 36
Music Corporation of America (MCA), 125, 254
Music Reporter, on "Gambler's Love," 189
"My Life Has Been a Pleasure," 212
"My Little Baby," 189, 251
"My Little Darling," xii

"Nashville Now," 256
National Barn Dance, 40, 119, 138
Negro spirituals, 6, 7
Nelson, Ken, 194, 199; on Lula, 179–180; recording with, 177, 178, 189, 193; rock & roll and, 179; Rose and, 212, 215, 223
Nelson, Richard A. "Dick," 64, 65
Nelson, Willie, 183, 247
Nettles, Bill, 118
Newman, Lee, 193
"New Mule Skinner Blues," 152, 226
Newton, Wayne, 160
Nichols, Roy, 112, 121, 129, 140, 141, 190, 195, 199, 201, 222, 238, 248, 258; departure of, 126–127; on Duncan firing, 114; Fiftieth Anniversary and, 252, 253; on Fred, 110–111; gags and, 113; on Henry/Don, 123; hiring, 108–109; on Lula, 126; playing by, 111, 114–115, 227; recording with, 115, 247; on Rose, 44, 215
"Nightingale Song, The," 149
97th Street Corral, 97, 145, 175
"No Help Wanted," 144
"No Help Wanted No. 2," 144
"No More Time," 152
"North to Alaska," 200
Norwegian elk hound: adopting, 235–236

Oakland Tribune, Maddox family in, 20
O'Day, Mollie, 83, 99, 100, 119
"Oh, Susannah," 34
"Oklahoma Hills," 133
"Old Man from the Mountain," 161, 238
"Old Shep," 97
"Old Slew Foot," 207
"1, 2, 3, 4, Anyplace Road," 169
One Rose, The, 192–193
On the Air, Volume One, 247
Owens, Bonnie, 184
Owens, Buck, 92, 160, 178, 183, 190, 196, 220, 222, 258; & the Buckaroos, 209, 227; club appearances by, 227; duet with, 199, 211; on Fred, 227–228; Maddox Brothers & Rose and, 95–96; Rose and, 209, 211, 221, 230
Owens, Fuzzy, 195
Owens, Laura Lee, 120
"Ozark Jubilee," 167

Painted Post, 96
Parton, Dolly, 160
"Party Girl," 190
"Patty Cake Patty Cake," 112
Paul, Les, 128
"Pay Me Alimony," 91
Pearl, Minnie, 103, 165
Peebles, Hap, 197, 198–199, 202
Peer, Ralph, 8
Penny, Hank, 233
Performing: dedication to, 43, 72–73, 76–77
Perkins, Carl, 154, 241
Perkins, Luther, 196, 197, 203
Petrillo, James, 133; jukebox strike and, 64, 87–88, 90
"Philadelphia Lawyer, The," xi, xiii–xiv, 37, 99, 104, 121, 122, 133, 159–160, 192; recording, 90–91
Phillips, Bert "Foreman," 53–54
Pierce, Don, xiii, 69, 90, 96, 101, 104, 131; on Daily, 98; 4 Star and, 64–65, 89, 98–99, 100; "Hillbilly Swing" and, 71; on jukeboxes, 88; on Lula, 76, 95; on Maddox Brothers & Rose, 99–100; on "Oklahoma Hills"/"Philadelphia Lawyer," 133; on Rose, 223; on Satherley, 132; on Tyler/McCall, 65
Pierce, Webb, 131–132, 138, 141, 152; on Lula, 140; "Opry" and, 104
Pipe City, 20
"Pistol Packin' Mama," 65
"Please Help Me, I'm Falling," 193, 194
Popularity, 94, 251; increase in, 45, 68,

Ramblin Rose: The Life and Career of Rose Maddox was designed and composed electronically in Sabon with Goudy Sans display type by Kachergis Book Design, Pittsboro, North Carolina. It was printed on fifty-pound Glatfelter Supple Opaque Recycled Natural paper and bound by Thomson-Shore, Inc., Dexter, Michigan. Cover design is by Lauren Finney. Copublished by The Country Music Foundation Press and Vanderbilt University Press.